WAR THROUGH CHILDREN'S EYES

HOOVER ARCHIVAL DOCUMENTARIES
General editor: *Milorad M. Drachkovitch*

The documents reproduced in this series (unless otherwise indicated) are deposited in the archives of the Hoover Institution on War, Revolution and Peace at Stanford University. The purpose of their publication is to shed new light on some important events concerning the United States or the general history of the twentieth century.

HERBERT HOOVER AND POLAND
George J. Lerski, compiler

NEGOTIATING WHILE FIGHTING: THE DIARY OF ADMIRAL C. TURNER JOY
Allan E. Goodman, editor

PATRIOT OR TRAITOR: THE CASE OF GENERAL MIHAILOVICH
David Martin, compiler

BEHIND CLOSED DOORS: SECRET PAPERS ON THE FAILURE OF
  ROMANIAN-SOVIET NEGOTIATIONS, 1931–1932
Walter M. Bacon, Jr., translator and compiler

THE DIPLOMACY OF FRUSTRATION: THE MANCHURIAN CRISIS OF 1931–1933,
  AS REVEALED IN THE PAPERS OF STANLEY K. HORNBECK
Justus D. Doenecke, compiler

WAR THROUGH CHILDREN'S EYES
Irena Grudzińska-Gross and Jan Tomasz Gross, editors
Ronald Strom and Dan Rivers, translators

War Through Children's Eyes

The Soviet Occupation of Poland and the Deportations, 1939–1941

edited and compiled by
Irena Grudzińska-Gross
Jan Tomasz Gross

foreword by
Bruno Bettelheim

introduction by
Jan Tomasz Gross

translated by
Ronald Strom
Dan Rivers

HOOVER INSTITUTION PRESS
Stanford University, Stanford, California

www.hoover.org

Hoover Institution Press Publication No. 247
Hoover Institution at Leland Stanford Junior University,
Stanford, California, 94305-6003

The photographs on pages 60 and 83 are courtesy of Dr. Zdzisław Stahl. The photographs on pages 45, 96, 113, 126, 151, 168, and 214, taken at Vrevskoe, are from the Władysław Anders Collection and the Polish Government Collection at the Hoover Institution.

First printing, 1981. First paperback printing, 1985
25 24 23 22 21 20 19   9 8 7 6 5 4 3 2

Cataloging-in-Publication Data is available from the Library of Congress.
https://lccn.loc.gov/80083832
War through children's eyes : the Soviet occupation of Poland and the deportations, 1939–1941 / edited and compiled by Irena Grudzińska-Gross, Jan Tomasz Gross ; foreword by Bruno Bettelheim ; introduction by Jan Tomasz Gross ; translated by Ronald Strom, Dan Rivers. Stanford, Calif. : Hoover Institution Press, Stanford University, ©1981.
xxvii, 260 p. : ill. ; 24 cm.—(Hoover Institution Press : Hoover Archival Documentaries series ; 247)
Includes bibliography, illustrations, and index.
ISBN 978-0-8179-7471-8 (cloth: o.p.)
ISBN 978-0-8179-7472-5 (pbk.)
ISBN 978-0-8179-7473-2 (ePub)
ISBN 978-0-8179-7477-0 (mobi)
ISBN 978-0-8179-7478-7 (ePDF)
D810.D5 W36
940.53/161

Design by Elizabeth Gehman

Contents

List of Documents   vii

Foreword   xiii

Note on Sources   xix

Preface   xxi

Acknowledgments   xxix

INTRODUCTION   1

ILLUSTRATIONS   29

DOCUMENTS   43

Białystok Voivodeship   45

Lwów Voivodeship   60

Nowogród Voivodeship   83

Polesie Voivodeship   96

Stanisławów Voivodeship   113

Tarnopol Voivodeship   126

Wilno Voivodeship   151

Wołyń Voivodeship   168

Refugees   214

Notes   239

Bibliography   255

Index   257

List of Documents

BIAŁYSTOK VOIVODESHIP

Białowieża County
1 Hanka Świderska   46

Grodno County
2 Leon M.   48
3 Walenty M.   49
4 Walenty P.   50

Łomża
5 Antoni C.   51

Sokółka County
6 Tadeusz S.   53
7 Mieczysław M.   53

Szczuczyn County
8 Czesław B.   54

Wołkowysk County
9 Kazimierz S.   55
10 Stanisław R.   56

Wołków County
11 Józef J.   58

LWÓW VOIVODESHIP

Drohobycz County
12 Zdzisław K.   61
13 Jadwiga O.   61

Lesko County
14 Adam R.   62

Lubaczów County
15 Mieczysław D.   63

Lwów
16 Wiesław R.   64
17 Stanisław H.   67
18 Marian K.   69
19 Zygmunt B.   70
20 Danuta G.   74
21 Jadwiga B.   75

Mościska County
22 Tadeusz M.   77

Przemyślany County
23 Bronisław A.   78

Sokal County
24 Bronisław R.   79
25 Eugeniusz S.   80
26 Feliks J.   80
27 Grzegorz K.   81

Żółkiew County
28 Franciszek O.   82

NOWOGRÓD VOIVODESHIP

Baranowicze County
29 Stanisław J.   84
30 Władysław T.   87
31 Henryk S.   88

Lida County
32 Unidentified girl   88
33 Władysław M.   90

Nieśwież County
34 Władysław P.   91

Nowogródek
35 Zygmunt C.   93
36 Sergiusz M.   93

Słonim County
37 Stanisław W.   94

Stołpce County
38 Kazimierz S.   95

POLESIE VOIVODESHIP

Brześć County
39 Ryszard S.   97
40 Witold S.   98

Drohiczyn County
41 Stanisław K.   99
42 Jerzy W.   100

Kamień Koszyrski County
43 Julian M.   101

Kobryń County
44 Jan S.   104

Kosów County
45 Józef S.   107

Łuniniec County
46 Antoni D.   108
47 Andrzej W.   110

Pińsk County
48 Mieczysław B.   112

STANISŁAWÓW VOIVODESHIP

49 Stanisław J.   114

Dolina County
50 Stanisław Skwirzyński   114

Kałusz County
51 Janusz K.   115
52 Alfred P.   116
53 Eugeniusz P.   118

Rohatyn County
54 Jan M.   118
55 Józef M.   119

Stanisławów County
56 Czesław S.   120

Stryj County
57 Stanisław K.   121

Tłumacz County
58 Piotr N.   124

TARNOPOL VOIVODESHIP

59 Jan K.   127

Borczów County
60 Tadeusz M.   127

Brody County
61 Adolf N.   129
62 Czesław K.   129

Czortków
63 Urszula B.   130

Kamionka Strumiłowa County
64 Maria W.   131
65 Józef C.   132

Kopyczyńce County
66 Józef J.   133
67 Bolesław S.   134
68 Kazimierz F.   136

Przemyślany County
69 Marian H.   138

Radziechów County
70 Antoni P.   139
71 K.S.   139

Skałat County
72 Mieczysław P.   140

Tarnopol County
73 Franciszek S.   141
74 Janusz N.   142

Trembowla County
75 Stanisław B.   143
76 Józef N.   145

Zaleszczyki
77 Henryk N.   147

WILNO VOIVODESHIP

Dzisna County
78 Nikodem U.   152
79 Andrzej K.   155
80 Adam P.   156

Oszmiana County
81 Wacław K.   159
82 Mieczysław K.   160

Mołodeczno County
83 Irena Ł.   160

Wilejka County
84 Stanisław C.   163
85 Franciszek K.   164
86 Leon K.   165
87 Tadeusz S.   167

WOŁYŃ VOIVODESHIP

Dubno County
88 Tadeusz L.   169
89 Roman J.   170

Horochów County
90 Leon M.   171
91 Ludwik K.   172

Kowel County
92 Zygmunt Z.   173

Krzemieniec County
93 Elżbieta P.   174
94 Sław R.   178
95 Jan M.   180
96 Paweł P.   181
97 Kazimierz Żołyniak   182
98 Zdzisław Jagodziński   183
99 Natalia Makarewicz   190
100 Jan B.   191

Łuck County
101 Wacław P.   191
102 Czesław B.   192
103 Roman M.   193
104 Witold T.   194

Równe County
105 Henryk S.   197
106 Roman Baranek   197

Sarny County
107 Marian K.   199
108 Stanisław S.   201

Włodzimierz Wołyński County
109 Czesław J.   203

Zdołbunów County
110 Apolinary H.   205
111 Ernest K.   210
112 Romuald Kozłowski   210
113 Tadeusz B.   212

REFUGEES

114 Kazimierz W.   215

Warsaw
115 Helena F.   216
116 Zbigniew R.   217

Majdan Kolbuszewski
117 Józef B.   220

Izbica
118 Eliezer H.   224

Leżajsk
119 Zeev F.   230
120 Eliezer K.   234

Throughout history civilizations have been destroyed when invaders imposed their way of life on conquered populations. The vanquished can only hope that they will be able to regain their independence later. Literate peoples have left accounts of what this terrible experience meant to them: how they managed their misfortunes; how they tried to cope with the sudden collapse of their world; what they learned from it about themselves and the invaders. But these were the reports of adults. I know of no example other than the one presented here where the collapse of one civilization and its replacement by a radically different and inferior one has been reported from the perspective of children.

True, we have some sketchy testimonies of Jewish children about their experiences under Nazi domination. *The Diary of Anne Frank* is probably the most famous of these; there are also the writings of Jewish children in Polish ghettos into which they had been herded in preparation for their extermination and of young inmates of German concentration camps. But their situation was quite different from that of the Polish children whose stories are collected in this book. Despite the courageous efforts of Jewish children to carry on, they and their parents knew that they were doomed. The intention of their masters was not to change their way of life, but to end it. Jewish children and parents tried to survive despite the horrible conditions in which they were forced to exist, but they did not expect that their lives would continue in a different form under Nazi domination. The hope to which they clung as long as they could was that one day they would be freed and then resume life as they had known it before imprisonment or before they went into hiding. This was the hope of Anne Frank and of her family. As long as they lived, the Franks planned for a life exactly as they had known it; Anne even tried to educate herself for it.

Things were very different for the children who experienced first the collapse of Poland and the Russian invasion and later deportation into

Russia. It is the accounts of those who were deported that are presented in this book.

This was not the first time Poland had been partitioned, nor the first time that part of Poland had been absorbed by Russia. But previously Russia had not made a deliberate and concentrated effort to destroy the existing fabric of Polish society and replace it with an alien one. During the earlier occupation, the indigenous society had continued, although in reduced form. Under such conditions it was often the children who were the first to cope successfully with the changed situation because their roots in the cultural past were not as deep as those of their parents.

When Russia invaded Poland in 1939, it was not only that an alien and inferior civilization extended its rule over a large part of the country. What took place was a ruthless attempt to destroy, in the shortest possible time, a way of life. Despite the superiority of Polish culture, the Russians intentionally destroyed it and forced their victims to live under conditions incredibly inferior to those they had known all their lives. When Germany attacked Russia, an unexpected and tenuous alliance between Russia and the remnants of the Polish state was signed. The children whose stories are given here were freed and could tell of their experiences. These are their recollections of their nightmarish existence, recorded after their virtual slavery had ended. Nevertheless it was still fresh in their memories; the events had been so horrible that they were impressed indelibly in their minds.

These children had been forced to exchange their accustomed way of life for an entirely different one suddenly; they had been robbed of all that had given them security, and their methods of coping were no longer effective—within hours their easy existence gave way to a life of terror. Together with one or both parents, the children were rounded up and shipped in cattle cars to distant reaches of Russia, to perform what can only be called slave labor, under the worst possible conditions. The children's stories render a vivid picture of their life of starvation, unrelieved sickness, of the death of their parents and brothers and sisters.

The remarks introducing these reports stress that most of the occupying Russians were friendly, provided they did not meet with a, to them, incomprehensible resistance to their efforts to impose the "correct" order of things. The editors rightly stress that "the crucial point is that the Soviets' behavior in occupied Poland and in their own country was similar. They, and their families, had experienced the same hardships to which the population of the newly liberated territories were now being subjected. 'You'll get used to it or else you'll croak,' they used to say, not maliciously, but merely summing up the commonsense wisdom life had taught them." And they were right, from their point of view. But how can a people who had once known a very different way of life, had cherished freedom and valued the individual, make such wisdom their own?

This clash between dissimilar ways of life was exacerbated by the natural resentment of an occupier who confronts a vastly higher standard of living than his own. I speak here of a natural resentment. As long as one is not forced to recognize how inferior one's living conditions are, compared with those of a subjugated population, one does not consciously suffer. But it becomes a painful insult to one's national pride to realize that a population that one had been told was inferior, that one had considered inferior, and that had demonstrated this by the ease of its defeat seems to have had a much higher culture and certainly lived incredibly better than one had thought possible. Even once settled in the interior of Russia, the superior habits of the Polish strangers and their disgust with the life the Russians had forced on them were an insult to the natives since it made them feel more keenly the miserable conditions under which they lived. The Russians had expected the Poles to accept this way of life as the correct one and to adjust to it without resentment.

Two stories must stand for many. In Document 8, a child describes how his mother and one of his brothers went on a two days' trip, trying to exchange some of their last belongings—their own badly needed clothes—for some flour to bake a little bread to sustain the starving family for a few days. Day after day those family members who remained behind waited and worried about what might have happened to their mother and brother. On the fifth day "one woman comes over and says that one woman with a boy froze to death. We all cried at once dad walks around the barracks like crazy." The father asks the camp authorities for a horse and wagon to bring back the corpses but is denied the use of a horse because it is needed for farm work, which is viewed as more important. After a day or two (the time span is unclear from the child's report), "Dad comes back . . . and says that Mama is frozen we started crying even worse. Older sister fainted . . . two kilometers away from the village Mama was sitting on the sleighs and holding my brother in her arms." Both had frozen to death.

It is a tale of nightmarish quality that reminds one of the worst fantasies in fairy tales. Only these are not fantasies, but real events witnessed by children who will have to carry the memories of such outrage with them all their lives.

Children see their parents disappear; they do not know where they went, whether they are still alive, or already dead. They watch their mothers and fathers, their brothers and sisters, die of overwork, starvation, and mistreatment, helpless to prevent it. The objectivity and absence of emotional expression with which these events are related may seem astonishing to those not acquainted with such deprived conditions. But emotions require a great deal of energy; the greater the demands made on one's resources for sheer survival, the less energy one has available to experience feelings. These children were exhausted by starvation and by the need to work long hours at unaccustomed and killing labor to earn completely inadequate food rations. Little wonder that Stanisław J. (Document 29) writes: "On May 8 dad died of typhus . . . Mother's despair didn't help and the crying of the children didn't help, of my brothers and of my sisters. A man is born only once and only dies once. And so it happened."

This is not an expression of callous indifference. Despite the seemingly philosophical remark about man's destiny, this is a statement of utter desperation. In childish language, it says that things were so terrible that the boy resented the open expression of grief on the part of brothers and sisters because it was more than he could bear. All he could do was to try to restrain his own grief, so that he could go on working to receive the handful of grain that might keep all of them alive for another day. Under such conditions, the most natural emotions become a luxury one cannot afford, but must repress.

This, then, is the cruelest story these tales convey: the children could not afford to feel because if they did, they, too, would perish. The stories do not tell of hope; they tell only of desperation, mistreatment, and death. Since they were written soon after the children had reached freedom and security, it would seem reasonable for them to have spoken of their hope for liberation, if they had any. The absence of such statements suggests that they had none. These children were robbed of the freedom to vent deep and normal feelings, forced to repress them in order to survive for barely another day. A child who has been deprived of any hope for the future is a child dwelling in hell. He can record what occurred after he regained liberty, but becoming able to feel and hope again may take a lifetime—or may never be possible.

In all wars—with the possible exception of wars between civilized nations during the past few centuries—the "spoils" of the victor include the right to do unbearable injustice to the vanquished. What to the Russians was the imposition of their system, which was obviously superior because they prevailed in the war, meant to the Poles the destruction of their ancient culture and often also of their lives. The testimonies of these children are a warning to all of us, about what would happen to our culture, ourselves, and most of all our children, if an alien power and system were to gain ascendancy. We think that this is impossible; so did the Poles. The fate of these children shows that a firm belief that such things cannot happen does not prevent them from happening. Let us hope that the warning inherent in the children's writings collected in this book receives the attention it deserves.

Bruno Bettelheim

Note on Sources

The Polish Government Collection, the Władysław Anders Collection, and the Poland, Ambasada (USSR) Collection at the Hoover Institution Archives contain over twenty thousand transcripts of interviews conducted with Polish citizens deported to the Soviet Union between 1939 and 1941. Soon after the Poles were released from captivity following the resumption of Polish-Soviet diplomatic relations in July 1941, they were asked to recount their recollections of the Soviet occupation of Poland and their life in exile after deportation to Russia. In late October 1943, the Polish Ministry of Information and Documentation established a study center for the purpose of preserving existing and collecting additional information on these subjects. Individual interviews (now deposited in the Polish Government Collection) were sorted and arranged according to the territorial divisions of eastern Poland. Later, based on these interviews, reports describing the process of sovietization in each county were written.

We quote from both individual interviews and county reports in the Preface and Introduction. Whenever reference is made to an individual interview, we identify the archival box, the place of origin of the interviewee, and the number appearing on the interview schedule (for example, HI, PGC, Box 200, Lwów: 4261). Sometimes, if there is no interview number, we identify the name of the interviewee. Whenever we refer to a county report, we identify the county and the page number on which the pertinent information appears (for example, HI, PGC, Postawy: 20). Abbreviations used in the references and documents:

AC	Władysław Anders Collection (HI)
DGFP	R. J. Sontag, ed., *Documents on German Foreign Policy*, vol. 8 (Washington, D.C.: Government Printing Office, 1954).

DPSR	GSHI, ed., *Documents on Polish-Soviet Relations*, vol. 1, *1939–1943* (London: Heinemann, 1961).
GSHI	General Sikorski Historical Institute (London)
HI	Hoover Institution
KOP	Frontier Defense Corps
MSZ	Ministry of Foreign Affairs
PAC	Poland, Ambasada (USSR) Collection (HI)
PGC	Polish Government Collection (HI)
PSZ	Polish Armed Forces Collection (HI)

Preface

The documents in this volume are preserved in the Polish Government Collection and the Poland. Ambasada (USSR) Collection deposited at the Hoover Institution on War, Revolution and Peace at Stanford, California. Both collections contain a variety of documents concerning twentieth-century Polish history, including over twenty thousand transcripts of interviews conducted with Polish citizens deported to the Soviet Union between 1939 and 1941. In addition, about 2,300 school compositions written by children who shared the fate of their parents are preserved in these two collections. These testimonies were collected from Polish citizens and their children soon after they were released from captivity following the resumption of Polish-Soviet diplomatic relations in July 1941. From among the children's compositions we have selected 120 for presentation.

The events described here took place as a result of a little-known episode in the modern history of Europe, communism, and the Second World War—the Soviet occupation of Poland between 1939 and 1941. In order to provide the necessary background, the Introduction describes the imposition of the Soviet regime of occupation on the southeastern half of Poland, which began on September 17, 1939. Here we briefly introduce the sequence of events that led to the writing of the compositions presented in this volume.

During the first two years of the Second World War, from September 17, 1939, until June 22, 1941, the territory of Poland was partitioned between two occupying powers—Hitler's Germany and Stalin's Russia. The Soviet authorities introduced drastic political, socioeconomic, and demographic changes (see Introduction) in the area under their control and, among other measures, subjected the local population to mass deportations into the eastern and northern parts of the Soviet Union. In the early phase of the Russo-German war, as a result of vigorous diplomatic action by the exiled Polish government in London under the premiership of Gen. Władysław Sikorski, several hundred thousand former citizens of the Polish republic were released from labor camps, prisons, and forcible resettlement in the Soviet Union, and over one hundred thousand were allowed to leave the USSR for British-controlled territories in the Middle East. The Polish embassy in Moscow was authorized to organize an independent network of "men of confidence" to provide welfare assistance to this mass of people, and Polish military authorities were permitted to build an army from these people. Both the army and the embassy provided a modicum of protection for their political rights. This all began on July 30, 1941, with the restoration of Polish-Soviet diplomatic relations, and ended on April 25, 1943, when the USSR severed relations.[1]

When the Soviet government recognized General Sikorski's government and agreed to the formation of a Polish army on Soviet territory, it granted amnesty to all Polish citizens "deprived of their freedom on the territory of the USSR either as prisoners of war or on other adequate grounds" and recognized that "the Soviet-German treaties of 1939 concerning territorial changes in Poland have lost their validity" (*DPSR*, pp. 141–42). Two ambiguities were left in the text of the agreement: there was no definition of Polish citizenship, and the Soviets did not renounce their territorial acquisitions in eastern Poland—they merely annulled Soviet-German treaties concerning Poland. Motivated by the desire to rescue the deported Polish citizens, General Sikorski signed the agreement, despite its failings, over the objections of several key ministers in his cabinet and the president of the republic.

No precise count of the number of Polish citizens deported to the USSR is available. The Soviet authorities, undoubtedly in possession of such statistics, never made them available to the Polish government. Deputy Commissar of Foreign Affairs Andrei Vyshinsky once quoted 387,932 as the total number of Polish citizens in confinement or forced resettlement in the USSR at the outbreak of the Russo-German war (*DPSR*, p. 180). But according to estimates by Polish authorities, over 1.2 million persons were resettled in the Soviet Union from southeastern Poland during the first two years of the war. Of that number, 880,000 were forcibly sent to Russia during the four waves of deportations in February, April, and June of 1940 and in June of 1941; about 150,000 Polish citizens were mobilized into the Red Army; 180,000 were taken into the USSR as prisoners of war; and about 20,000 went there to work. About half of the deportees (440,000) ended up in labor camps and prisons. The other half were dumped into settlements (*posëlki*) all over the Soviet Union (see map, p. 30). About one-quarter, some 220,000 to 250,000, were children fourteen years of age or younger.[2]

The population of Soviet-occupied Poland was unprepared for the cruelty that characterized the deportations. People were usually awakened in the early morning hours by squads of soldiers and local militiamen, given little time to pack, and quickly driven to the nearest railway station (Docs. no. 9, 23, 54, 104). There, freight trains awaited them. They froze in unheated cattle cars in February and suffocated in the June heat four months later. They were locked in for weeks with only meager rations of food and water, with a hole in the car's floor for all facilities. Men, women, and children of all ages were mixed together. Because even the sick and aged, as well as newborn infants, were put on the trains—there were no exemptions from the deportation order— many died, and corpses traveled with the living before being discarded at some railway stop (Docs. no. 5, 23, 25). Almost every testimony in this volume contains some terrifying details of these involuntary journeys into Siberia. Although ethnic Poles constituted an absolute majority among the deportees, no social category or ethnic group from the area was spared. Almost one-third of the forcibly deported population was Jewish (52 percent Poles, 30 percent Jews, and 18 percent Ukrainians and Belorussians). A similar fraction of the deported, almost one-third of the total, consisted of peasants and workers.[3]

But the horrors of the journey were only a prelude to the misery of everyday life that awaited the deportees at their destination—filth and overcrowded living quarters, hunger, cold, disease, and slave labor. Most of the deported survived until the amnesty by selling piecemeal to the local Soviet population the few possessions they had brought (Docs. no. 11, 31, 62, 97). In addition, until the outbreak of the Russo-German war, the deportees could receive parcels from friends or relatives.[4] When the amnesty finally came, the deportees were dying and sick and in need of help (Docs. no. 14, 52, 109, 114). In the "Report on Polish Refugees in Persia," a British officer, Col. A. Ross (HI, PGC, Box 420, File "Ewakuacja obywateli polskich z ZSSR. 1945."), described the state of health of the refugees after their evacuation from the Soviet Union:

> The physical and mental state of the refugees on arrival in Teheran was generally very bad. The most prevalent diseases were dysentery, diarrhea, deficiency diseases due to prolonged malnutrition, many malarias imported from Russia, and typhoid: 40% of the refugees were malaria cases. A visit to any of the hospitals at the beginning of the first or second phases of the evacuation was sufficient to create on the mind an indelible impression of unmerited hardships and physical suffering.

General Anders [commander of the Polish army established in the USSR] stated on his arrival from Russia that he expected 25% of the refugees to die after their arrival in Persia. The number of deaths among civilians had in fact been 2,119 up to the end of 1943, or just under 5%.

The death rate among the Poles in Russia was much higher. Among children, it was estimated at around 20 percent (HI, PAC, File no. 266, "Note Concerning Children Deported into the USSR," Irena Wasilewska, Teheran, October 27, 1943; see also Docs. no. 27, 57, 61, 96).[5]

Small wonder, then, that the deportees greeted the amnesty as an act of heavenly justice and a long-awaited reprieve. The prospect of joining the Polish army electrified them more than anything else, for they hoped that this would allow them to leave Soviet territory altogether.

The area originally designated for organizing the Polish army in the USSR was located near Kuibyshev, the city to which the Soviet government and foreign embassies, including the Polish, were evacuated from Moscow. The newly created Polish 5th Infantry Division was billeted in Tatishchevo and the 6th Infantry Division in Tockoje. Army headquarters were located in Buzuluk, and various auxiliary formations were organized in Chkalov and Kotlubanka. In January and February 1942 all Polish army personnel were evacuated south to a new area designated for army organization. The Poles were distributed over a long strip of territory stretching through the Kazakh, Kirghiz, and Uzbek republics. (Tashkent is located roughly in the middle of this area.)

From February 1942 until the final evacuation to Iran six months later (there were two evacuations—in April and in August of 1942), outfits of the Polish army were stationed in Yangiyul, Dzalal-Abad, Shakhrisabz, Kermine, Tchok-Pak, Margilan, Lugovoe, Guzar, Vrevskoe, Velikoe-Alekseevskoe, Karabalti, Otar, and Kara-Su. From the evacuation base at Krasnovodsk on the Caspian Sea, people were taken by boat to Pahlevi in Iran. Into the area occupied by the Polish army units flocked newly amnestied Polish deportees from all over the Soviet Union. The geographical names of these locations, often distorted beyond recognition, can be found in nearly every testimony, for they were memorized and repeated frequently since their true meaning was freedom.

In terms of climate it was an inhospitable region, and various contagious diseases were endemic. In addition, the area was crowded with refugees from European Russia who had been relocated to avoid the rapidly advancing German army. Supply shortages plagued the Polish military authorities. They were issued only 44,000 food rations, although their military contingent was nearly twice as large. Hungry, sick, and destitute Polish citizens poured in continually, and the army, though sharing what little food and medication it had, could not provide adequately for many. People were dispersed, therefore, among the neighboring kolkhozes, where they had to work in exchange for meager subsistence and shelter—hence the grim memories of this final period in the Soviet Union before evacuation (Docs. no. 30, 42, 80, 96). The mortality rate among the Poles during these last six months of captivity in Russia was staggering. Between February and August 1942, Polish army hospitals registered 49,411 cases of contagious diseases. At any given time, the morbidity rate among Polish army personnel hovered around 25 percent; 2,020, or roughly 4 percent, of the hospitalized died of contagious diseases.[6] And these were mostly young men, who had joined the army and had the benefit of at least some medical care in army hospitals. It is chilling to think that Polish citizens deported to kolkhozes, state farms, and settlements throughout the USSR simply shared the hardships of ordinary Soviet citizens—by 1940 the Soviet economy could not provide even a starvation diet to the majority of its citizens (Docs. no. 91, 100, 116).

From the beginning the Soviet authorities were reluctant to implement the agreement signed with the Polish government; many Poles were never informed of the amnesty, others were not released from confinement (Docs. no. 13, 36, 58). The personnel of the welfare organization established by the Polish embassy were harassed and often arrested; obstacles were put in the way of conscription into the Polish army—it did not receive enough equipment or food rations to sustain and train the conscripts.[7] In the end, Polish leaders decided to evacuate the army and the soldiers' families to Iran, where British authorities could outfit the army for combat and provide decent living conditions for the destitute population.[8]

Polish authorities also tried to evacuate a large number of orphaned or lost children from the USSR, but in vain. England, Canada, and the American Red Cross agreed to help resettle fifty thousand children, and on June 12, 1942, the Polish ambassador called on Deputy Commissar Vyshinsky to obtain his government's permission to proceed with the evacuation. Vyshinsky rejected the Polish request, alleging difficulties in transportation. An evacuation would be pointless, he added, because "the welfare of the children is assured by the Soviet authorities" (HI, PAC, Box 25, Folder 269).[9] In the end, only fifteen to twenty thousand children were evacuated to Iran.[10] Once in Iran, they were dispersed in displaced person camps throughout the British-controlled Middle East, chiefly in Palestine, Egypt, and Iraq.

The Polish authorities had given special care to children's needs ever since the embassy in Moscow established the network of welfare assistance for Polish deportees. While the deportees were still in the USSR, nurseries, schools, and orphanages were created (behind the proud names on embassy personnel reports a very humble reality was hidden—warm shelter, two or three meals a day, adult-supervised activities, learning a Polish poem or song [Docs. no. 1, 29]). These centers continued to function even after the evacuation of the Polish army and the accompanying civilian population to Iran (HI, PAC, Box 16, "Assistance and Care Given to the Jewish Population in the USSR"). In January 1942 Polish military authorities established the first Junaks' school, in Vrevskoe (after the evacuation, the British authorities called the Junaks "Young Soldiers" and considered them personnel of the Polish army in the East). With time the institution evolved into a complex school system, with ten boys' and five girls' schools dispersed throughout several locations in the Middle East. In the boys' division the schools were known as Junaks' Schools (Szkoły Junackie), in the girls' division as Schools of Young Volunteers (Szkoły Młodszych Ochotniczek) (HI, PSZ, Box 2, Folder 10/206). Most of the boys who wrote the compositions published in this volume studied at the Junaks' School of Cadets (Junacka Szkoła Kadetów) at Barbara, while the girls attended any one of several Schools of Young Volunteers at Nazareth.

We could not ascertain the precise circumstances under which the school compositions translated here were written. In some cases children must have been asked to answer a specific set of questions—this is especially true of the compositions preserved in the Poland. Ambasada (USSR) Collection. In other cases it was probably an open-ended assignment very much like one given children all over the world after a prolonged absence from the classroom, say, after summer vacation.

The process of selecting the compositions included here was difficult. On the one hand, the great majority of manuscripts were too similar to discriminate among easily. On the other hand, even the most typical ones had some little, unique details that we found interesting and important and did not want to exclude. There was also a distinct group of compositions, written by younger children, that were much shorter and focused on the one episode or event that had the greatest impact on the young author. Essentially, the selections in this book are a mixture of these two kinds. We have omitted very general and uninformative testimonies, as well as those (very few indeed) whose author's intent was to conform to the standard of a "good and patriotic" school composition. We also strove to preserve variety—there are stories from the taiga, from the steppe, and from the deserts; by boys and by girls of anywhere between ten and eighteen years of age. We have arranged the documents according to the original area of residence (voivodeship) of each author.

The London headquarters of the schools' alumni associations helped us locate some of our authors.[11] Surnames as well as exact dates (month and day) of birth of unlocated children are omitted. The vast majority of the testimonies in the Hoover collections came from Polish Catholic children; four of the few Jewish depositions we found in the Hoover Archives are placed at the end of this volume in the section of refugees' testimonies. Unlike other documents in this volume, all of which were handwritten, the Jewish depositions were typewritten and therefore, we assume, either translated from Yiddish or dictated.

Although a year in Polish schools may have colored the children's accounts,[12] the compositions constitute a unique historical, sociological, and literary document, enabling us to study living conditions in eastern Poland under the Russian occupation, the deportations, life in Russia, schools, work, and propaganda through small, funny stories no adult would include in his recollections. The compositions show where the deportees were directed and the "local" population they lived among (these populations were composed mainly of people deported one, five, or fifteen years before the Poles arrived; see Docs. no. 108, 116). They are micro-history as told by young and perspicacious authors.

Another unusual quality of the compositions is their language. Under the German occupation, the authorities essentially did not try to germanize the population; the Russians, however, made an enormous effort to russify the children both while they were still in Poland and after the deportation. Eastern Poland was an ethnically mixed area, and the majority of children knew some Ukrainian or Belorussian; when deported, they were either in Russian schools or workplaces. Their teachers and supervisors made every effort to detach them from their family, religion, and language.[13] Too young to have attended Polish schools for long, many children, particularly the youngest ones, lost a sense of the division between the two languages. Some of the older children wrote in a nice, polished style, but the majority, writing the way they spoke, with no attention to spelling or word order, used a strangely attractive mixture of Polish, Polish dialects, and Russian. The quality of this combination could not be rendered into English. However, we decided to translate the misspellings and awkwardness of the children's writings, considering them an integral part of the original documents.

A special category of mistakes is due to the unexpected encounter with the new, adult reality of war. Words like "amnesty" ("Poles got vacation") or "citizenship," for example, were written in a variety of ways. The second major problem for the children was the lack of an adequate vocabulary to describe the Russian reality. The terms for work discipline and punishment, for the miserable quarters they lived in, for the military organization of life had to be incorporated into Polish from Russian. No Polish linguistic equivalent was to be found for *progul* (severe punishment for tardiness of work), *posëlok* (settlement for deportees), or *kizjak* (bricks of dried manure used as fuel). This reality was alien and incompatible with the children's language, experience, and expectations.

The children's essays are in a way repetitive. Since the lives of our authors were woven around the same historical events (Soviet occupation, deportation, forced resettlement, release from confinement), they were all structurally identical. This superficial repetitiveness is not superfluous, however, for it reveals that 120 strangers from varied social backgrounds and different geographical locations were exposed to the same—yet in each case individual—hardships. Clearly the Soviet domination adversely affected the *entire* society.

War, deportations, the death of loved ones, starvation, and hard labor were the life story of all the children whose compositions we read. And yet only a few of them showed in their writings signs of severe psychological and emotional disturbance. Perhaps those with less resistance did not survive; those who did had three powerful allies: family, religion, and patriotism. But since the writers of these compositions were children and not soldiers or politicians, the war's cruelty and random violence was not transformed into mythology. Confronting this unprecedented experience is, in fact, the problem of all literature about the Second World War.[14] The testimonies collected in this volume, with their austerity, helplessness, and suffering, are, we think, closer to the core of what happened than many a volume of sophisticated writing. No heroes, no victors—only death, nightmare, and daily misery.

Acknowledgments

We wish to express our gratitude to the Hoover Institution Archives and in particular to its director, Dr. Milorad M. Drachkovitch, who made this book possible. We are very grateful to the alumni of the Junacka Szkoła Kadetów (School of Young Soldiers) and the Szkoła Młodszych Ochotniczek (School of Young Volunteers) who spoke with us about their experiences. Our special thanks go to Dr. Zdzisław Jagodziński, Jerzy Kulczycki, Danuta Polniaszek-Kossakowska, and Hanna Świderska, who were especially generous with their time and patience. The Concilium on International Studies and the Junior Faculty Griswold Fund at Yale University offered financial assistance that enabled us to travel to Stanford and London during the preparation of this book.

Introduction

Introduction

SOVIET-NAZI DIPLOMACY

On September 17, 1939, at daybreak, the Red Army unexpectedly invaded Poland across the entire length of the Polish-Soviet frontier. Although European political observers unanimously recognized that the signing of the German-Soviet Treaty of Non-Aggression in August had encouraged Hitler to start the war, no one had considered it a prelude to Soviet military expansion as well. No one, that is, except the signatories of the treaty, which included, as was later discovered, a secret protocol. In this addendum to the treaty, Stalin and Hitler agreed on the northern frontier of Lithuania as the dividing line between their respective spheres of interest in the Baltic states and partitioned the territory of Poland along the line of the rivers Narew, Vistula, and San.[1] Then, in barely two sentences, they settled the future of Bessarabia.

But the secret was well kept, and—with the exception of German and Soviet leaders and the generals preparing marching orders for the Red Army and the Wehrmacht—few people foresaw that the revived spirit of Rapallo would lead to Soviet-Nazi military collaboration. In any case Poland was unprepared in September 1939 for a military confrontation with its eastern neighbor. The Frontier Defense Corps (KOP), whose task was to defend the eastern Polish border, had no battle plans or emergency orders in the event of war with both Russia and Germany.[2] The KOP had no artillery, only a few antitank weapons, and numbered roughly eleven thousand soldiers (GSHI, Orlik-Rückemann [KOP commander], 1940)—an adequate frontier police force, perhaps, but no match for a regular army of one million.

Not that it mattered militarily, for on September 17 Poland had already lost its war against Germany and the Polish government was about to abandon the territory of the country—but the Soviet attack indeed came as a surprise. There was little advance warning of the coming invasion except, perhaps, for a September 14 article elucidating "internal reasons for the destruction of Poland during the war," displayed prominently on *Pravda*'s front page in the place reserved for important editorial statements. The disintegration of Poland, the article argued, was due less to the technical and military superiority of the German army and more to Poland's multinational structure (40 percent of its population, *Pravda* stated, was composed of national minorities). Poland's "leadership circles" had ruthlessly oppressed these national minorities, particularly in the "Western Ukraine" and "Western Belorussia," where the Polish government's record was no better than that of the tsarist government. No wonder, therefore, that Poland could not withstand the confrontation with Germany; like tsarist Russia twenty years earlier, it disintegrated from within. In a somewhat changed and amplified version, the article was handed to the Polish ambassador in Moscow three days later and then broadcast all over the world as Molotov spoke on the subject to the Soviet people.[3] Indeed, some circumstances surrounding the Soviet government's communication of its intended action against Poland, as well as the content of the Soviet note, are revealing.

At 2:15 A.M., on September 17, the Polish ambassador in Moscow, Wacław Grzybowski, received a telephone call from Deputy Commissar Vladimir Potemkin of the Soviet Commissariat for Foreign Affairs, asking the ambassador to appear at the Commissariat at 3:00 A.M. (*DPSR*, p. 87). At 2:00 A.M., Soviet leaders granted another interview. Stalin, Molotov, and Voroshilov summoned the German ambassador in Moscow, Count Friedrich Werner von Schulenburg, to the Kremlin. Stalin informed Schulenburg of the impending Soviet invasion of Poland and read a note about to be delivered to Ambassador Grzybowski. "The note contains a justification for the Soviet action," reported Schulenburg in a "most urgent" telegram to Berlin. "The draft read to me contained three points unacceptable to us. In answer to my objections, Stalin with the utmost readiness altered the text in such a way that the note now seems satisfactory for us." (*DGFP*, p. 80.) Thus, what Grzybowski heard one hour later was a joint product of Soviet-Nazi diplomatic collaboration. The ambassador was informed that the Polish state no longer existed, that it had "disintegrated," and that, therefore, all treaties between the USSR and Poland were void. The march of the Red Army into Poland was not a belligerent act, for it did not violate the now non-existent Polish sovereignty. The Soviet government simply decided to launch a rescue operation on behalf "of its blood brothers, the Ukrainians and the Belorussians inhabiting Poland, who now have been utterly abandoned to their fate and are defenseless." At the same time, the note stated, the Soviet government intended "to take

War Through Children's Eyes

every step to deliver the Polish people from the disastrous war into which they have been plunged by their unwise leaders and to give them the opportunity to live a peaceful life." (*DPSR*, p. 46.)

Even though the Germans participated, through Schulenburg, in drafting the Soviet note to Poland, they were dissatisfied with their ally. They wanted to publicize their collaboration and issue a joint communiqué concerning the situation in Poland. But at the insistence of the Soviets the close collaboration between the two governments was kept secret (*DGFP*, pp. 3, 4, 12, 14, 15, 34, 35, 44, 60, 61, 68–70, 76, 77). The USSR wanted at all costs to avoid the appearance of acting as an aggressor. Having invented the argument about the need to protect its blood brothers in eastern Poland, it clung desperately to this justification. "This argument," said Schulenberg, "was to make the intervention of the Soviet Union plausible to the masses and at the same time avoid giving the Soviet Union the appearance of an aggressor . . . Molotov conceded that the projected argument of the Soviet Government contained a note that was jarring to German sensibilities, but asked us in view of the difficult situation of the Soviet Government to stumble over this piece of straw." (*DGFP*, pp. 44, 77.)

And so it was only on September 18 that the world learned from the Soviet-German communiqué (published in *Pravda* the following day) of the joint presence and role of Hitler's and Stalin's armies in Poland. The document is a remarkable specimen of the Orwellian doublethink:

> In connection with the circulation of all kinds of rumors about the alleged tasks of the Soviet and German armies now in Poland, the governments of the USSR and Germany inform *that the activities of these armies do not involve any task that would be contrary to the interests of Germany or the Soviet Union or that would be incompatible with the letter or the spirit of the Non-Aggression Treaty concluded between Germany and the Soviet Union* [italics added]. On the contrary, the task of these armies is to establish peace and order in Poland, which were disturbed by the disintegration of the Polish state. Their task is to assist the population of Poland to reconstruct its statehood.

Like many texts of this kind, this one—contrary to the wishes of its authors—also reveals their true intentions. Indeed the fourth partition of Poland was the direct consequence of both the spirit and the letter of the Nazi-Soviet Non-Aggression Treaty concluded in August 1939.

THE FIRST ENCOUNTER WITH THE RED ARMY

The population of the territories occupied by the Red Army was utterly confused. For some time, the inability of local administrators to obtain instructions from their superiors, rumors that immediately began circulating widely (Docs. no. 15, 77, 98), and the campaign of disinformation by invading Red Army soldiers (who themselves might have been confused about why and where they were marching) left the population wondering what was happening. The KOP, for instance, received no orders from its headquarters after the Soviets marched into Poland. The KOP commander, Gen. Wilhelm Orlik-Rückemann, decided to fight the invaders, but for a day or two, the information forthcoming to him through the police and the postal service and in the form of rumors indicated that the Red Army had entered Poland as an ally and was on its way to fight the Germans (GSHI, Orlik-Rückemann, 1940). Many villages through which Soviet soldiers marched were left with the same impression (Docs. no. 2, 64, 77, 104). In some instances the local authorities (for example, county prefects in Tarnopol, Zdoł-bunów, and Zbaraż) instructed the population to be friendly toward the Red Army because it was Poland's ally (HI, PGC, Box 10, Lwów: 3102, 3409; Zdołbunów: 3).[4]

Some of this confusion did not originate in the simplistic minds of Polish citizens, who could not conceive of such a prompt, practical implementation of the Nazi-Soviet Non-Aggression Treaty, but was the result of Soviet activities. The Russians dropped leaflets explaining that the Soviet army was assisting Poland against Germany, a statement repeated by many Soviet soldiers in conversations with the local population while they marched through hamlets and villages (HI, PGC, Łuniniec: 2, 3; Kostopol: 3; Kowel: 1; Szczuczyn: 1; Postawy: 3; Wilejka: 3; Dzisna: 1; Brasław: 1; Box 10, Lwów: 6348). Simultaneously with this campaign to assuage, as it were, the fears of the populace, another, very different propaganda theme, designed not to quiet down but to stir up the inhabitants of the area, called the Ukrainian and Belorussian masses into action under the banner of national liberation from the yoke of their Polish masters.[5] Leaflets urged Belorussian and Ukrainian peasants to grab pitchforks, axes, saws, and scythes and overwhelm the Polish landlords (Docs. no. 85, 98, 104). Appeals were made to soldiers to turn their guns on the officers who made them fight an unjust war. As the Red Army moved through the countryside and villages, political commissars and soldiers told the local peasants to take all they wanted from the landlords and the rich farmers. Much blood was shed without the Soviet Army's firing a single shot.

The confusion of the first day slowly gave way to certainty—Poland had lost the war. No one really knew what the new order would be like, but this did not matter since at the moment there were scores to settle in the area , where mutual suspicion and even outright hatred between the different nationalities had accumulated over the years. The Soviet appeal to Belorussian and Ukrainian nationalism, combined with the collapse of political and administrative order after Poland's defeat, released the destructive force of long-downtrodden pride and repeatedly injured sensibilities. The day of reckoning came, and in the countryside it was marked by death, fire, and destruction.

Ethnic antagonisms were exacerbated in the immediate past. Throughout the 1918–1939 period, politicians of the Second Republic (as the Polish state created after the Versailles treaty was called) pursued an ambitious goal of national unification. The challenge was to create a unified state from three territorial units that for over a century had belonged to three different empires (Russia, Germany, and Austria-Hungary) and were, therefore, economically developed and administratively integrated in conjunction with and in response to different state organisms, social needs, and political traditions. In addition, the new state comprised within its borders various ethnic groups, which, in view of the ideological saliency of nationalism in interwar Europe, added another irredentist factor that impeded the task of national unification.

Especially in southeastern Poland, where ethnic Poles were a minority, this became a burning issue. Although ethnic minorities comprised one-third of the Polish population of 35 million, in the southeastern voivodeships of the country they constituted a significant majority—over 60 percent of the population (from 85.5 percent in Polesie voivodeship to 31 percent in Białystok voivodeship).[6] Among the 13 million Polish citizens who found themselves under Soviet occupation in September 1939, there were about 5.2 million ethnic Poles, according to the official Polish census (HI, AC, Pack 109, Biuro Dokumentów, "Polska Wschodnia okupowana w latach 1939–1941 przez ZSRR. Dane statystyczne"). The pursuit of the legitimate goal of state unification, the latent xenophobia of the colonels' regime (increasingly more visible after Józef Piłsudski's death in 1935), and the aggressive nationalism of the largest political party in Poland, the National Democratic party, combined to exacerbate ethnic antagonisms in the country. With the exception of the left, public opinion was more or less unanimous that the Jews, almost 10 percent of the country's population, were an alien element that should be denied access to or opportunities for further expansion into the professions, the economy, or the state administration. Nor was the Polish government able to find an acceptable formula of accommodation for burgeoning Ukrainian national aspirations. Violence between the Polish state and Ukrainians residing in southeastern Poland was frequent. Twice, in 1930 and in

1936, the Polish army brutally pacified the area.[7] In 1934 Ukrainian nationalists killed the minister of the interior, Bronisław Pieracki. There were countless incidents of arson, beatings, and isolated killings between the two national groups during the *dwudziestolecie* (twenty years, 1918–1939). This tension exploded during the transition from Polish to Soviet rule and smoldered long beyond the time of uncertainty over the area's political future. For the Soviets immediately initiated a social revolution in this territory, and class warfare, as they discovered, could be most effectively nurtured by encouraging ethnic hatred.

The Polish farmers brought into the area in the 1920s and 1930s by the government as so-called military colonists suffered the brunt of the ethnic minorities' wrath in southeastern Poland (Docs. no. 64, 73, 99, 103).[8] They had always been seen as intruders, as standard-bearers of the enforced polonization of this territory. From among them was recruited the majority of local administrators, who carried out the prejudiced policies of the Polish government. They assisted the army in its pacification programs in the 1930s against the Ukrainian peasantry and infringed on customary rights of the local inhabitants in carrying out their duties in the deeply resented Forestry Service.

In September 1939, individual Polish soldiers wandering in search of their detachments or simply returning home were often killed by hostile local peasants or, more frequently, stripped of their uniforms and beaten and then released, naked and bruised (Doc. no. 77). Small army units were often shot at or ambushed. But as the Soviet army quickly marched forward to reach its objective—the demarcation line agreed on with Germany—larger detachments of the Polish army trying to reach the Romanian or Hungarian border and avoid captivity put to fire and sword hamlets where a day or even a few hours earlier such incidents had occurred. According to the recollections of a lieutenant marching with a larger KOP detachment, "every night there is shooting. Soldiers are afraid to march in the rear guard because the Poleszczucy [local inhabitants of Polesie] are firing at the rear detachments. A special company from the navy carries out executions in the villages. Often burning fires mark the path of the army." (GSHI, File "Brygada KOP 'Polesie.'") In the last two weeks of September the gap between the Poles and other nationalities living in the area widened into an abyss.

According to many Polish witnesses, from different areas of eastern Poland, the Red Army behaved very well in its initial contact with the local population (HI, PGC, Białystok: 5; Kobryń: 3; Szczuczyn: 3; Stryj: 8, 9, 11; Brasław: 3; Wilejka: 5; Postawy: 6; Dzisna: 5, 6; Zdołbunów: 9; Kowel: 8, 9, 10; Łuniniec, 6: Box 10, Lwów: 4014; Box 501, File "MSZ

War Through Children's Eyes

1940," December 24, 1939). But then, except for sporadic skirmishes with isolated and disorganized units of the Polish army, it encountered little resistance in the area,[9] and the local inhabitants received it, on the whole, very well. It was the rule rather than the exception for villages and towns to greet Red Army units with the traditional symbols of hospitality—a group of peasants offering, in a centuries-old gesture, a loaf of bread and a measure of salt; flowers thrown at passing soldiers; "triumphal arches" hastily erected across the road, as on a festive day, or, in communities better informed politically, a display of red banners (easily prepared by cutting the white stripe off the Polish flag). Sometimes Ukrainian national colors were flown by the cheering population. (HI, PGC, Box 10, Lwów: 7129.)

Such improvised manifestations of goodwill and friendliness were not to everyone's liking. Again the dividing line of ethnicity became apparent—the Polish population of the area, subdued and frightened in this hostile environment, remained aloof and resentful of the celebrating Jews, Ukrainians, Belorussians, or, as they very often called themselves, the "locals." Not every non-Polish person, however, welcomed the Red Army units (HI, PGC, Włodzimierz Wołyński: 3–4; Zdołbunów: 4; Lida: 3). Older peasants, for instance, who remembered the 1920 war, were suspicious of the "Bolsheviks," and many were altogether suspicious of any change. But even a small group of enthusiasts was enough to make a visible display of hospitality, and such groups were plentiful throughout the area.

Even before the Soviets entered, citizens' committees or militias were spontaneously formed in many places to replace the local Polish administration, which had either fled or lost the ability to enforce order (HI, PGC, Skałat: 4; Lida: 4; Kowel: 4, 5; Kobryń: 2, 3; Brasław: 2). These committees often acted as hosts to Red Army units. This process of filling the vacuum of authority attracted a wide variety of people, who for a few days were left in charge. Then, slowly, they were weeded out or put under the firm control of NKVD operatives or party organizers. But in the first moment of encounter, the Soviet commanders relied on such welcoming committees and militias. The Soviets armed them or authorized them to carry the weapons that they had already acquired and entrusted them with protecting their communities against "class enemies." Their primary immediate task involved ferreting out hiding Polish officers and policemen.

These first militias were a strange lot. In some areas, particularly in the larger towns where the majority of the 1.7 million Jews living in this territory dwelt, they were predominantly Jewish, often organized by communist sympathizers. Sometimes they were formed by the activists of the Ukrainian nationalist movement—for a few days some militia detachments in Lwów, wearing yellow and blue (the Ukrainian colors) arm bands, rode in cars belonging to the Ukrainian milk cooperative, Masłosojuz, flying Ukrainian flags (HI, PGC, Box 10, Lwów: 4352, 9722). In other cases local peasants, who had already been ambushing Polish soldiers and colonists in the area for a day or two, exchanged, more or less willingly, their vigilante status for the respectability of official squads enforcing law and order. Numerous militia units, all over the "liberated" territory, included common criminals in their ranks (Docs. no. 15, 100).[10]

It is not surprising that the Soviets should utilize criminals to subdue the conquered territory and the potentially hostile population since they used criminals in camps throughout Russia as auxiliaries and treated them better and trusted them more than politically suspect people. Common criminals were viewed in the USSR as "class allies" whose cooperation in the effort to stamp out the *social'no opasnyj* (socially harmful) element, that is, class enemies, was most welcome.

The Red Army broke open jails along its way—Who else could have been kept there but class enemies of the Polish "masters"?—a logical deduction since during the first days of the war scores of Ukrainian nationalists and communist sympathizers had been arrested in Poland. Red Army commanders, on their westward march, had no time to ask for character references from everyone ready to assist them in organizing the new order. Front-line soldiers and officers of the Red Army knew that the old order in the conquered territory had to be inverted, that those on the top and on the bottom of the social scale would trade positions. Naturally, prisoners of the Polish government were more trustworthy than those who had not been in jail; a coachman was a better candidate for town office than a civil servant or a politician; a doorman was better fit to run a large enterprise than an engineer; a porter made a perfect railroad stationmaster; and the poorest peasants were promoted over everyone else to village committees (HI, PGC, Box 10, Lwów: 4107, 5156, 8656; Łomża: 13, 16; Łuniniec: 21; Postawy: 42).

But it would be wrong to attribute all the violence of the early days to internecine struggle among the local inhabitants. Although their actions toward each other were probably more devastating than the executions carried out by the Red Army,[11] Soviet conduct was by no means as innocent as many witnesses reported. The army did not turn randomly against the population but committed numerous murders, primarily of Polish officers and policemen (Doc. no. 19). These were not isolated killings, perpetrated hastily on the march against more or less accidentally encountered individuals, although such incidents did occur (Docs. no. 3, 33, 70, 74).[12] In many instances whole detachments or their officers, already in captivity, were killed indiscriminately.[13]

The first visual contact between the Soviets and the population of eastern Poland revealed something that neither side anticipated. The Red Army was, of course, an army, but there was something odd about its makeup. True, its tanks rolled proudly along streets and country roads, but then horsemen and horse-drawn supply carts came. Most of the animals appeared to be on their last legs. Soldiers poured in endlessly—there were thousands of them—but some had saddles and some did not; some had shoes, but others only cloth wrapped around their feet; some wore long coats, others short ones; some had belts, while others had only strings attached to their rifles (Docs. no. 17, 19, 43, 110). And there was a strange look on their faces—a mixture of suspicion, incredulity, and joy. For they literally could not believe their eyes when they saw those immense, unbelievable riches. Take, for example, the peasants' horses and cattle, all so well fed and well kept. Many a Red Army soldier jumped on a grazing horse and sped away. Many swapped their nags for the healthy and strong horse of a helpless peasant. Then, too, there was food, in dazzling amounts and varieties: orchards bearing fruit to which they freely helped themselves, food offered in peasants' huts, including delicacies rarely seen in their kolkhozes or home-towns—butter, sour cream, meat, sausage, eggs, cheese. But perhaps the greatest revelation came when they reached the towns with their material objects and commodities: shoes, clothes, fabrics, and industrial products of all sorts—watches, for example, were a great wonder. And all this could be seen in the shops; it could be touched, bought, appropriated.

It was a very confusing experience for Red Army soldiers who knew they had come to liberate their oppressed blood brothers from the masters' yoke. For they also knew that the masters, by definition, were a small minority and that everyone else was suffering deprivation. But where were the masses if everyone lived so well? (This is even more ironical since the eastern half was the poorest part of Poland, which itself was rather poor by contemporary European standards.)

Before being ordered into Poland, Red Army personnel had been warned of propaganda tricks that would be pulled on them in this foreign country, and they were taught how to protect themselves and how to behave (HI, PGC, Box 423, File "Okupacja Sowiecka").[14] There were even standard phrases to memorize such as "*U nas vsë est'* " (we have everything) and "*U nas ètogo mnogo*" (we have plenty of that). But as the soldiers saw many commodities for the first time in their lives, they blundered repeatedly and made fools of themselves. Soon the boldest young pranksters in Lwów and other towns were entertaining audiences by engaging soldiers in conversations about Soviet factories that produced oranges, Greta Garbo's, and Amsterdams (Doc. no. 77).[15]

ECONOMIC CONSEQUENCES OF THE "NEW ORDER"

Like most conquering armies, the first orders of the Soviet military authorities imposed an all-night curfew and instructed everyone to return to work without delay. During the next few days, a number of regulations that established the general framework of the new order in the conquered territories were issued. The one with the most immediate impact on life in eastern Poland was the introduction of the ruble as legal tender in the occupied areas, with a value equal to that of the Polish złoty (Doc. no. 98).[16] This regulation was issued jointly with another ordering that all shops stay open and that merchants sell their stock at prewar prices.

Ostensibly, the primary consideration behind these decisions was concern for the welfare of the local population, since artificial shortages, hoarding, and subsequent skyrocketing prices add a heavy material burden to the sufferings of ordinary people whose lives are already disrupted by warfare. But this was neither the motivation behind nor the practical consequence of the Soviet decrees. These regulations were part of a comprehensive policy to exploit the newly acquired territories. They also served to prevent any outburst of uncontrolled behavior and anarchy among the occupiers themselves. The Soviet authorities must have realized that Red Army soldiers, seeing the abundance of foodstuffs and material goods, would be unable to resist temptation and would loot everything in sight unless provided with other means of acquiring goods, as indeed they were. Soviet officers and soldiers bought inordinate amounts of commodities once they found—much to their surprise—that sales were unrationed and that quantities were unlimited. They did not even bother to ask about prices.[17] The evidence is unequivocal: it was not so much the panicky conquered population but the greedy conquering army that frantically bought up everything (Docs. no. 19, 46, 78, 94).[18] Added to this was outright theft, requisitions, and, ultimately, expropriation of private and state-owned property.

The radical redistribution of material property that soon took place in eastern Poland undercut nearly everyone's material basis of existence. Within a few months, landowners, well-to-do peasants, industrialists, petite bourgeoisie, craftsmen, merchants, professionals, civil servants, and police and army personnel had their property confiscated or found themselves unemployed (and often unemployable) as a result of the dissolution of the Polish state and regardless of ethnic background. The bulk of the material resources seized by Soviet authorities either went to maintain the occupying army and the constantly growing police and administrative apparatus imported from the USSR or was simply shipped to the Soviet Union (Docs. no. 19, 74, 80, 85). Factories were dismantled and shipped to Russia: almost the entire Białystok textile industry was transported east. Stocks of supplies and finished products were carted away. Government buildings were demolished and sent piecemeal to Russia (wooden floors, doors, stoves, brass and iron handles, tiles, and military barracks were particularly susceptible to deportation). Hospital and school equipment, furniture—anything that could be of use—was shipped (HI, PGC, Box 10, Wilno: 7966; Szczuczyn: 10, 11; Kobryń: 21; Brasław: 8, 9; Wilejaka: 19; Postawy: 15; Dzisna: 17; Kostopol: 11; Zdołbunów: 14; Kowel: 26, 27; Stryj: 20, 21; Białystok: 29; Łuniniec: 20; Równe: 18; Box 10, Lwów: 10976, 6613, 7588).[19] Oil, food-stuffs, and cattle, on the other hand, were shipped through Przemyśl to Germany in accordance with the economic cooperation clause of the Friendship Treaty with Hitler (HI, PGC, Box 10, Lwów: 8793).

From the first day, Soviet economic policy in occupied Poland was clearly exploitative. The redistribution of goods consisted of a takeover of resources by the Soviet state. The heaviest burden fell on the well-to-do strata of Polish society, simply because they had things that could be taken away. But neither the peasants nor the working class of Western Belorussia and Western Ukraine benefited from the new economic system. True, for the first few months after the village committees were organized, the poorer peasants were encouraged to help themselves to property expropriated by the new authorities from land-owners or Polish military colonists.[20] But they were soon as heavily taxed as everyone else; they were ordered to repay all back taxes due the Polish state, subjected to corvées (chopping or transporting wood or constructing roads), and periodically called on to make "gifts to the Red Army"—food, meat, hay, poultry, or whatever they "decided" during meetings organized by the village committees (HI, PGC, Łomża: 91; Skałat: 37; Równe: 17; Dzisna: 14; Box 10, Lwów: 7301; see also Docs. no. 4, 106). Even the inventories that individual peasants were allowed to retain were not truly their own. The village committees compiled detailed registers of livestock and household goods and imposed severe restrictions on their use; nothing could be sold or transferred without committee authorization (HI, PGC, Łuniniec: 19; Kobryń: 18; Bras-law: 8; Wilejka: 17, 18; Postawy: 14; Zdołbunów: 10; Kowel: 24; Lida:

10; Równe: 16; see also Doc. no. 46). Similarly, peasants had to secure a special permit to kill a calf, pig, or chicken. Property rights were effectively suspended.

There is nothing surprising in this, considering that long-range Soviet plans called for agricultural collectivization in this territory. Once the Soviets decided to incorporate Western Ukraine and Western Belorussia into the USSR, no other solution to the agrarian problem could be considered. But since this decision surely predated the invasion, one must assume that the peasants' fate was predetermined—they were soon to be collectivized.[21] The land redistribution that occurred in the initial days and primarily benefited poor Ukrainian and Belorussian peasants was only a temporary arrangement. It was, most likely, a propaganda device to elicit the active participation of the lower strata of local society in transforming the social structure.[22] Behind the slogan of retaking land from the rich, vigilante groups in every community could be mobilized to make the rounds, taking away inventory and livestock from some, killing a few others, and assisting in the parceling of land. But the majority of people were suspicious of land redistribution since it was carried out hastily and without formality. Few, if any, planted the plots they received from the village committees. In some instances, peasants returned to former owners various objects that had been redistributed from landed estates (HI, PGC, Box 10, Lwów: 3949). Redistribution, it seems, served first of all to terrorize the local population, to create an atmosphere of insecurity and fear—a necessary prerequisite for the smooth future implementation of radical social revolution. The great atrocities and pervasive lawlessness of the time profoundly shook all communities, rendering them susceptible to demands that otherwise would have been considered intolerable.

On the one hand, the Soviet authorities encouraged and directed this popular retribution (Docs. no. 64, 103). But on the other hand, they curtailed it when they thought fit to do so. They executed many militiamen and committeemen for committing excesses, which, in their line of work, so to speak, were commonplace (HI, PGC, Box 10, Lwów: 7492, 7301; Równe: 8581; Box 501, File "MSZ 1940: Okupacja sowiecka w Polsce"). It was as if the Soviets were letting the population know that they could unleash or curtail terror as they pleased. It was a very persuasive lesson in intimidation.

Among the working classes, living conditions did not improve under Soviet rule. Workers were subject to a ruthless system of work discipline (Doc. no. 107),[23] and remuneration was contingent on fulfillment of quotas that were often established in a random and capricious manner.[24] Redistribution of material resources belonging to the propertied

14   *War Through Children's Eyes*

classes of Polish society and to the Polish state did not raise the living standard of the Polish worker, who was not a beneficiary of this transfer of goods. If anything he was a victim: he lost his job or his savings.[25] The general impoverishment of the population disproportionately affected those who had very little to begin with.

Within a few months drastic shortages developed,[26] and very little could be bought through the official network of retail stores (misleadingly called "cooperatives" although they were state-owned shops), since the only commodities that the Soviets brought into the occupied territories were salt, kerosene, matches, and tobacco (*Pravda*, October 13, 1939). Consequently people had to sell their possessions in order to buy food and fuel on the open market; those who had nothing to sell could not afford to buy (Docs. no. 19, 98, 104).[27] As a result, the man who had little to spare before the Soviets came found himself in dire need of basic necessities after their rule was established.

Nearly everyone recalled queues in front of the few shops that sold goods, mostly bread, at prices people could afford (Docs. no. 19, 43, 83, 99). But as the supply was insufficient due to meager production and expanded demand (in most cities the population doubled because of the influx of refugees from the German-occupied area), people stood long hours, often in vain. Many queued overnight to make sure they could buy some food the next morning. And then there were the Soviet soldiers who, ignoring the lines, went into the stores and bought as much as they wanted. Militiamen often accosted and arrested those in queues whose clothing or looks betrayed their upper- or middle-class origin.

There were scores of homeless people all over eastern Poland. Some, fearing for their lives, fled their households and villages. Hundreds of thousands of refugees rented rooms or stayed with family or friends, while many literally had to live in the streets—in Białystok, for instance, which was packed with Jewish refugees (Docs. no. 19, 44, 56, 104). In every town and village the Soviet occupiers took over living space simply by requisitioning apartments. Many families were ordered to abandon their dwellings, leaving their furniture and household utensils behind for Soviet officers, administrators, and party officials (Docs. no. 63, 94). In Równe whole streets were emptied of their local inhabitants, and newly arrived Soviet families moved into the vacated houses or apartments (HI, PGC, Równe: 12). As one of the Ukrainians interviewed by Milena Rudnycka said at the time: "Everyone lived, ate, and dressed worse than before."[28]

One quick glance was sufficient to note the substantial deterioration in the quality of life. Many recalled the sensory experience of the Soviet presence—images, sounds, and smells—as the most persuasive and startling evidence of the dramatic change in living conditions. The threat of arrest and deportation or the necessity to hide one's political past complicated many people's lives. But the immediate and all-pervasive realization that a new society had already been installed came from the new look of houses and streets and the people in them; from the new songs, music, and propaganda broadcast full blast over speakers mounted in the streets; from unfamiliar odors, like that of the tar with which the footwear of Soviet soldiers was impregnated.

The visual change was the most striking. "Within a week our town was completely changed: dirty all around, no one caring to keep it clean, heaps of refuse thrown away by the army disintegrating in the streets. Sidewalks, trees, lawns all destroyed by trucks and tractors." (HI, PGC, Włodzimierz Wołyński: 39; see also Doc. no. 77.) There had been a war in the area, but the brief military operations caused relatively little destruction to life and property. The new look was more a result of the occupation than of the war itself, and it promptly passed, as if by contagion, from things to people. The population suddenly became acutely aware that external appearance was indicative of social origin. Dressing in certain ways or carrying certain objects increased the probability of being stopped in the street by militiamen and invited snide comments from supporters of the new order, as well as curiosity from Soviet soldiers. It took only a few days for the population in the streets to change its look and undergo a rapid process of outward, external proletarianization. Soon everyone looked more or less like a worker going to or from work. No one wore extravagant colors or fancy clothes; ties rapidly disappeared from men's wardrobes; and scarves replaced hats on women's heads. People instinctively started to care less about external appearance. They went out, indistinguishable in the large crowd of similar men and women, unkempt, hurried, and color-less.[29] On this subdued proletarianized backdrop, a new reality was systematically imposed. Various symbols of Polish statehood and cul-tural tradition were slowly eliminated—memorial plaques, monu-ments, Polish eagles. "Lwów jest już bez lwów" (Lwów is now without lions) wrote a high-school friend to Danuta Polniaszek; the occupiers had removed the stone lions in front of the town hall. Street signs were rapidly changed, the Polish names in Latin characters replaced by Ukrainian inscriptions in Cyrillic.[30] Towns and villages were decorated with portraits of Soviet leaders, which appeared everywhere in all sizes, the biggest ones perhaps six by eight meters, on office buildings oc-cupied by the new administration. Banners with inscriptions and posters were hung in public places, some ridiculing the former Polish govern-ment, some showing despicable silhouettes of Polish officers or, for contrast, advertising the beauty and happiness of the lives of Soviet citizens (HI, PGC, Kowel: 2; Postawy: 20; Box 10, Lwów: 5723, 8479, 10190). On Hetman's Embankments in Lwów enormous red billboards with excerpts from the Soviet constitution written in gold were erected (HI, PGC, Box 10, Lwów: 6119).[31] Red stars popped up here and there, replacing old crosses, eagles, and, sometimes, the traditional rooster-shaped windvanes. The physiognomies of Soviet leaders invaded the interiors of buildings as well; in lieu of the familiar faces of Polish politicians, holy pictures, or small wooden crosses, they appeared on the walls of restaurants, offices, and classrooms (Doc. no. 40).[32]

People in the streets changed not only their appearance, but also their behavior. For one thing, the pace of street life changed. Rather than strolling leisurely or aimlessly, people pretended to walk quickly toward a specific destination. They avoided meeting each other in the street and engaging in conversation. "On October 21, I was walking down Żyblikiewicz Street with Mrs. Wanda S. We were talking about some family matters. Suddenly two men separated us brutally and proceeded to question us about the subject of our conversation. Since our answers were identical, we were released. But I know of people who were arrested in this manner." (HI, PGC, Box 10, Lwów: 3469; see also Lwów: 4100.) It was safest to walk alone, briskly.

There was also less courtesy, chivalry, and politeness in crowded tramways or public places, and women received less of the recognition and respect traditionally granted them. This was partly due to the overcrowding and shortages and the fatigue and irritation typical of situations of prolonged stress. But to a large extent it was another consequence of the law of mimicry, for the occupiers were, most conspicuously, lacking in social graces: "Their conduct was one of the main reasons why we looked upon them as if they were of a different mentality, as if they belonged to a different spiritual formation." To understand the experience of the Bolshevik occupation, one would have to know "how they moved, how they walked, how they sat, how they waved their hands."[33]

THE ADMINISTRATIVE REORGANIZATION

The initial regulations issued by the occupying authorities were essentially the same throughout the entire territory. Occasional local variations were of secondary importance: in some places people were required to register their radios (Równe), in others they had to turn them in (Skałat); Russian, Ukrainian, and Belorussian were made official languages, although in some villages (Krzywe, near Skałat, for example) zealous committees issued ordinances forbidding people to speak Polish. But the fundamental orders were identical everywhere: to turn in all weapons; to refuse shelter to Polish officers and policemen; to refrain from gathering in groups; and to remove all Polish state symbols and official portraits. Freedom of travel without official authorization was denied; confiscation of landed estates and larger industrial property was decreed (though this decision was "legalized" only at a later date, after the convocation of the national assemblies of Western Ukraine and Western Belorussia); all credits and loans from banks, merchants, or loan associations had to be repaid; and then—a request that was to be repeated many times over the next year and a half under many different pretexts—the population was ordered to register (Docs. no. 64, 112).[34] Many people were arrested when they registered, military personnel, including reserve officers, in particular. Finally, everyone was asked to return to work, and a statement was issued announcing that no one would be prosecuted for holding office under the Polish government. But this promise was consistently violated.

For the next few months the occupiers proceeded to overhaul and expand the administrative structure of eastern Poland. They wanted to create a system to identify and keep track of every individual in the territory. Registration was insufficient for this purpose—the supply of information on all citizens had to be steady and constantly up-to-date, rather than intermittent.

The Soviet decision—made before the invasion—was to annex all conquered territories, which accounted for the speed and efficiency with which the new public order was introduced. The decision was formally implemented within roughly six weeks of the invasion, but the scenario of the so-called plebiscite, in which the population allegedly expressed its wish to join the "happy family of nations" federated within the USSR, must have been prepared beforehand, given the tremendous organizational effort that went into it.

The Soviets had some genuine supporters among the ethnic minorities, but their motivation derived more from an appreciation of what the Soviet arrival prevented than from an espousal of communist ideals. The Jews saw in the Soviet occupation a lesser evil than Nazi occupation, and the Belorussians and the Ukrainians rejoiced mainly over the end of Polish domination. But the new Soviet "national" policy led to considerable confusion. For even though the minorities at first experienced a sense of relief at the end of Polish rule and welcomed the de-polonization of the local administration, the economic redress against Polish landowners, and especially the rapid growth of minority-language schools and cultural outlets,[35] with time it became more and more obvious that those who thought seriously about an ethnic Ukrainian, Belorussian, or Jewish revival under the Soviets fell very easily into the poorly defined and dangerous category of "nationalists."[36] Furthermore, the economic expropriation of small businessmen, craftsmen, and merchants affected mainly the local Jewish population for whom these pursuits, rather than agriculture, were traditional. The Poles themselves reported that the national minorities' initial feelings of welcome, which led to a warm reception of the Red Army and collaboration with the Soviet authorities, cooled toward the end of the occupation (HI, PGC, Box 10, Lwów: 3926; Łuniniec: 60,61; Wilejka: 64; Białystok: 99; Postawy: 48; Kowel: 71, 72; Stryj: 60; Szczuczyn: 50; Lida: 50; see also Docs. no. 77, 104).[37]

In 1940 considerable numbers of Ukrainian nationalists fled to the Generalgouvernement (the German-occupied part of Poland) or moved there legally, aided by the German repatriation commission sent to Lwów in accordance with the Russo-German Boundary and Friendship Treaty.[38] Perhaps even more telling, this commission was besieged by tens of thousands of Jews who wanted to return home to German-occupied Poland, which they had fled in panic a few months earlier (HI, AC, Box 38: 10560, 10580, 10584; Box 40: 14017; see also Docs. no. 117, 118, 120). This Jewish population of refugees from west-central Poland constituted the bulk of the June 1940 deportation into the USSR.

In any case, the initial collaboration of ethnic minorities allowed for the effective penetration of local society. The effect of this collaboration on the occupier's administration cannot be overestimated. And it is to the Soviets' credit as practitioners of revolution that they were able to appreciate and nurture such local support as long as they needed it. They were carrying out a social revolution in eastern Poland, which could not be accomplished without *local* support, as experience in their own country had shown. A battle could be won or pacification achieved with imported manpower, but not a social revolution. There were not enough professional revolutionaries to tip the scale by sheer weight of numbers—the population (guided, cajoled, or coerced) had to subdue itself to a new pattern of allegiance and life in common.

A new administration was quickly established in the conquered territories. In the countryside it took the form of a network of committees—village, *gmina* (the smallest territorial administrative unit), and county. Typically, a visiting Soviet official would call a meeting of the village population to "elect" a village committee.[39] In higher administrative echelons, the *gmina* and county committees, either Soviet officials or Polish communist sympathizers (usually Jews) always held supervisory positions. In addition to committees, militia detachments were formed, which were soon subsumed under the command of NKVD (the Soviet secret police) operatives. This was the network through which the social and political transformation was to be implemented.

In the first phase of the takeover, committees were used mainly for expropriations and arrests. But the Soviets soon gave them a more important task: a mass mobilization of the local population in support of the new regime. On October 22, barely one month after they crossed the Polish frontier, the Soviets organized a plebiscite in eastern Poland. The entire population was called out to vote for candidates to the national people's assemblies of Western Belorussia and Western Ukraine. The enormous effort that went into this election required manpower and an organizational network capable of contacting and bringing to the ballot box every individual in the conquered territory. Thus, the committees' task was never limited to the simple routine of daily administration. After assisting in the initial exercise of intimidating the local population, the committees were then supposed to draw the inhabitants together and mobilize them on behalf of the new regime. From the beginning the purpose of the new administration was not to restore peace and order to the conquered territory so that it could be quietly governed and exploited, but to prepare it for incorporation into the Soviet Union, in other words, to lay the groundwork for the installation of Soviet society there.

In larger villages and towns the replacement of the Polish administration followed a slightly different pattern. A temporary administration was put in charge, with Soviet military, party, or police officials at the head. Sometimes a prominent post was filled with a newly promoted representative of the people, such as Karmazyn, a coachman from a Lwów brewery, who was appointed deputy chairman of the Lwów Temporary Administration. But initially, as a rule, most Polish functionaries (except policemen, judicial officials, and titular heads of administration) were left in office until their replacements learned their duties (HI, PGC, Box 10, Lwów: 1594, 8656; Równe: 10; Zdołbunów: 17; Kowel: 55; Białystok: 8, 13). Only after the new Soviet substitutes had acquired the necessary skills were the Polish officials dismissed—a well thought-out strategy, for revolutionary fervor cannot replace expertise on short notice.

This somewhat greater reliance on trained personnel previously employed in the local Polish administration did not seem to jeopardize the Soviet goal of penetrating urban social milieus, where the reorganization of either residential or work communities offered greater opportunities. Indeed, as a mandatory condition for employment one had to join the appropriate labor union (*profsoyuz*) organized by every factory, office, or professional association. Each person had to fill out a detailed questionnaire or relate his autobiography at an open meeting where he could be challenged or questioned by any of his workmates.[40] At the same time very close supervision was initiated in places of residence. All inhabitants had to register with the authorities, and doormen were made responsible for ensuring that everyone complied with registration regulations. Doormen were periodically called in to militia head-quarters to report on the tenants living in their houses.[41]

During the pre-election campaign, mobilization within neighborhoods and at work was used to generate support for the new regime. The apparatus of city administration was too distant from the lives of ordinary residents to be used as an instrument of social revolution. Instead, the intimacy of the workplace and residential area was invaded, so that no one could hope to hide from the new regime and its supporters.

THE PLEBISCITE

There is some confusion surrounding the circumstances under which the call for organizing elections in the occupied territory was launched. The first mention of the elections in *Pravda* appeared on October 11,[42] but the decision must have been made in Moscow, most likely several weeks before being publicized in the press. As early as September, party and propaganda personnel were being dispatched rapidly into the conquered territories, on the heels of the front-line army detachments. The first secretary of the Belorussian Communist Party, Pantelejmon Ponomarenko, in an interview with *Pravda* on October 7, spoke of the fraternal assistance offered to Western Belorussia—by that date about eight hundred party and Komsomol (the Soviet youth organization) activists had been sent from the Belorussian republic. One hundred journalists and three hundred specialists in "education, health care, finance, and commerce" had also arrived.[43] Most likely Western Ukraine was equally well supplied by Khrushchev, who was at the time Ponomarenko's counterpart in the Ukrainian republic. "Newspapers," wrote *Pravda* as early as September 23, 1939, "have begun to appear in all community and district centers." Using Red Army personnel, local supporters, and professional party workers, the Soviets constructed an extensive and reliable network for the propaganda and mobilization necessary to assault the population with an unprecedented election campaign.

For the first three weeks of October, everyone was preoccupied with the elections (Doc. no. 98). On the streets people could not miss the pre-election banners and posters or the propaganda broadcasts; every other day at work, they were called for a pre-election meeting; late in the evening they were often herded into an apartment to listen to a neighborhood agitator. The very word "meeting," as part of Soviet political parlance, was so deeply ingrained in the minds of the population that even barely literate children, three or four years later, would list "meetings" along with night house searches, hunger, arrest, and deportation when enumerating the plagues that afflicted their families under Soviet rule (Docs. no. 46, 104, 110).

The entire territory of Western Belorussia and Western Ukraine was divided into electoral districts of about five thousand people each. These electoral districts were in turn subdivided into much smaller units for the purpose of compiling voters' registers and organizing propaganda meetings three or four times a week.[44] An agitator chose a spacious apartment, house, or peasant hut and assembled everyone entrusted to his or her political guidance when they returned home from work. Attendance was mandatory and checked against a list of inhabitants.[45] These lists were prepared with great care because they later formed the basis of voters' registers.[46] People were also made to attend propaganda gatherings at work, school, or university. If they were called to a meeting during working hours, they had to work overtime on other days in order to make up the lost time (HI, PGC, Białystok: 34).

Strangely, despite the intensity of the pre-election campaign, most voters compelled to cast ballots confessed to not knowing what, or even whom, they were asked to vote for (HI, PGC, Box 10, Lwów: 3340, 3962, 8238, 9707; Łomża: 44, 71; Skałat: 31; Łuniniec: 38; Jaworów: 24; Kobryń: 22; Szczuczyn: 30, 31; Lida: 16, 17; Brasław: 13, 14; Wilejka: 40, 41; Postawy: 32, 33; Dzisna: 36; Kostopol: 12, 13; Stryj: 37, 38; Kowel: 55; Zdołbunów: 17; Białystok: 55; see also Doc. no. 32).[47] The issue of uniting Western Ukraine or Western Belorussia with the Soviet Union was rarely, if ever, raised during the pre-election campaign.[48] Instead, a variety of themes were routinely discussed: that England and France were "political prostitutes" and warmongers;[49] that the Red Army and the Soviet Union were invincible and would soon conquer the rest of Europe (Doc. no. 113); that life in Russia was beautiful, while people had been miserable and downtrodden in Poland before the war.[50] No wonder, then, that the pre-election meetings were dreadfully boring, particularly since there were so many of them and they could not be avoided.

The sole concern throughout the campaign was to make people

realize that they must vote. Direct threats were made against anyone who considered not voting. People were told that they would be dismissed from work, arrested, or sent to Siberia if they did not (HI, PGC, Łuniniec: 25; Wilejka: 24, 25; Łomża: 42; Dzisna: 23; Kostopol: 14; Kowel: 36, 37; Białystok: 35), and the intimidation and coercion concomitant with the pre-election meetings made these threats highly credible. At the same time the population was cajoled into participating by promises of benefits.[51] Just before the election food supplies in the towns improved significantly. There also seemed to be fewer arrests and night searches.

Ideological propaganda in the form of speeches about the decay of capitalism and the good life in the Soviet Union was added to this combination of threat and bribery. Readings of the Soviet constitution were frequently organized by agitators who often spoke only Russian— a language that few of the tired and angry participants understood (HI, PGC, Box 10, Lwów: 4450, 5146; Łomża: 41; Białystok: 32).

A distinct portion of the meetings was devoted to presenting or electing candidates. Most of the candidates were unknown to their constituencies (Docs. no. 78, 79, 95); they included Soviet military commanders and party functionaries (HI, PGC, Box 10, Lwów: 2577, 11262; Dzisna: 36; Kostopol: 16; Kowel: 40, 41; Stryj: 29; Szczuczyn: 21–23; Białystok: 39, 40; Skałat: 29; Łomża: 71). Some familiar local people among the candidates were identified with scorn as "a thief," "a housemaid," "a farmhand," or "a woman of dubious reputation" (HI, PGC, Łomża: 57; Brasław: 17, 18; Zdołbunów: 20, 21; Kowel: 41, 42; Szczuczyn: 21; Łuniniec: 29; Skałat: 29).[52] Among the candidates were also some randomly chosen, unsuspecting citizens. Adam Polewka, for example, a writer who later fled to the Generalgouvernement, was visited one morning by three grim-looking Soviet officers. He was convinced that they had come to arrest him. They proceeded to interview him, checking his answers against a file they had brought along. When they finished, the senior Soviet inquisitor shook Polewka's hand and announced proudly to him, "You will be a deputy to the National Assembly!"[53]

The meetings at which candidates were elected faithfully followed a simple scenario. The agitator-chairman would introduce a candidate and either read his autobiography or let the candidate do it himself. Then he would ask the sacramental question: Who is *against* the election of this candidate? Typically, there would be silence and no show of hands, at which point the meeting would be closed.[54]

The pre-election mobilization was utterly confusing. It sufficiently cowed the people so they could be processed through the voting station on election day. It also showed that the Soviets had the ability to reach everyone—people realized that they would be severely punished if they did not show up for the election. Still they were very confused about their purpose,[55] but that benefited the organizers of the new order. For although the cost of not participating was hammered into people's minds during the pre-election campaign, the consequences of participating were foggy and unclear to them, and thus less feared.

This immense propaganda effort bore fruit on October 22. On October 23, *Pravda* reported: "The population of Lwów went to vote in a friendly atmosphere. Many people arrived together, organized in columns . . . In Białystok people gathered during the night in front of the polling stations, before they opened . . . No one has to force the electorate to go to the voting stations. Everyone went willingly of his own accord." As usual, these reports were a mixture of lies, half-truths, and misinterpretations. It was true that many voters arrived at the polling stations in marching columns, but they did so precisely because few were willing to go on their own (HI, PGC, Box 10, Lwów: 3874, 7585, 10396).

From 4:00 A.M. on election day (that is, two hours before the curfew ended), doormen were reminding people that they must vote. Later, each hour, some civilian would arrive, demanding that those whose names had not yet been crossed off the eligible voters' list promptly fulfill their citizen's obligation. Around noon militiamen showed up to inquire who had not yet voted and why. From early afternoon on people were escorted to the voting stations (HI, PGC, Box 10, Lwów: 10193; Łomża: 57; Brasław: 19; Wilejka: 34, Postawy: 27; Dzisna: 30; Kostopol: 16, 17; Zdołbunów: 21, 22; Jaworów: 25; Kobryń: 32; Lida: 25; Kowel: 45).[56]Equally popular was another method of persuasion, which may explain the eagerness of some in Białystok to vote early: food was used as an inducement. Throughout the occupied territory each polling station had a buffet where, after voting, people could treat themselves to a glass of vodka or tea, to a sandwich, a piece of sausage, some sugar or candies, tobacco or cigarettes. Latecomers risked missing the choicest items.[57]

Election organizers went out of their way to make sure that everyone voted. The local authorities sent cars or carts for the elderly or for those who were (or pretended to be) sick (Doc. no. 83); soldiers with ballot boxes toured hospitals, collecting votes from bedridden patients (HI, PGC, Kowel: 52; Kobryń: 37; Box 10, Lwów: 3761, 7977); a ballot box was brought to Jews praying in the synagogue on Żołkiewska Street in Lwów, and their votes were recorded in less than an hour (HI, PGC, Box 10, Lwów: 9663). Electoral commissions were empowered to enfranchise anyone they thought fit (Red Army personnel voted in several locations), and thus even those who traveled or who were away from home were not excused. Needless to say, others, going from one voting station to another, voted several times (HI, PGC, Box 10, Lwów: 3166).

Militiamen, Soviet officials, or soldiers in uniform were visibly present at all voting stations. Each voter was checked against a list. Then he was handed a ballot and instructed to deposit it in the ballot box. If the voter wished to cross out the candidate's name (this was a plebiscite with basically only one candidate on the ballot in every precinct, who could be either rejected or accepted), he could withdraw to a specially designated place behind a curtain, but that, he was informed, was not necessary if he wanted to vote for the candidate. Also, the polling station was arranged so that anyone seeking privacy was highly visible—he had to go to another room or to a distant corner (HI, PGC, Box 10, Lwów: 2233; Dzisna: 32; Szczuczyn: 27; Lida: 26; Białystok: 48). The ballots often had to be put into envelopes first and then dropped into the ballot boxes. Many voters noticed that the envelope was numbered before being handed to them. It can be assumed that the number corresponded to the one beside their name on the voters' list (HI, PGC, Łomża: 58; Wilejka: 35, 36; Postawy: 29; Zdołbunów: 23; Kowel: 51; Stryj: 32, 33; Szczuczyn: 27; Białystok: 46, 47). In some places the procedure was further simplified. People were handed sealed envelopes and told to deposit them in the ballot box (HI, PGC, Łomża: 60; Włodzimierz Wołyński: 28). Peasants in Wołuck village were told to sign ballot cards before returning them; in Tauste village they were asked to sign a list on which the names of candidates appeared at the top (HI, PGC, Skałat: 34, 35; Włodzimierz Wołyński: 28). In the village of Lips, the organizers, openly addressing all present in the voting station, announced that since so and so could not come, they were voting for them (HI, PGC, Łuniniec: 38). Such stories go on and on.

Yet despite the threatening visibility of the Soviets and their minions, many people did not yield to them. Some crossed out candidates' names or wrote obscenities on the ballot;[58] quite a few managed to stay away altogether. More important, there were entire hamlets and villages that refused to vote. Communities in which no one sided with the occupier found strength in their collective will to resist the new masters.[59]

After the election things moved rapidly to the foregone conclusion. On October 26 and 28, the national assemblies of Western Ukraine and Western Belorussia met in theaters in Lwów and Białystok. The oldest deputies—Prof. Kirilo Studyński in Lwów and some poor old peasant in Białystok—delivered opening speeches. Both national assemblies were called to vote on three issues: the incorporation of the province into the USSR; the confiscation and redistribution of land held by the church and large landowners; and the nationalization of banks and big industry.[60] Then delegations of deputies went to Moscow for a special session of the Supreme Soviet of the USSR, which was highlighted by Molotov's speech. On November 1 and 2, the Supreme Soviet, graciously consenting to popular demand, incorporated the occupied territories of Western Ukraine and Western Belorussia into the Soviet Union.

SOVIETIZATION VERSUS NAZIFICATION

After October 22 the sovietization of eastern Poland proceeded with new vigor. Arrests of "socially alien" elements increased dramatically, and mass deportations of the population were organized. Approximately 900,000 people (about every twelfth person living in the territory) were transported into Russia in four big waves under conditions that have only one parallel in history—the Nazi deportations to ghettos and concentration camps.

When Hitler attacked the Soviet Union in June 1941, the German army encountered a society in Western Ukraine and Western Belorussia significantly changed from barely two years before. For one thing, it had been decapitated, its leadership stratum, whether Ukrainian or Polish, eliminated through arrests and executions and its population depleted through deportations; it was materially exhausted and spiritually subdued as a result of the confiscations, exploitation, terror, and constant exposure to numbing propaganda; ethnic prejudices were exacerbated, especially anti-Semitism in reaction to the active Jewish participation in the local administration and militia.[61] The Soviet occupation shook the local society and set it in motion. People were displaced in both social and physical space.

But although the Soviet record in eastern Poland—measured by the impoverishment of the local population, by the number of those arrested and tortured (Docs. no. 40, 69), and by the scope of resettlement or deportations for forced labor or execution—was no better than the Nazi record for the same period in the western and central parts of the country, there was a difference in style and atmosphere between the two occupations. The pervasive contempt that the Nazis displayed towards the Jews and the Poles was absent under Soviet rule. The Soviet occupiers did not permanently stigmatize the local population as a group of outcasts. Many Soviets were nice and likable enough and had good rapport with the locals.

The crucial point is that the Soviets' behavior in occupied Poland and in their own country was similar. They, and their families, had experienced the same hardships to which the population of the newly liberated territories was now being subjected. "You'll get used to it or else you'll croak," they used to say, not maliciously, but merely summing up the commonsense wisdom life had taught them. They looked with forbearance on the frantic activity of this population, which was trying with great ingenuity to avoid the inevitable. But they knew better. "There are three categories of people in the Soviet Union," they tried to explain to their new co-citizens, "Those who were in jail, those who are in jail, and those who will be in jail."[62] And they did not mean this malevolently; rather, this was the story of their own lives.

This attitude was important in preserving a semblance of humanity under these altogether inhuman conditions. The Soviets in the occupied territories felt they were not exploiting, but sharing; they did not interpret their actions as discriminatory, but rather as bringing redress and equality; their intentions were not vicious or evil, but routine; they did not wish to humiliate or subdue, but to teach proper ways.

But let there be no mistake: the population of eastern Poland was brutalized, exploited and—there is no reason to avoid the word—massacred.[63] The organizers of the new order viewed this as normal, routine procedure, which does not in any way justify their actions. But it carries an additional message, one that could easily be overlooked but must be recorded and considered: the real hero, or martyr, of the stories told here by Polish children is not just the population of eastern Poland. Here is the fate of all the peoples of Soviet Russia. This is the story of Ukrainians, Russians, Lithuanians, Jews, Poles, Georgians, Tatars, Uzbeks, and of many others.

Illustrations

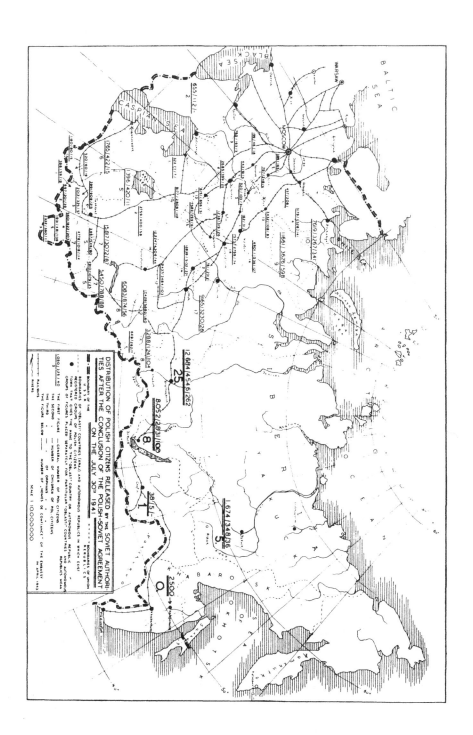

DISTRIBUTION OF POLISH CITIZENS RELEASED BY THE SOVIET AUTHORITIES AFTER THE CONCLUSION OF THE POLISH-SOVIET AGREEMENT ON THE JULY 30ᵗʰ 1941

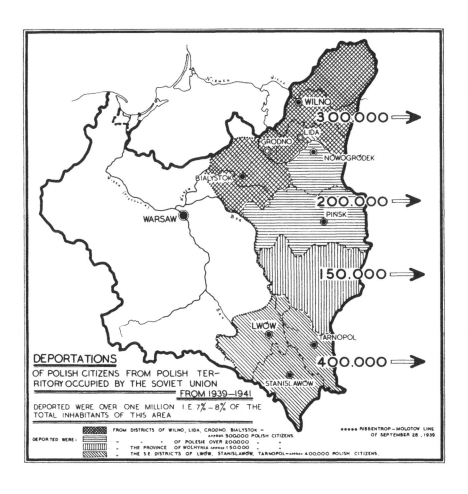

DEPORTATIONS

OF POLISH CITIZENS FROM POLISH TER-
RITORY OCCUPIED BY THE SOVIET UNION
FROM 1939—1941

DEPORTED WERE OVER ONE MILLION I.E. 7% — 8% OF THE
TOTAL INHABITANTS OF THIS AREA

DEPORTED WERE:
- FROM DISTRICTS OF WILNO, LIDA, GRODNO, BIALYSTOK — APPROX 300,000 POLISH CITIZENS.
- " " " OF POLESIE OVER 200,000 " "
- " THE PROVINCE OF WOLHYNIA APPROX 150,000 " "
- " THE S.E. DISTRICTS OF LWÓW, STANISLAWÓW, TARNOPOL — APPROX 400,000 POLISH CITIZENS.

••••• RIBBENTROP—MOLOTOV LINE OF SEPTEMBER 28, 1939.

Two maps prepared by the Cartographic Service of the Polish Army in the
East. (HI, PAC)

An identification card of a Polish girl, issued for the 1938–1939 school year in Wilejka. (HI, PAC)

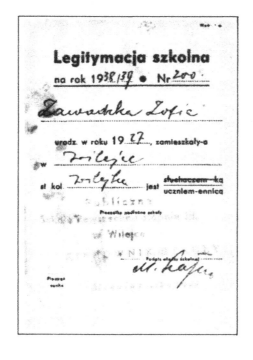

Identification card of a militia member from Lwów. One can see that the original Citizens' Guard, established by the Polish authorities, was later transformed into a Soviet militia, which illustrates the confusion of the transitional period during the Soviet occupation. (PAC)

A poster from Śniatyń announcing the contamination of the town's water supply with typhoid fever bacteria. It advises citizens to boil water before drinking. (HI, PGC)

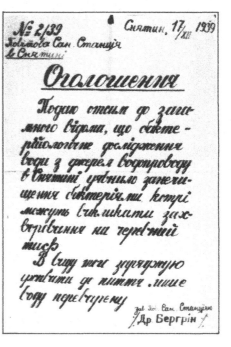

Kl. II a.

Zygmunt z Nowogródka

Więziony do Archgielska

Chodziłem po burówki i zapadałem
do błota jeszcze był śnieg a ja musiałem
iść pobawówki żeby zamienić na chleb zo
cały kosz pół pudowy dostawałsmy kilo
chleba. A Mamusia pracowała ciężko
jeszcze mamusia była chora musiała
pracować. Była u nas taka nęda że wszy
gryzły.

Document 35. (PGC)

Drawing by Ryszard S., first grade, ten years old. *Top:* "This is our settlement. And this is our hourse." *Bottom:* "I am pulling wood on sleds for mommy to kook dinner."

Zdzisław.

Zamieszkałem w Polsce w Przymyślu województwo Lwowskie powiat Drohobycz zostałem wywieziony z mamusią do Uzbekistanu do Bucharskiej obłaści Rejon Gurar.

Najsmutniejszym moim dniem był ten dzień w którem moja mamusia zachorowała w nocy. Niebyło lekarza ani nikogo tylko ja sam. Musiałem stać i grzać wody. Ale niebyło drzewa. Poleciałem na podwórze i znalazłem kawałek szczapki. Zapaliłem i zagrzałem wody bo bardzo kłuło matkę koło serca. Ale to nic nie pomogłoby musiałem iść do szpitala znowu aż do drugiego posiłka. Na drugi dzień gdy matka była w szpitalu poszedłem po lipiorki ale rosyjanki nie chciały sprzedać. Powiedzieli mnie że matka nie pracuje to niedadzą chleba. Ja odszedłem z płaczem i siadłem na okna. Siedziałem na oknie i skrobałem się bo bardzo gryzły wszy. Poszedłem na bazar i musiałem kraść marchew. Gdy matka szła ze szpitala to po drodze zemdlała bo była bardzo głodna. Ja siedziałem na oknie gdy zobaczyłem mamusię to poleciałem do niej. Ja opowiedziałem wszystko matce to matka poszła do komendanta a on jej odpowiedział że mu jemu do tego. Potem gdy było nabożeństwo i było wojsko Polskie to Rosjanie wyśmiewali się że my chodzimy na nabożeństwo. Szczęśliwy jestem że już wyjechałem z tego piekła.

Kozłowski Zdzisław uczeń Kl. III^a

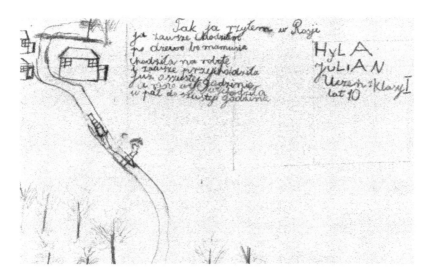

Drawing by Julian H., first grade, ten years old. "I thus lived in Russia I always went for wood because mother went to work and she always returned at six and in the morning she left at half past five." (HI, PGC)

Drawing by Zbigniew P., born 1931, in Lwów. "As it happens sometimes in Russia." (HI, PGC)

Ernest.

KLASA II A.

Wywieziony z osady Tajkury.
Powiat Zdołbunów Województwo Wołyńskie
do ross. Archangielskiej Obłaści.
rejon Siezynga. Mamusia i Siosrczysk
i brat zarobiliśmy po 10 rubli
tatuś został w Krakowie.
nas wszystkich było 7.8 troje. Chodziło
do roboty a dzieci było w domu
czasem chodziliśmy na jagody.
za dwa kilo jagod dawali dwa rubli
i tak na tym żyli. jak mamusia
zachorowała to my nie mieli co
dać, w zimie niemieli drzewa marzli
ja i brat chodzili do szkoły nas
w szkole bili zamiast uczyć obracał
się byłem wszystko mówił do rosjanów
uczył żeby nas bili w rossi siostra
chodziła do ochronki rosianny biły
i pruzni pojechała do szpitala.
my jusz wyjeżdżali to umarła
mnie w rossi zęby bolały nie nie leczyły.
—

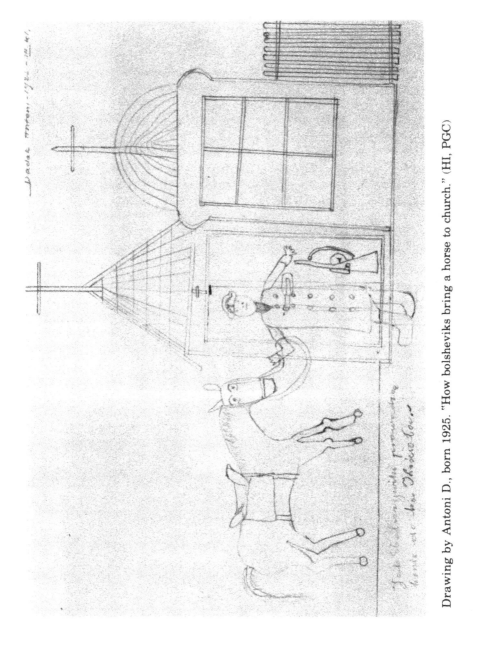

Drawing by Antoni D., born 1925. "How bolsheviks bring a horse to church." (HI, PGC)

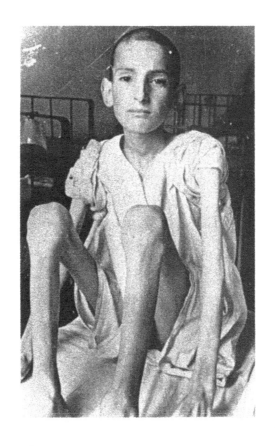

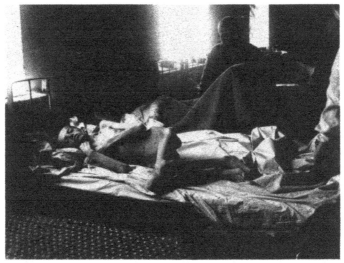

Drawing by Adam J., born 1928, from Stanisławów. Inscription on the drawing reads "Bolsheviks are chasing the civilian population away from cars train cars in which they were deporting the Poles . . . This is the picture we saw from the cars." (HI, PGC)

This photograph and those on opposite page were taken at the small hospital at Vrevskoe. They illustrate the desperate physical condition of many of the children. (HI, AC, and PGC)

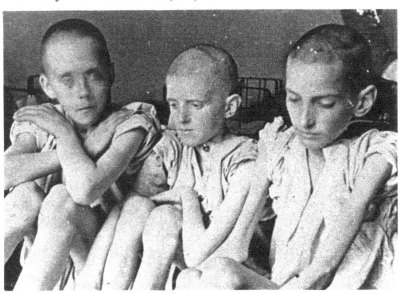

Documents

Translators' Note
Several documents reproduced in this volume were written by barely literate children. In an attempt to preserve the quality of the originals, some punctuation, grammatical, and spelling errors were left in the translations. Russian words in the text reproduce the Russian words in the original. Editorial additions are in square brackets.

Białystok Voivodeship

HANKA ŚWIDERSKA
Born 1930
Białowieża county
Białystok voivodeship

Before the war we lived in Białowieża, where Daddy was an inspector of state forests.

On the first and following days of the war the Germans directed air raids against Białowieża. On the first day the Germans wanted to bomb the military hospital, but they hit a nearby Orthodox church instead. Then they only flew over, but none of them dropped bombs. This is how it was until the Russians came. They came in very carefully, because units of the Polish Army were hiding in the forest. Their first act was to hang their flag on the president's palace and paint over the bronze statue of Marshal Piłsudski in red. They took away our new school and made a Russian school out of it. But a Polish school was found for the Polish children. On November 7th all the management employees had to parade [to celebrate the October Revolution]. There was also some election during that month. On that day they sent a militiaman for my Daddy three times. The "Soviets" behaved seemingly decently, but the jails were becoming full. A "boyetz" [soldier] bought an alarm clock from a peasant and took it to the watchmaker, asking him to change it into a wristwatch. The Russians bought up everything literally by the bagful. Bacon, shoes, and fabrics enjoyed the greatest popularity, so that Białowieża, which did not have many stores, became empty. The new director, a Russian, sent to the management, refused to live in the clerical colony since "the Polish gang is sitting there."

On February 11, 1940, a lot of activity began. The "Soviets" lined the roads leading to the forest with soldiers, so that no "Polish master" could run away. There was a lot of snow that winter, and the temperature fell to 30 some degrees below zero.

Two "leytienants" [i.e., lieutenants] and a militiaman came to our house. The "leytienants" were dressed in uniforms, and over them they wore Polish civilian coats. Both of them carried revolvers. They gave us half an hour to pack our things and searched the whole house. They rushed us to the station and pushed us into a freight car that was already overfilled. This was the first time we rode in a cattle car. This was when they deported the whole administration of the Białowieża Forest. During the whole month we were on our way we were let out twice. There was often a lack of water in the cars. At the stations the local people came begging for bread, with an expression on their faces that told us a lot. Although we were going "into the unknown," they already knew what fate awaited us. On the way we observed through the little windows of the train how Russia looked. Poverty peered out from people's houses and faces. The people were poorly dressed. The houses were old and dirty, sometimes they adjoined solid government buildings. We saw very few cattle. The forests were devastated.

On March 8, 1940, they brought us to the Oktiabrski "settlement" in the Novosibirskie province, county of Tisulska, 600 kilometers from the Mongolian border, 150 from the Tiazyn station. The "settlement" was situated in a taiga where there were gold mines. The adults were forced to go to work, since otherwise they had no right to buy bread. The children were hustled off to a Soviet school, where they had to listen to nonsense on the subject of Poland and the faith. No Polish child attended the lectures of the "bezbozhnik" [godless] circle, and detained by force— escaped at every opportunity. When for the first time they gathered us no one knew what for, and the teacher (Katierina Ivanovna) began to say that our parents were fooling us, because there was no God, one of the boys stood up and walked out, and behind him the whole class, so that, brochure in hand, the teacher stood there facing empty benches. The director of this school was a man of Polish descent, a certain Bułhak, a very fervent communist. People sold their last remaining things, and this is how they lived, since Daddy working hard at the mine could not even make enough for bread. We lived in a moldering hut where water froze in the winter and hoarfrost covered the walls completely. Wood had to be carried from the taiga on one's own back. Mommy went to clear the taiga of woods for growing potatoes.

After the amnesty, October 10, 1941, we happily left the "settlement" forever. As I heard, there were sometimes cannibals in the area. To leave, we had to sell everything we could get along without.

Because they would not take Daddy in the the army, because he had been a cavalry man we traveled south. After a long period of roaming, with lice and hunger (people ate dogs) we stopped at the Uzgen kolkhoz "Pravda" (70 kilometers from the Chinese border, 60 kilometers from the Kara-Su station).

On the way to Uzgen, in the huge troop train there began to rage infectious diseases caused by hunger and cold. There was a shortage of medical help. People were covered with ulcers.

Only in the Uzgen kolkhozes typhus broke out in full force. The local hospitals became overfilled with Poles. Whole families died. Our route in Uzbekistan was marked with hundreds of graves. After a week, Mommy and I went to the hospital for typhus. The conditions there were terrible. Lice, cold, bad food, and lack of medicine sent people off into "the other world."

After a month we returned from the hospital. Papa was called into the army. (9th cavalry division, Gorchakovo). We were left alone, not quite recovered yet. When they deported us, I was attending the III class in elementary school. Now I practiced reading and writing, as much as the shortage of paper allowed, in order not to forget what I knew.

We got 40 dekagrams of flour per person per day at the kolkhoz. Later there was not even that, because from the moment work in the field began, the kolkhoz administration ordered me, since I was 10 years old [,] and Mommy to go to work.

There was nothing to heat with, so we went every day into the fields of the kolkhoz to pick "pakhta" [dried branches of cotton plant] for fuel. A real misery started for real.

After Daddy's telegram calling us to Gorchakovo, we left Uzgen with great difficulties. We did not find Daddy there, because a few days earlier the army had gone abroad. There were lots of military families in Gorchakovo. As in every large gathering of emaciated people there was hunger and sickness here, not to mention vermin. People ate dogs and weeds, since the "soviets" refused to give the people bread.

After some time, following the last unit of the 9th division we went to Guzar. This was even worse than Gorchakovo. Along with a heat wave and hunger, there was an outbreak of dysentery. Mommy found work at the Karkin-Batash orphanage. (In Uzbek—Valley of Death, 8 kilometers from Guzar). The orphanage was in a treeless and waterless vicinity, in an old, ruined kolkhoz, where snakes, tarantulas, and scorpions ran rampant. Lizards crawled on people, and in the night the mosquitos did not let people sleep. The "kibitkas" [clay huts] were ruined, without doors or windows. There were great difficulties with water. Poor nourishment caused dysentery and pellagra, of which several children died each day. On August 18, 1942, together with the orphanage, we left Russia, with the wish never to see it again!

DOCUMENT NO. 2

PGC/Box 120

LEON M.
Grodno county
Białystok voivodeship

The entry of the red armies into Poland

On the morning of September 17 1939 the red armies entered Poland. When the forces entered Poland they said that they were

Poland's allies. This was all untrue, they went occupied towns, smashed up shops and stole the merchandise. We thought they were animals out of the woods, on the second day at 5 in the morning on Saturday we are asleep in our beds someone knocks at the door at our neighbor, daddy thought they were hunters. And then I heard someone shout otkroj dzviery [open the door]. Mommy got frightened they came and shout get ready in 25 minutes. And they even did not say where we were going. They put us into a railway car like dogs into a doghouse. They closed the door. All the people were hungry, every family wanted to eat, all the Polish families were crying. There was a train to Siberia and to the Ural we thought we were going to Siberia but no[,] God directed us to the Ural: There was nothing to eat there people died and even daddy died February 10 1941. Mommy almost died from grief. Later mommy was chased to work in the forest to clear the land And we were chased to a Russian school, we didn't want to learn Russian. They called us to the club and commendant Akatziev. said that Poland was rotten and it would be no more. And three weeks later director Uvicki. came out onto the stage and said angrily that there was a Poland and there would be. And Mr. Rużniakowski came out onto the stage and ordered the Polish people to sing Poland has not perished so long as we live [the Polish national anthem]. The Russian people nearly ate us from anger. Our people did not go to work in the forest, the Soviets did not want to give us bread, on the next day two passenger cars came for our fathers to take them to the Polish army. Later after 2 weeks a petition came from our fathers to the office that they should give horse carts for our Polish families. We went to Bobranka to the port, the port was already being closed and we still made it. The last boat was leaving for Kuibyshev, and took us. We traveled under the floor of the ship it was called Kurier we slept on benches, we fell down to the floor. We arrived at the podstiapki kolkhoz, later I joined the junaks.

DOCUMENT NO. 3

PGC / Box 122

WALENTY M.
Born 1927
Grodno county
Białystok voivodeship

Bloody Autumn

While entering Poland the bolsheviks murdered Polish colonists and foresters. Well[,] after entering the Lerypol settlement in Grodno county the bolshevik NKVD men in disguise arrested the colonists and led them in the direction of the nearby forest. Suddenly we heard shots. So my older brother and his friend ran in the direction of these shots. Near the forest they saw corpses, among which was my father. The news spread throughout the entire settlement that bolsheviks murdered the colonists of that settlement. At this sight crying and lamentations of widows and orphaned children.

But this was not the end of it.

On a frosty day on February ten at daybreak they deported us to syberia.

DOCUMENT NO. 4

PGC/Box 124

WALENTY P.
Grodno county
Białystok voivodeship

Experiences in the soviet state during the war

The invasion of soviet troops aroused fear in the Polish nation. When the troops came all the way to my very house, I immediately found out that we were not afraid of them in vain. At the beginning they started searching for weapons, leading the family into corners "at gunpoint." Afterward they took away the best cows and pigs, for which they gave us receipts (they said that money will be given for these receipts). Finally they started taking wheat issuing receipts for it. In schools they were breaking all the portraits, broke down crosses, arrested teachers for being Polish, and sent their own. Those taught to sing songs against God and against Poland and other unheard-of things.

On 2.10.1940 towards the morning the soviets burst into the house and ordered us to pack things, watching father with a gun and not letting us walk around, only to sit. But they didn't let us pack our better things. After packing up things we left. They didn't let us eat breakfast before leaving. The trip was hard. There was no place to relieve oneself. One had to relieve oneself on the floor and then we threw it out when someone was going out to get water. There wasn't even anything to wash with, because there wasn't even enough drinking water. It was cold in the cars because they didn't give wood for fuel. Lice bit mercilessly. After arriving on the spot, we were placed in barracks in which there were many bedbugs. Father, I, and mother went to work. Everyone who could walk had to work, because they would say that "kh'to nyerobotayet ten nye kushayet" [who doesn't work, doesn't eat]. If someone got ill they went to the doctor. The doctor didn't give sick leave because he wasn't familiar with illnesses and he was afraid of superiors. The natives who remembered the Tzar's reign were not content with communism [,] and the youths, who were taught about what was going on in the country, didn't know how people in other countries live. We had to walk a few kilometers to get potatoes. At work people died or mutilated themselves, in "stolova" [dining halls] there were meals cooked with horsemeat, some potatoes, and water. For an entire month of work you could survive for 4 days on that soup and 800 grams of bread. They didn't allow praying, and if a woman said something against that, they locked her up in a cold cell. One day they ordered women to work with horses. A few women died because of horses. After the amnesty it was a little better, you didn't have to go to work under compulsion. Afterward we wanted to leave, but the commander didn't give horses, so we carried on our backs 30 kilometers to the station, from which we rode to Kujbyshev, where there was a Polish outpost. From there we left for a kolkhoz. In the kolkhoz it was worse yet so we had to steal, because we would have died. The city of Samarkand was not too far away, so I went with my brother to get bread. Lines were big, so people pushed ahead without standing in line, and because brother and I were smaller so I would steal into the store between the legs. Once they almost trampled me under their feet, but it happened that I stole something or bought something. On 1.1 shops were closed because there was no bread. At the kolkhoz younger brothers let cattle and sheep graze, because we went to pick up or steal. Afterward I and father joined the army and brought the family to Karmine.

DOCUMENT NO. 5

PGC / Box 119

Antoni C.
Born 1928
Łomża
Białystok voivodeship

Deportation to Russia

In 1941 at three o'clock in the morning the Soviets came to the house and began to ransack things. Everybody woke up and mama wondered what they wanted and one NKVD man went up to mama and hit her with the butt of a rifle and she fell down. When they searched everything then they said get out! everybody cried and there was no time to pack up only fifteen minutes to pack the things. In a while a wagon came and we got on the wagon and it went to the station and they packed us in a hog car where they carried pigs where it was dirty. It was very stuffy there were fifty people and most of all there was no water. They took us under German bombs and there was fire because people began to burn up in the cars. There was shouting to let them out but they didn't let them out but only unhitched the cars that were burning, and kept going on like that for thirteen days, there was nothing to eat because the bread got moldy and they didn't give provisions because they didn't have any themselves, only Polish people brought food to the stations and handed it to the cars. Very many people died from desiring water and food. The train only stopped a little and they threw the dead people out the window. There was no medical help. When we got to the place where we were to zgruzhat' [unload,] wagons requisitioned from the kolkhoz came immediately and we started to nagruzhat' [load] on the little wagons. We traveled two days by wagon to the kolkhoz, on the way there was no water because it was a dry steppe only pricking grass grew, and only the camels ate it. They brought us to the kolkhoz and started forcing us out to work at once but everybody was tired and couldn't work, most of all they didn't give us anything to eat, people ate beet leaves. The next day mama went on the road for bread with my sister and I stayed with my two brothers who are younger then me and I kept house by myself.

It was very hard to get bread there were such lines that you had to get in line at night to get a kilo of bread. Mama and my sister was three days and she began to come back and the road was hard the nights cold they had to sleep on the steppe there were no houses there wasn't even a place to hide from the rain. But again at noon it was hot so that their clothes smoked from the sun, they didn't have anything to drink because the bottle broke and the water poured out. They came home at night tired and ragged they didn't have a place to lie down because there were no beds only a clay stove so they slept on that. There were very many flea-beetles, fleas, and ants because there was no tub so you could wash somewhere and most of all there wasn't any soap. That's how it was in our kolkhoz in that Russian paradise without bread, without clothes, without soap.

DOCUMENT NO. 6

PGC/Box 119

TADEUSZ S.
Born 1927
Sokółka county
Białystok voivodeship

Departure to the South from Siberia

After the amnesty the Poles escaped everyone where he could. Our family decided to go south. We stayed at the station for six days to buy a ticket. Finally we were loaded onto railway cars which had been used to transport pigs and cows. We could not stand it in the car because there was a terrible stench and when we opened the door the cold bothered us. Then we procured a small stove at first we put this stove in the corner so no one would see it because for such a crime we would be arrested. Then we chopped up the bench we slept on and lit the stove. We did not have one piece of bread and we traveled dying of hunger. In our car seven people died of hunger. We were traveling through unpopulated areas so at a small station we were told to unload the cadavers. There was no morgue anywhere so we put them down in the snow. As we continued on our way lice appeared from God knows where and bothered us terribly and there was no possibility to bathe. After agonies such as a cultured person could not imagine we arrived in Bokhara this is in Uzbekistan. At this station we bought oil cakes, which in Poland the pigs refused to eat we had to eat them, because we were in danger of dying of hunger. There were robbers roaming the town who took away people's money and better belongings and whoever resisted was threatened with death.

DOCUMENT NO. 7

PGC/Box 124

MIECZYSŁAW M.
Born 1927
Sokółka county
Białystok voivodeship

When they brought us to Uzbekistan they ordered us to go to work that very same day. They didn't give us nothing to eat for 5 days only they mocked us and cursed us 'o ty morda Polska" [you Polish mug]. They rushed small children to work and they mistreated them. They rushed us to work like dogs and they would murder us by starvating us. After a few weeks two children died and two elderly people died of hunger. Afterward my father got ill and mother went to ask for a wagon to take him to the doctor, so the "prasyedyatel" [village head] said "nyedayu vozu pust podikhayet" [I won't give any wagon. Let him die]. We were living in mud huts in which sheep were kept and the ceiling leaked.

DOCUMENT NO. 8

PGC / Box 117

CzesŁaw B.
Szczuczyn county
Białystok voivodeship

My experiences in the USSR

Mnesty

We found out that we were released from compulsory work and could leave there. Then we started getting ready for the trip. We started drying bread for the trip. And we would go around the Soviet villages exchanging clothing for flour. One day mama and dad with my brother went to the village and took sleighs with her on the sleighs she put a big pot, a pillow, and fabric she still had from Poland her own clothes and she went off in the evening and when she was going away she will come back in two days. that she'll sleep over at a "russka" woman. Mama with brother went on monday said goodbye and went [.] one day passed and another its cold outside and had to stand on line for bread third and fort day passed we worry why Mama isn't comin back on five day that is on friday this one women comes over and says that one woman with a boy froze to death. We all cried at once dad walks around the barracks like crazy and thinking how she could have froze. Dad went to the commander on the second day to give us a horse and wagon to bring frozen mama and brother. Commander says no horses they went to work Dad cam back home took bread and coffee and went to the kolkhoz and a friend went together with dad. . . . [periods in original] we wait at home for dad to come back and guessing what couldave happened with them dad comes back sunday night and says that Mama is frozen we started crying even worse. Older sister fainted dad says she is lying frozen in the village at a farmer's house on a stove.

That when they were going to get hay and found two kilometers away from the village Mama was sitting on the sleighs and holding my brother in her arms. They took them on the wagon and brought to the kolkhoz Dad says that on monday they will bring mother and brother both frozen.

We all sitting by the stove and saying how we will live now without Mama and thinking in our minds about Poland to our sisters so they would not lucky for them know what would they be doing then. We went to sleep by the stove Dad was thinking all night and couldn't sleep we were thinking too but we fell asleep quickly. We slept through the night in the morning we got up and we straightened up the place and waiting for Mama and brother to be brought back on the sleighs.

My sister ran over crying and sayin that they are bringing Mama and brother. Then we all started cryin then dad and dad's friend started carryin Mama and Tadzik from the sleighs and they put them on the table the whole body stiff and then one woman started warmin up the bricks and warmin up the body and started taking mama's clothes off they washed her and dressed her up in a new dress and dressed brother in his travel suit dad went to a carpenter to make coffins. He made coffins for tuesday and we put in the coffins Dad hired one man to dig a grave. In the evening we led mommie and Tadzik from the barracks then my sister fainted the second time and stayed behind in the barrack we led mommie to the cemetery we buried mommie in one grave with the brother we covered it with sand and prayed over the grave and we came to the barracks my sister was lying on the bed sick. That was my worst day in Russia.

DOCUMENT NO. 9

PGC/Box 122

KAZIMIERZ S.
Born 1928
Wołkowysk county
Białystok voivodeship

Imprisonment

It was a day memorable to all, February 10, 1940. In the morning at 4 o'clock someone knocked at the front door. Mama jumped up from the bed and unbolted it, and from the outside came two shtyki [bayonets] of krasnoarmyeytzy [Red Army soldiers]. Their first words were "where are the weapons," afterward they stopped off at the little room where the son of my aunt, who came to visit us two days earlier, slept. We were all rounded up in one room. They sat us down on the floor against the wall and in front of each one a bolshevik stood with a shtyk against our chests, and they started the search. They searched the room my cousin slept in the most because he was 20 years old so they evidently thought he had some sort of weapons factory. because they even tore the cardboard off of the walls and chopped up the floor. They had to look through each one of about a thousand Polish books, and then they burnt them. After the search they gave us 20 minutes to pack up and announced that they would move us to another voivodeship at these words mama immediately fainted. The Russian soldier first had to look through everything I picked up in my hands and feel it from all sides. After all they only let us take what we had and they themselves put it on, all the better things the communists immediately stuffed into their pockets, and when their pockets were full then they went behind the house and threw them into backpacks, and then went back to get new trophies. Afterward they took us to the station and put us into freight cars.

DOCUMENT NO. 10

PGC/Box 117

STANISŁAW R.
Born 1927
Wołkowysk county
Białystok voivodeship

The arrival of Russians in Poland was sad, and joyful. For some Jews, Byelorussians, and Ukrainians it was joyful. And for the Poles it was sad and hard. Bolsheviks called meetings of all the farmers and ordered them to vote on the taxes and to give up their cows, horses, swine, chickens, and many other things whoever had a surplus those who had 6 cows then 4 for the army and 2 for the farmer. Whoever didn't agree and didn't want to give they would take it by force and the farmer would be arrested or killed. Many Poles were sentenced to prisons. On February 10, 1940, they started deporting our people to work in unknown territories. The journey was hard, there was a lack of food of water because packing took 15 minutes more they wouldn't give more and those who turned back would be beaten with rifle butts and threatened with death. We were only allowed to take what we had on us and 50 kilograms of food together with bed linnen and other things. During the journey they didn't allow us to leave the train cars in which it was dark dirty and it stank because they transported cattle in them before us.

Every 3 days they would give 100 grams of bread a bit of soup and oats per person. There were many illnesses and corpses because of lack of medical care. The journey lasted 2 weeks. After bringing us to the Ural they gave us tiny apartments for 2 families and rushed us to work from the age of 13 up to hard labor I was to load wood onto cars and to cut peat by hand.

Father worked in an ore mine and he was so beaten by a stone which fell off that he was taken by car out of the mine, he went to the doctor and the doctors declared that the damage was slight after which he was punished by losing 25% of his pay for 6 months, after 4 days they took father to the hospital and he lay there for 14 days after the injury to his head and back it was difficult with food and it was hard to get. They gave 600 grams of bread per worker and those who didn't work got 20 grams. Each worker got 500 grams of flour for 5 days, 500 grams of oats, 100 grams of lard, and those who didn't work got nothing.

They didn't allow any of the Poles to go to the market, and if they catch someone then they immediately take him to prison. I was punished with 7 days of arrest for buying cabbage, potatoes, and a kilogram of bread at the market. I worked at sawing peat. The pay was low from 100 to 200 rubles a month. Poles were treated with filthy words because they are poles and catholics. They said you will see Poland and churches like I can see my own ear without a mirror, they ridiculed and cursed poles and religion as they only could. They wouldn't let letters and parcels from Poland through and they abused us as best they could. After the amnesty they didn't abuse us as much as before, but they didn't want to pay up the money we earned. In 1942 we were riding closer to the Persian border, in the meantime they turned in a completely different direction to Juznokazakhstan to work in kolkhozes because of lack of kolkhoz hands. There they gave us a mud hut without a furnace, doors, or windows. Life was hard and difficult there, when we wanted to bring some hay for bedding and fuel, they didn't want to give horses so we had to carry it on our backs from the distance of 2 kilometers. After a month we got sick with enteric fever. We lay there in that mud hut without any medical or human care. There we were robbed during our illness, nobody cared about us because they had sent us away from our relatives and friends over a dozen kilometers. The neighbors (kazakhs) didn't want to help us with anything, there was only one woman who brought us water and hay to burn for fuel, and nobody else.

After 16 days of illness I had to get up in spite of the illness and tiredness and I had to go to work, I was the oldest in the family. Father and mother were very ill for 2 months so I had to work hard for living expenses and clothes. I worked 12 hours at the kolkhoz without lunch and at home after work I would fix shoes trying to earn a morcel of bread and some clothes, because we walked around in rags like bums. I earned 20 kilograms of flour, 2 kilograms of meat, 50 decagrams of sugar, and 1 kilogram of salt monthly. If there was some of it they would give it and if not then not, and no soup. Sugar and salt could be gotten only by those who worked well.

In 1942 on April 13 I joined junaks, in spite of leaving Father, mother deaf after the enteric fever, 2 younger brothers, and a 6-year-old sister.

I had the most recent news from my parents while at the junaks in Shachrisyab [.] they wrote that it is very difficult for the reason that they lowered the pay in the kolkhoz and they don't give what they used to give.

DOCUMENT NO. 11

PGC/Box 120

JÓZEF J.
Wołków county
Białystok voivodeship

When they took us to the settlement then my father got sick with pneumonia the next day. A woman doctor was there but there were no medications. And when she came she saw father and she said it was nothing and it would go away. So she came in a few times every day but medications could not be bought anywhere. And none of us were able to earn money for bread. So mother would sell things she still had from Poland and she would support us. But one day she caught a cold and got sick. So then when the parents were sick some water had to be heated up. When the water was boiling I was taking it out of the furnace water was hot and I burnt my hands. Blisters popped up on top of the burn and my hands hurt a lot. Tomorrow morning Father had to get himself up and prepare food even though he himself was not well yet. After that father got sick even worse and they took him to the hospital. But he did not stay in the hospital for a long time because it was cold in the hospital and there were no windows because windows were broken. Afterwards when we were traveling south for seven days they didn't let us buy anything to eat. When we come to a station we go to buy some soup or bread and the train would go away and all those who stood on the line for soup and bread had to catch up with it by another train. Only when we got to Vołogda we bought bread there and for a lot of money too. And

War Through Children's Eyes

whoever ate more of it would get sick with dysentery because the bread was a bit raw and sticky. I went to get water in Vologda, and there you had to climb up a platform. That platform was covered with frozen water and there was ice. That's why when I was climbing up top on the ice my hands got cold. When I was carrying water our train wasn't there. But I found it on another track when I walked into the car my hands hurt a lot from the cold. I am happy that I broke away from that damned Russia even though I don't know if my parents broke away from that hell.

Lwów Voivodeship

DOCUMENT NO. 12

PGC/Box 120

ZDZISŁAW K.
Drohobycz county
Lwów voivodeship

My saddest day was the day when my mama got ill at night. There was no doctor or anyone only me by myself. I had to stand and heat up water. But there was no wood. I ran to the courtyard and I found a piece of a wooden chip. I set a fire and boiled some water because mama had a very piercing pain about her heart. But this didn't help any because I had to go to the hospital at night as far as the next settlement. Next day when mama was in the hospital I went to get lepyoshki [flat bread] but the russian women didn't want to sell. They told me that mother isn't working so they won't give bread. I walked away crying and sat down on the window. I was sitting at the window and scratching because lice bit a lot. I went to the bazaar and had to steal carrots. When mother was walking back from the hospital she fainted on the way because she was very hungry. I was sitting on the window when I saw mama I ran towards her. I told everything to mother so mother went to the commander and he replied to her that it wasn't his business. Afterward when there was a mass and there was the Polish army then the Russians were ridiculing us that we go to mass. I am happy that I alread left that hell.

DOCUMENT NO. 13

PGC/Box 124

JADWIGA O.
Born 1925
Drohobycz county
Lwów voivodeship

On 4.13.1940 I was deported to Kazakhstan with mother Maria and brother Jerzy to a kolkhoz, in which they forced us to work under threat of starvation. I was not able to support the family on the money earned, which was the reason for very frequent fasting, and also of declining health. Work conditions were very difficult for me, because I was only 15 years old, and I had to do the hardest labors, wanting to support the family after a fashion. Mama almost did not work, because mama's age did not allow her to work, and my brother still as a child (10 years old) also could not work, so I could not count on the earnings of mama or brother. I worked everywhere in the fields, in the garden, and in the stables. The work in the field was hard, because every day I had to walk to my work place, and it was about 5 kilometers, one way, for being late to work one was threatened first of all by losing one's job and being tried by a court. After the case was decided in court, one is usually threatened with a few years of prison. As far as housing conditions were concerned, they were very poor. I lived in an old and neglected little house, which leaked on your head after the smallest rain, not to mention what went on during the thaw. I worked in a horse stable all winter long, it was not a light job. All by myself I had to feed and clean 53 pieces, and that included 15 oxen and 4 camels. At first it was very hard for me, because not having had anything to do with horses, oxen, and even less so with camels before, all of a sudden I had to work there by myself. Not once and not twice I was kicked by a horse, a camel spit, and an ox stuck me with a horn; once I even had to lie in bed for two weeks because of a broken rib. But after recovering they again forced me to work not caring about consequences. I withstood everything calmly, consoling myself that this will not be forever. We lived in terrible misery consoling each other that it has to end. Finally the day we awaited so very patiently arrived, the day the amnesty was announced. But after the amnesty was proclaimed they didn't want to release us from work and their treatment of us had not changed; there was one terrible thing that they didn't want to let us leave the kolkhoz. I saved my family from further suffering by an escape at night. Those who did not manage to escape stayed there and they are still suffering, and those are: Jadwiga Jastrzębska, Maria Jastrzębska, Jadwiga Jastrzębska and Józek Jastrzębski, Olga Wnók, Anna Wnók, Jerzy Wnók, M. Malinowska, Stanisława Łykowska, Kazimiera Łykowska, Jadwiga Ruczkowa, Irena Ruczkówna, Aleksander Ruczka, Kazimiera Trybalska, and her mother died. I lived through all this in Kazakhstan.

DOCUMENT NO. 14

ADAM R.
Born 1927
Lesko county
Lwów voivodeship

In the kolkhoz where they took us and three other families we worked at the cotton plantation. You had to work twelve hours a day, and producing the assigned norm we got two hundred grams of rice flour. Aside from that we didn't get anything else, like food, the same for clothes or money. The attitude of the local people (Uzbeks) was very hostile. They made no difference between us and the Russians and they took it out on us any way they could, for the Bolsheviks (NKVD) having taken away their grain and cattle and for deporting their sons for work. All this is why living conditions were very hard. A kilo of wheat flour cost 156 rubles, a kilo of salt 35 rubles, at private price, for the government prices only factory workers could buy 600 grams of rye bread (85 kopecks per kilo) per day. In addition we lived in low mud and straw huts, with no windows at all. The only way light got in was through the door, and instead of a stove there was a hearth that let the smoke out through a hole in the roof. On account of these circumstances health conditions were very disagreeable. Because of the lack of food various diseases broke out, like e.g., enteric fever, spotted fever, dysentery, and most of all malaria. During my stay in the kolkhoz I never saw any doctor at all. And in the government hospitals, people died mainly of hunger and not from illness. Of the families who were with us in the same kolkhoz the following died: the whole Wołoszyn family, i.e., father, mother, and two grown sons, in the Worotyłek family (Ukrainians) six people died, fate spared an 8-year-old girl Hela, whom the Polish government agency took care of later, in the Misiewicz family the father and seventeen-year-old Franek died. My father went off looking for mushrooms and the Uzbeks killed him only because he had new Polish boots on. Mama died leaving me and four sisters in the kolkhoz. All these disagreeable and very painful memories bind me to the "Soviet paradise."

DOCUMENT NO. 15

PGC/Box 117

MIECZYSŁAW D.
Born 1927
Lubaczów county
Lwów voivodeship

After the retreat of Polish troops to Lwów. The rumors started circulating about the arrival of Russian armies and the populace was very frightened and was very unhappy. And they started hiding everything to secure themselves against an attack. And only in two weeks they came to us and started letting the worst criminals and murderers, who were awaiting them and greeted them with great joy, out of prisons.

After letting these criminals out they started giving them the authority of so-called militiamen who together with the Russian militia helped to oppress Polish citizens.

And so they started taking cows, chickens, pigs, grain from the farmers. From Jewish merchants merchandise from the stores.

From the others on the other hand clothing and other things. After a few months passed they started forming different councils the people didn't want to go to these councils so the militia picked them at gunpoint threatening with prison or the penalty of death. Afterward they ordered to vote for a representative who was to go to moscow to join the polish land to russia. people did not agree with this. And those who did not agree they took away to prison and in that company they took my father.

On 4.13 1940 me and mother were arrested at night and ordered to pick up our things for the road better things they kept for themselves and worse things they gave to us. After packing they drove us to the station and put us in freight cars the cars were dirty and not heated. The journey was very difficult and uncomfortable. Namely the toilet was arranged so that in the middle there was a hole. Women had to relieve themselves in front of children and men. after a few days of the ride great crying and lamentation prevailed, because there was great hunger and thirst because the Russians didn't give either to drink or to eat, to get this we lowered pails through the windows and begged for water.

So we rode on for 14 days until we arrived at a certain station where we were ordered to get off and drove us by cars to the kolkhoz where they let us off and ordered us to look for housing so the people lived under open sky for a few days until they found housing. After two weeks they rushed us to work and ordered us to fulfill a norm. Those who fulfilled a norm got five rubles and 300 grams of bread. For 5 rubles one could buy two handfuls of sunflower seeds. And those who didn't fulfill the quota got 100 grams of bread. And they forced my mother to do this kind of work she worked at 60 degrees without having the clothing and she froze. to death. And the three of us were left without any care and we had to go begging we lived from begging until the amnesty.

DOCUMENT NO. 16

PGC/Box 122

WIESŁAW R.
Lwów
Lwów voivodeship

On 9.22 the entry of Soviet troops on Lwów took place. Polish soldiers laid down their guns, ammunition, and machine guns on a pile with tears in their eyes. Machine guns on wheels moved along the pavements under the escort of Soviet soldiers, and heavy tanks, with guns distrustfully directed towards the local people who were passing nearby, were rumbling down the streets. On the same day army officers were called in by the D.O.K. [military garrison command]. Mother and I bid farewell to father. We knew what awaited them—deportation. I went with father to the command post and there I saw a terrible sight: wives and mothers crying and saying farewell to their husbands and sons. From time to time a shot could be heard, it was the officers who couldn't stand those sights and didn't want to submit themselves to captivity taking their own lives. But this didn't last long, they were loaded into cars and driven in the direction of Łyczakowski train station, from which they were taken in the direction of Russia in freight cars, with many dozen persons in each car. There they were divided up and placed in concentration camps such as: Starobielsk, Kozielsk, and Ostaszków. We received news from there, we were amazed that they were allowed to write to their families, but that was only a stratagem on the part of the Soviets, in this way they caught out all officers' families. Already by March we did not receive any more news, and they disappeared without a trace, until today we don't know where they are and whether they are alive. In the meantime new order was established in the city. All signs were changed to the Russian language, the civilian population was urgently assigned Soviet officers as tenants, etc. Shortages of bread, sugar, soap, meat, and other products were beginning to be felt. Soviet soldiers and officers, by dozens, bought drawing compasses, buttons, piles of notebooks, and kilograms of soap. Shops with fabrics were emptied in a few days. Russian women were seen at the theater wearing "our" nightshirts, and the officers would wash themselves up in toilets and were surprised why water was running so fast. We had to stand in lines to buy foodstuffs, many times from 2 in the morning, and that food was dispensed in grams. Shortages of wood and coal forced the local people to take trips to the nearby grove for fuel, from which such adventurers often never returned. In schools Russian and Ukrainian languages were introduced along with Russian history, and religion and Latin were abrogated. They started persecuting religion, enormous taxes were put on churches, for which reason they had to stay closed. On the other hand, we as high school students would betake ourselves to the Cathedral, as conspirators, and listen to the priest's lectures. But what we so-called "peace" did not last long. Numerous arrests and deportations started, the first such transport of civilians left on February 10. On the night of April 12/13 I was awoken by energetic ringing and knocking at the doors. I sprang to my feet and opened it. A Soviet officer, a Ukrainian militiaman, and two soldiers with bayonets stood in the doorway. I guessed that they came to do a house search. My mother, frightened, showed them around the rooms and I stayed, watched by one of the soldiers. After a careful search we were given an hour to pack up our belongings. When asked where we were going, they replied to Stanisławowo. After we were packed they put Grandma, mother, and me on the car, together with our luggage, which at the same time they advised us not to take because where we were going "vsyo yest" [there is everything]. It was dawn, as we rode through the streets I saw dozens of cars parked at the entrances to apartment buildings. I knew, that tenants of these buildings were going to share my fate. We arrived at the station. Over a dozen freight trains were standing at the the station, some of them were already loaded, and the platform was covered with cars packages and people. We were loaded into the cars 30 persons or more in each car. The cars were locked and secured with wires immediately. One person at a time would be allowed out to get water under soldiers' escort. We stood at the station for 2 days watching (through the little windows with gratings on them) the new unfortunate people, who were being continuously brought to the station in cars. Living conditions were terrible in these cars. Women together with men the toilet was in the shape of a wooden pile protruding outside. The crowd lack of bread and heat drove people mad, already on the second day of the journey two women lost their minds and were placed in a special car. When we were crossing the Polish-russian border sadness and crying prevailed. We knew we were entering the country of poverty misery and hunger, and we had little hope of ever getting out. This journey lasted 17 days, along the way we left behind corpses of elderly people and children who didn't survive the journey. We were traveling through cold areas where everyone would freeze or through deserts and steppes where there wasn't enough air women would faint from the heat and from lack of water. On May 1 we arrived at a small station in Kazakhstan, there they loaded us into cars at night and we were driven to nearby farms. There they stuck us in stables and Cossack mud huts, taking no interest in us and not even asking us about food. We had to sell out our things and for that money get wheat or other products. Me and the other boys were rushed to work immediately under threats of sentencing and "lagier" [camp]. We rode with the tractor brigade out into the fields where tedious summer labors started. Cutting the grass, gathering it, stacking it up in mounds, and then picking up the hay in country wagons pulled by a pair of stubborn oxen. Terrible heat lack of water and negligible amounts of bread let themselves be felt. Our shoes wore out quickly and our clothes got torn, so we walked around barefoot and in rags. Work started before the sun was up and ended after sundown. The heat often reached 66 degrees Celsius. Burnt from the sun, hungry and clenching our teeth, we worked with just one consolation, that our mothers were not working on the farms, that they were not rushed and cursed as we were. After this so-called "haymaking" work with the soil started. We worked on so-called "pritzepy" [trailer] attached to tractors sowing machines and harrows. Afterward came "khlebovuborka" [harvesting]. Hard work, on a tractor or on a combine driver. The summer was over. The winter was even worse. Frost 70 degrees Celsius, and we don't have either shoes or clothes. We worked with frostbit cheeks under the threat of prison NKVD, removing snow from the road and from around giant tanks of oil. We had to walk 24 kilometers to pick up the mail, from a nearby farm on which there was a post office. And to get wheat we had to travel 40 kilometers all the way to the city, if only the "oopravlayushchy" [supervisor] was in a good mood and gave us a wagon with oxen, which happened very rarely. They put us on tractors, because Russian tractor drivers were taken to the army, and at that time the amnesty took place. Our fate improved a bit, they treated us in an uncertain manner, for they didn't know what rights they had with regard to us. A short time after the amnesty I left with friends and with my mother to the Polish Army which was being formed. The NKVD men looked at us angrily, that such a tasty morcel of "loodzie robotchi" [workers] who are so much in demand now, is slipping away from them, for the tractors would come to a standstill without us, and the Cossacks were not familiar with the engines. Before our departure my grandmother died because of lack of medications and of doctors and because of inappropriate living conditions.

DOCUMENT NO. 17

PGC/Box 50

STANISŁAW H.
Born 1932
Lwów
Lwów voivodeship

On September 1 1939 the terrible war with the Germans started. It was terrifying. Dad went to war. The Germans attacked us without declaring a war. Poland was defending itself for 18 days, but still it had to surrender to the immense strength of the enemy. When Polish refugees were leaving the Western areas of Poland, Germans terribly bombarded trains which carried them. Bombs fell like hail on the defenseless civilian population, it is indescribable. In panic and fright we ran to the cellars escaping bombs and to gardens. In our village a refugee committee was formed. My mama belonged to that committee. The first days of war were very depressing. Suddenly we were hit by another terrible news like a bolt from the blue: the bolsheviks fell like locusts on the Eastern territories of Poland. Finally on September 24 we look and on our communal building there is a red flag with a hammer and sickle. Their army entered town on September 24 in the morning. The army was terrible, torn uniforms dirty coats hands and faces, they washed their boots in puddles, they picked papers off the streets and rolled cigarettes. They were pitiful. The troops arrived in our school courtyard with cars with messes and other vehicles. Their army did not meddle with the population. But their civilian authorities also poorly clad started their "administration" with arresting those whom they wanted to destroy, with taking away human conveniences, houses and other things, they effected a great depression and fear this way! They would call people to meetings under bayonets and there they spat on everything which was precious to us. On 4.13.1940 they arrived at our place at night picked us up in a truck and took us to the "Rudki" station. There they loaded us into a freight car. Those moments were very unpleasant and depressing. We traveled for 13 days they gave us bread black as earth they didn't give us water and if they did it was dirty like hogwash. They treated us like criminals they locked us up with a bolt. We arrived in a region town "Martuka." in Kazakhstan they threw us into a burrow. The next day they drove us to the settlement "Andre-jevsk." We got to the store, because mama wanted to buy bread and the salesman said that it was only sold to workers, mama was very surprised that in such a large country one couldn't even get bread and it frightened us. Afterward they put us in apartments so-called "kvatery." Mama volunteered for work right away as a "shchotovod" [accountant]. She worked at M.T.S., that is "Mashinno-traktornaya-stancya" [tractor and machinery center]. I saw people collecting cow and bull manure we got very surprised for what they were collecting this, we found out that it was the only fuel for the winter. Mama wanted to take her own life and ours so as not to live in such torment, but when I told mama that I want to see dad and that I want to return to Poland mama's spirit rose again. People in the U.S.S.R. did not have clothes so only this saved us, because from this handful of clothes which we were allowed to take mama exchanged some for bread, butter, and eggs to nourish us. We suffered want, there were few vegetables and no fruits at all, one had to beg and exchange for materials when one wanted to secure something to eat. We lived poorly cold and misery hurt us. Our consolation was letters from home, which uplifted us that all evil will pass, not to lose our heart. For instance they wrote to us before the war with the Germans, that Adolcio [Hitler] slaughtered all the poultry and only red color was left for him to slaughter. And these words came true, because Hitler, who anyway was a great ally of Russia declared war on it on June 22,1941. Entire Russia was one big hypocrisy; one was afraid of the other, not to be thrown in prison. In front of Poles they said how they "like" Stalin very much and that whole idea. They wished that entire U.S.S.R. fall apart into tiny pieces and that "chort" [devil] take Stalin away. But I departed from my subject for I am supposed to be describing my own experiences. I was making "lepyoshki" [flat cake] from "kizyak" [dried manure] and picked up "kizyaki" every day. When we wrote to Poland about "kizyak" that it was cow manure which cost much and served as fuel, because there is no other kind; they were very surprised. Mama had a lot of troubles for not having sent us to a soviet school, only taught us herself at home. Finally on July 30 we were granted amnesty. What a joy it was. Many Poles were set free from prisons and labor camps at that time and the Polish army was beginning to form. Thanks to general Sikorski we got to Iran on September 8, 1942. We are living on the free Iranian land. Our government is taking care of us, we have everything from it. I just completed fourth grade. I owe everything to the Polish Government; I thank it from all my heart and wish to grow up to be a brave pilot, to serve Poland.

DOCUMENT NO. 18

PGC/Box 117

MARIAN K.
Born 1925
Lwów
Lwów voivodeship

I was arrested in Lwów on June 23, 1941, at 9 in the morning. After a two-hour interrogation in the 7th militia detachment I was taken in a prison van to the railway station, from which they deported me across the border. After a journey of several days I reached a Kiev colony for minors. The next night about 2 o'clock a guard called me for interrogation, although I wasn't confessing to any of the charges they accused me of I was forced to sign a sentence against myself. On that occasion they beat me unconscious, with double blows of the pistol butt the guard is knocking out teeth and crippling my face. A few days after that incident the whole prison colony was evacuated. They loaded us on freight cars at the Kiev station. So many of us were packed in, in one car there were 128 of us prisoners. Right after loading they closed the doors and windows. People in a car like that were in a very sad position because of lack of air, no room, and thirst. At 3 o'clock at night the transport set out on its journey. As soon as we left the city one of the guards in the car came up to me and took 485 rubles from me and took my shoes off my feet and said you're not allowed to have it and then he said look if any of *our* prisoners has money good footwear or clothing and you're not allowed to have any either. We went for three days without getting anything to eat only the fourth day they gave us 200 grams of bread each and a pot of water. During that period of hunger two of my companions died, I don't know what from. Two weeks later we reached Kirov, and from there they made us walk to Korynstroy, 25 kilometers from Kirov. When we got to the place we saw barracks without windows and without floors to live in. Life in the lager [camp] also appeared very tragic. The first days had to be called famine, we got almost nothing to eat and that's why diseases broke out, like dysentery and night blindness (that's a disease of the eyes). Every day I went to work on the rafts. We didn't have any tools at work and there were fatal accidents because of workers crushed by logs, like for example, on September 1, 1941, Józef Nieżka was killed, crushed by a tree because of the lack of tools. Some time later the situation in the camp appeared noticeably worse because of the lack of linen. I didn't change my shirt since I got out of the freight car because I only had one, I slept and worked the whole time in one shirt and one pair of pants. At the beginning of September I ran away from work but they caught me and in Kirov they sentenced me to 5 years of prison, altogether I had to be in for 15 years. On the 8th of September, the day after I came back from the court in Kirov, I run away for the second time. A couple of weeks after escaping I reach Gorky and join the Polish army.

DOCUMENT NO. 19

PGC/Box 117

ZYGMUNT B.
Born 1926
Lwów
Lwów voivodeship

Nightmare days came to Lwów, it started with German planes bombing then battles with the Germans outside Lwów and finally the entry of the Red Army in Lwów. We were living in our old place, that is with mother, father wasn't there, he left with the police in the direction of the Romanian border. It was a dismal day for me the 23rd of October (I don't remember well), when the Red Army invaded [the correct date is September]. I saw the first Soviet soldiers on Grodecka Street, dirty and tired and unsmiling they walked in detachments.

The advance guard had grenades ready in their hands, because at any moment they might expect grenades or other surprises from the windows of the buildings. That same day the town swarmed with them, the stores were full of them, they bought everything there was. I saw an officer who bought a big armload of shoe leather and he was as happy as a child, saying he would send it right away to his wife in Russia. The next days the walls of buildings and houses were colored with different posters. But they all had the same substance. "The rule of the Polish masters has ended, the Red Army has liberated Poland." One poster particularly struck me because it hurt me, a Polish eagle was shown wearing a four-cornered Polish soldier's cap all stained with blood and a Soviet soldier stood over it sticking it with a bayonet.

The next day I went to school, I found out that lessons would begin soon. But there was a lot of commotion in the school, soldiers were in the corridors tearing Polish eagles and portraits off the walls.

There was a statue of Marshal Piłsudski in the office, one of the soldiers knocked it down and kicked it and naturally it shattered. And other soldiers were carrying books from the school library and throwing them in a car standing outside the gate like garbage when they were very valuable books. As I found out later from friends the books were burned outside town.

A few days later a friend dropped in and told me not to show myself at school because the Bolsheviks were looking for all the boy scouts in our school troop, fortunately we burned all the records so they couldn't find us.

In the month of November father came home all ragged, dirty, unshaven, and tired. He walked from Tarnopol, because the Bolsheviks there had defeated our police unit (including my father too), those who fled were lucky, because the rest when the Bolsheviks caught them were machine-gunned. My father turned gray when he saw it from where he was hiding. My father decided not to sleep at home because we knew for certain that they would look for him (my father was a police sergeant) and we could expect them at home at any moment.

Father didn't sleep at home, but every day he slept in a different house.

In fact the next afternoon we saw an automobile come to the house. They surrounded our house and a few came into the apartment their first question was where was father. Of course mother said she didn't know. They searched, they stuck all the mattresses with bayonets, threw everything around, then they found a little money's worth of things that they carefully wrote down and told us we were forbidden to sell them. Days full of uncertainty followed. Mass arrests began and deportations of whole families to the depths of Russia. I stopped going to school, because if I turned up there I'd never go back home again, the Bolsheviks were on duty there and they were looking for boy scouts, so I could easily have been caught.

In front of shops in the city there were kilometer-long lines to get bread and flour. Often one had to stand in the frost all day long to get a kilogram of bread or flour. The only thing one could get without standing on a line were matches and shag of which there was plenty in the stores. Ever more frequent visits of the N.K.V.D. and searches started. They were looking for father. The winter was hard, it was difficult to get fuel, cars loaded with wood stood at the station, but that wasn't for us because it was Polish wood which the bolsheviks were carrying away to Russia. I saw father very little because he had to stay in hiding he would sleep in various corners and secluded places. Lwów prisons were filled, every night long lines of cars in which the Polish prisoners were driven drew toward the station through the city streets, at the station they loaded them into cars and deported them to Russia and their places were filled by new ones.

As luck would have it father got ill (he got a cold) and had to stay at home. Until one night we heard knocking at the door, we knew who it was, it was the bolsheviks. Mother opened up the door, they entered the house at the sight of father lying in bed they drew their revolvers and ordered him to get up and get dressed in spite of mother's explanations that father was ill (that evening father had fever 39.8 degrees [39.8°C equals 103.6°F]). They ordered father to get up and get dressed and did a search. They made up some report (that father is under arrest) which they ordered father to sign at gunpoint and they took father away.

At that time I saw father for the last time and until this day I don't know what happened to him. One night we heard a strange movement of cars and wagons out in the streets. The following day we found out that that night there was a big police roundup, many men were arrested in their homes. Mama found out that it was possible to send prisoners the most necessary things (packages). When mama found where father was, she brought such a package over, she would hand it over in prison but each time she got a different signature on her receipt (mama carried these packages over a few times). As mama finally learned later father was deported a long time ago and the signatures were falsified by soviet

War Through Children's Eyes

soldiers who took the packages for themselves. It was getting worse with food, and even worse there was no money so mother started selling various things on which the bolsheviks threw themselves greedily. We expected that our turn will come soon, because the bolsheviks were deporting more and more families of prisoners. The city became terribly deserted, display windows and shops were empty in the streets there were plenty of portraits of Stalins Lenins and some other such daubs.

A few passed like this until on 4.13.1940 at night a number of N.K.V.D. men burst into our apartment they ordered us to pick up our things, one was only allowed to take 50 kilograms per person. We took the most necessary things. The entire property, the fruit of mother's and father's twenty years of work was now being left for some wife of a soviet officer or for some other soviet family.

On the basis of the report which was written up we learned that we were supposed to leave for Kiev, and that father is awaiting us there. Afterward we carried our things to the car and rode (guarded by a soldier) to the station. But passing through the streets I saw great commotion in the streets. Cars and wagons were driving through the streets and on all of them sat people with bundles. Long lines of these cars were aiming for the station, as our car was, and I understood: it was a roundup organized on a large scale. We arrived at the station there a traffic jam was created the masses of cars couldn't squeeze through a narrow passage. We entered the station, there already stood rows of cars and families were loaded into cars, in which cattle were transported previously. Our car was small over 60 persons were stuffed into it. Afterward doors and windows were bolted. We spent an entire day like this without water or any sort of food.

Afterward one window was opened, on the adjacent tracks I saw a transport full of families, there were 8 transports altogether and each one consisted of 50–60 cars pulled by two locomotives.

Soon we left Lwów we passed through Kiev, we understood that we were cheated. On the way we got some food very poor at larger stations we would get some warm soup or groats.

On the 12th day we crossed the Urals, we were already in Asia. On the 18th day of the journey we arrived at our place of destination. We were unloaded from cars, we saw a rugged desert. We were later driven to one of the Kazakh villages. We arrived there, we saw a few clay cottages. Soon a small group of slanted eyed people ran over to us. They looked at us with curiosity and greedily at our clothing and things. They themselves wore rags. We were distributed in old cottages in our one room 15 persons were suffocating. On the following day they chased us to work.

DANUTA G.
Lwów
Lwów voivodeship

Remembrances from Russia

The invasion of Soviets in 1939. When they entered Lwów the Russians treated the Poles as Russians are used to treat people. No wonder they don't know how to treat people. They carried everything away from Poland even tramways.

Deportation from Lwów. I was deported to Kazakhstan on April 15. We were taken through a trick. They were saying that we would go not far away from the city and that's it. They brought us to a kolkhoz in Kustanay oblast. In the kolkhoz I worked together with my brother because my mama was ill and even though they chased us she didn't go to work. In our kolkhoz there was a so-called "predsidyatel" [chairman]. Our life depended on his mood, if he wanted to give flour, he gave, and if he doesn't want to give there was nothing one could do he wouldn't give and that was the end of it. When I had to go to school I didn't go for long, because they wouldn't let me go, we were called bandits and some other names so I couldn't listen to that and stand that and I preferred not to learn and not to eat bread, but not to hear it. The Russians are terribly starved they don't have bread either and they crave it.

When Christmas holidays came there was nothing to eat not even a morsel of bread. Even though I didn't know how to beg I tried it. I went from cottage to cottage and sang and so I brought something home. I was shaming myself a lot but it couldn't be helped one had to go because in a poor kibitka [clay hut] mama and brother are dying of hunger. When spring came I worked everywhere even on tractors with a trailer ("pritzepshchik") I did everything just to earn money, but they stole my truda dni [workdays, basis for pay computation] and they didn't write all of them down. I weeded wheat and vegetables I scorched in the sun all day, and late in the evening I came back home tired I was 12 years old then I was still very little. I was not strong enough but it couldn't be helped I had to be. When I came back home to eat one thin flat pancake and lie down to sleep only to wake up tomorrow morning and go for a whole day to the field on just one flat pancake. They called us the worst names they could, in general we don't have enough words to describe what we went through. Everything that goes on in Russia is based on a lie really one doesn't know when a given Russian citizen tells the truth, and when he lies. They constantly spoke about work and those tractors, which work half a day and stand for one day it is all one propaganda. Every day in the summer we rode to get so-called kiziaki (cattle manure) in the steppes and we got a few grams of flour for picking it up or one big nothing. They didn't care if we were ill they rushed us to work and that was it. To survive a winter in siberia one has to have nerves of iron, because then there isn't even grass to boil. And water has to be carried a good half a kilometer and one has to flounder through waist-high snow. Empty in the stomach and one can hear one's own guts really make noises. When mother was bedridden and only brother went to work I wasn't allowed to stay by my bedridden mother and was forced to work. They only yelled "hoyda na robotu" [out to work] and one couldn't hear anything else fall from their lips always the same thing. The holidays I had in Siberia I will probably never have anything like this. There wasn't even a morsel of bread at home, Only misery and poverty looked into our windows. When I went out to beg sometimes I brought back a morsel of bread, and sometimes not even that. My longing was to put a good morsel of bread into my mouth. When we were riding South we saw people rambling about the stations and black from hunger. In our oblast the N.K.V.D. building served as the representative building, it served as the propaganda building. We really don't find the words to describe these experiences in Russia. It is impossible either to describe or to tell, only that person can understand it who felt it himself on his own skin. Otherwise no one will understand.

DOCUMENT NO. 21

PGC/Box 123

JADWIGA B.
Lwów
Lwów voivodeship

Exile

They transported us to a kolkhoz 250 km. away from town. A falling down mud hut without windows, without doors, with a hole in the roof over the chimney and a mud floor. At first we used straw for bedding, which we stole from the ricks, and we spread out the remains of the bedclothes we brought with us. As we got to know the neighborhood and got used to conditions we procured wooden bunks and slept on them almost until the end. 6 people lived in an isba [room] 3 x 3 meters in size and a chimney for cooking food, which we built with out own exertions. Lacking windows and doors we put up bags stuffed with straw or horse blankets. In case of rain, water leaked through the clay roof dropping together with pieces of wet clay. As for furniture nobody could even have dreamed of it; in the middle of the isba stood a "table" made of unfired bricks and around it 4 "benches" of the same sort. From the first day they forced us to physical work on the kolkhoz not taking any account of our strength or age. So everybody worked from 10-year-old to 70-year-old. The "brigade leaders" divided up the work, they didn't allow for illness (unless there was a dispensation from the doctor) or for work at home. All household work like washing, darning, and cooking had to be accomplished after a workday lasting from dawn till sunset, when it was allowed to leave the field of work, often several kilometers distant from the village. We received no compensation for work until harvest. Until that season they ordered us to live "by our own industry," the only help a worker got was 2 liters of milk daily that had already been through the separator. So to keep ourselves alive we sold off clothes and bedclothes in the regional town 30 km. away. We traded clothing chiefly for food, and that for very low prices, because the natives despite the great shortage of clothing and footwear couldn't give us more, they didn't have anything to put in their mouths themselves. After 3 months of work that was exhausting for organisms not used to it we received our first compensation, which amounted to . . . [periods in original] 100 grams of wheat, 100 grams of rye, and 100 grams of oats per "workday." The "workday" you could earn when you accomplished a certain assigned amount of work (on the average 1½ – 2 days work). This is how we found out about great misconduct, because each of us was short at least 10 – 15 "workdays." Compensation was so poor that what we got was used up in a few weeks, and then began slow death from hunger and cold. In the huts with snow up to the roof and with no heat provided at all and neither with warm clothes nor with food we awaited the deliverance of death. And it came more and more often taking the weakest. We prayed for them and we envied them. In every family it took someone, leaving the others in the hut swelling with frozen limbs. When hunger reached its greatest pitch and it seemed that no one would live to see the spring, they tossed several kilograms of grain to us like dogs to stay vanishing life a few more days. Spring came and communications were opened again with our "sales outlet" and a few more things were sold, the last pillow pulled from under the head of a sick child and taken to the bazaar and we begin to come back to life again. I say come back to life: because all winter we sat like badgers in a burrow, dying and in total consciousness staring approaching death straight in the face.

Hygiene? It was totally out of the question: a small muddy stream flowing through the kolkhoz served as a well, lavatory, laundry, and . . . [periods in original] watering place for cattle. You couldn't get soap at all; only occasionally (once in 2 months) they issued (if you had money) one piece of soap per family, with no account of the number of members. So it is not surprising that the amnesty and the rectification of living conditions found us in total misery, our bodies and nerves were exhausted.

DOCUMENT NO. 22

PGC/Box 117

TADEUSZ M.
Born 1927
Mościska county
Lwów voivodeship

On 10 of 1940 in February they deported me with the entire family to U.S.S.R. They arrived at 3 in the morning, woke everyone up at gunpoint they let us take nothing with us only what we had on and into the train car. My trip was very hard, they didn't give food and if sometimes they gave then it was some sour and rotten groats. They didn't give water when I jumped out through the window to get water a soviet soldier made me turn back and he still hit me with his gun. So we had to reach up to the roof of the train through the window with our hands for that dirty snow with soot to quench our thirst. They didn't give fuel in the car so it was bitter cold. Finally we arrived in ural to the station of Usfa there they threw us out of the car onto the snow only and after a few hours soviet sleighs arrived and started taking us to the settlement. There was big frost they gave us nothing to wear only what we had on. Small children froze along the way. We got a poor apartment not secured against the cold and in addition plenty of rats and bedbugs. Grandmama was already older so it was cold she lay in bed all the time but there were many bedbugs so they sucked up all the blood and after a few months grandmama died.

There was nothing to eat. People ate nettle and swelled up from it and they, left for the other world. They rushed us to the russian school compulsively because they didn't give bread when you didn't go to school. They taught us not to pray to God that there is no God and when after the lesson was over we all got up and started praying then the commander of the settlement locked me up in the tyurma [prison]. From there we left for Tashkent to a kolkhoz there too there was nothing to eat so we caught dogs and satisfied our hunger and from this people got ill with typhus my sister too. They gave us only 400 grams of wheat and you can do what you want with it and only to those who went to work and the ones who didn't work got 200 grams. My uncle had more children who couldn't go to work and uncle himself was working and after this little bit of wheat mixed in water he got dysentery and died, the late Jan M[——]. When I went to the market with my things the soviet police took them away from me and put me in prison. I had an eagle on my hat so they tore it off and threw it on the ground under the bench I wanted to pick it up so he struck my face and didn't let me pick it up he says I am wearing a rooster. in brief the end.

DOCUMENT NO. 23

PGC/Box 119

BRONISŁAW A.
Born 1927
Przemyślany county
Lwów voivodeship

The Most Terrible Days of My Ordeal

February 10th 1940 was the day of bidding farewell to the Polish land. On the night of February 10 something walks quietly under our windows and knocks on the door. We woke up with a start and look to see what happened. A dozen militiamen broke into the bedroom with the bayonets drawn on their rifles. No one dared to move because he would be killed on the spot. They tied daddy up with a chain, and the others searched for weapons and at the same time stole whatever was valuable. The oldest militiaman shouts that in half an hour we have to be ready to leave! We got up and prepared something to eat. Also they did not let us take down the cross which hung on the wall. They caught mommy tied her up and threw her on the sleigh and loaded us on the sleigh too and took us to the station. And the militiamen stayed behind to take and rob anything good that was there. We sat on the sleigh hungry without eating the whole day. Before evening the locomotive arrived they took from it hot water with oil and brought it to us to drink, the water stinks dirty and besides also with oil. A moment later another train appeared with freight cars made for carrying cattle. They put 70 of us into one small freight car closed off from below. And they locked it with a key and in a moment we felt a violent jerking of the train so that all of us fell down. In the car one could only hear the weeping of mothers and little children. It was cold in the car those who stood close to the door froze to the door and someone else who could not get up from the floor ended his life there. It was dark and cold in the car everyone was hungry, and in the car a stink because everything was melting people are choking because there is no access to fresh air. For two days they did not even open the car and for those two days none of us had anything to eat. Little children are crying dying from hunger and cold. On the third day they opened the car and half of the people were dead already, lying on the floor, frozen and starved from hunger and lack of air. They began to take out the dead and piled them on a large heap and later they covered them with snow so that it could not be seen that so many had died. When they had taken them all out and covered them with snow they put a guard on them dug a large hole and threw them into this common Soviet grave. But in our thoughts remained their dreams and their wishes. A moment later they brought us a soup annointed in this oil on which the engines are running today. And so every three or four days they brought us such food. And again they closed the freight cars and continued taking us to Siberia. And so the trip goes on who is curious and does not believe let him read this and he will believe for sure that it is really so.

DOCUMENT NO. 24

PGC/Box 124

BRONISŁAW R.
Born 1927
Sokal county
Lwów voivodeship

They brought us to the impenetrable taiga to the eternal mud and snow on March 2, 1940, that same night they drove us out to work at once. For 10 days they didn't give us absolutely nothing at all. The 10th day they gave 200 gr. of bread each and ½ liter of soup with some rice, but what a soup! sour and bitter. 2 grains of rice in the whole soup. People rebelled and didn't go to work. And an 18-year-old boy named Wiecheć even started to run away but he didn't get far. He got to a village the N.K.V.D. caught him and they beat him right away so he could hardly stand up. Then a few days later they drove him to the woods under a tree, they told him to dig himself a hole. But when he didn't want to dig a hole. The N.K.V.D. men were impatient and began to make fun of him sobache zhitie sobacha smert [you've lived like a dog, you'll die like a dog] and he tore into them. Then the N.K.V.D. started beating him with their rifle butts and they buried him half alive.

EUGENIUSZ S.
Sokal county
Lwów voivodeship

February 10. 6 Russian soldiers came to our house ordered us to pack up. I was scared and ran away to the stable and hid under the trough. Dad started to look for me. Finally he found me. After about 5 minutes they order dad to hitch up the horses and the Soviet sat on a horse. And we went to the station. They gave us a freight car. And they assigned 80 people it was very cramped. Right away the Soviet policeman locked us in the car a small child died. At the station they took him to the cemetery. When we got to the Vyeruska settlement they gived us a cold room. In two months my mama and brother died. Dad worked 98 kilometers away. Later the whole family joined dad a year later dad died.

Grade 2B
I am 13

DOCUMENT NO. 26

FELIKS J.
Born 1930
Sokal county
Lwów voivodeship

The Soviets came February 10 they said that we had to dress that they would take us to another locality because 50 kilometers from the border the Poles had to be evacuated. The Soviets said that we should take along food for one day because there we would have everything we would need. We got on the sleigh. We went to the train. The Soviets said they would put us into "tieplushki" [heated cars] and you will go. When we got into the cars we see what kind of cars they are and they were worse cars than we carried the cattle in. Cold. They put 20 families into one car. We stood there for 3 days and no water food if it hadn't been for what we had from home we would have died. As the transport left then for 27 days no water or bread when we got out half of the people had died. We came to the settlement and on the second day they drove us to work we had to work from dawn to night. When payday came for 15 days 10 rubles was the top pay so that in two day it was not even enough for bread. People had to sell their clothing if they brought any from home. They had to sell it and walk around naked. People were dying from hunger. They ate dead horses. This is how my mommy worked and got a cold because she had no warm clothing she got pneumonia and was sick for 5 months she got sick December 3. April 3 she went to the hospital In the hospital they did not treat her at all if she had not gone to the hospital maybe she would still be alive she came to the barracks at the settlement and died there was nothing to eat and so she died of hunger April 30 1941. My mommy was dying and I and my sister were at home. Daddy was not there he was at work and my mommy died when Daddy came home from work then mommy died and so my Mommy died of hunger. And then the amnesty came and we got out of that hell.

DOCUMENT NO. 27

PGC/Box 120

GRZEGORZ K.
Sokal county
Lwów voivodeship

On February 10 five Russian soldiers came they searched and ordered us to get ready for the journey. When we resisted they said that they would give us a cow in Russia and that it would be good there. We rode in a freight car. There were over fifty people in the car. It was cold. We rode for two months because the train would break down. We arrived in Arkhangielsk. It was cold in the barracks because they would not give wood and they didn't give bread. At school they didn't allow us to wear [religious] lockets. A teacher tore a locket from one boy and threw it into the garbage. The boy took the locket and put it back on his neck. They told us that we wouldn't go back to Poland. I stood in the line to get bread. I was freezing for three hours but I wangled my way in and got my portion and those who were last on the line would go back without bread. Almost 200 Polish people died. They died of hunger and hard work. They would rush us to the woods and often they wouldn't give bread for four days. Many children died too more than fifty. Father earned 20 rubles a week and a pood [about 36 pounds] of flour cost 100 rubles. Our granny and grandpapa died. I felt sad when I was sitting around hungry.

I am 12.

DOCUMENT NO. 28

FRANCISZEK O.
Żółkiew county
Lwów voivodeship

We were deported to Russia on 12.25.1940. When they were driving us from Poland they were *beating* us. Father was taken to *prison*. When we were in the train cars the Russians would laugh at us and say that we would die of hunger. They would *not give us* any food, and *locked up* the cars *with padlocks*. They did not give us any water. People *died* of thirst, they put *80* people in one car and when we arrived they put everyone into one big barracks. People were suffocating, bedbugs bit us and lice were there too. We spent two months in one place and they took us to Siberia. There we were sailing on a ship and it *rained*. Inside they took us to a settlement in the woods. At first there was bread and they would *rush us to work*. Two months passed and they gave us less bread. They would add years on paper to the *age* of the younger ones and would send them to *work*. I was in third grade at school. Father worked. Mother didn't work because she was *sick,* and when we prayed one evening the commander came over and said that he *would take father away in one direction and send my mother in another direction* to punish us for praying. When we regained independence they didn't give us a *wagon or a boat,* they gave us nothing, we *walked through the woods hungry for 5 days*. Then we took the train. *Lice* attacked us because there were many people. My two sisters died. Then they took us to the Polish Army.

War Through Children's Eyes

Nowogród Voivodeship

STANISŁAW J.
Born 1928
Baranowicze county
Nowogród voivodeship

On the day of September 17, 1939, when the Bolsheviks crossed the Polish border, arrests started. Not only were county clerks, and forest district administration arrested, but also superintendents and guards. The arrested were put in the communal jail. When leading them they spit in their faces and beat them on the face, they kicked them making games for themselves. Afterward plundering started.

The estate and the palace of count Potocki were completely robbed. Afterward the estate of Nowicka and the office of state forest administration. At that time came the turn for Zagórze where the wife of the forest administrator with some women refugees lived. After that they started robbing gamekeepers of state forests. In the nearby village under a stack of hay the bodies of about 15 murdered, naked soldiers were found. When the "Nyepobyedzimaya Krasnaya Armya" [victorious Red Army] was passing through Krzywoszyn on September 24 dad was arrested under espionage charges. But soon he was released because they couldn't prove anything about him. In October on the day of elections dad wasn't home. And the militia, as if possessed, came once in a while and looked for him. Finally before the evening came having seen him in the street, they captured him like wolves a sheep and led him to the election hall. Plundered furniture was collected at Baranowicze, and from there shipped deep into USSR. One day over a dozen cars with dogs were even sent. Cows horses and meat in great quantities were shipped out, and even animal heads which we saw entire carloads of as we went to the settlement. Fruit trees were destroyed and cut down and the woods were felled mercilessly and the wood probably went to Germany.

On the night from February 9 to 10 we were assaulted by militiamen with an N.K.V.D. commander in command, and from 2 to 4 and then from 5:30 until 6:30 they were doing a search at the pretext of looking for weapons. When sleighs arrived at the front of the house we were ordered to pick up our things, because we were supposed to be going for an interrogation. Only a few kilometers beyond the village we found out that we were being sent into the heart of the USSR to work. At the station we were loaded into cattle cars, and the doors were closed and sealed shut. We stood at the station for 3 days during the course of which we were not allowed to go outside. Finally the train started and we were taken past the station into a clear field and there the doors were opened for us for a moment. We ate snow like madmen because it was much better than white frost on frozen nails in the car. Riding for over two weeks, which seemed to be eternity, in cold cars, for they had holes in them and there was not enough wood because we even chopped plank beds for fuel, we twice got a loaf of bread for the family and twice soup with rotten cabbage. At the end of February we arrived in Vologda, and from there by cars to Vyelsk, in which we spent a few days. There were plenty of cripples and old men there. Many also had frostbit hands and legs, others yet were burnt from red-hot stoves in the cars. Everywhere one heard groans and crying. Some lay on top of others because there was no space. On the other hand lice big as bedbugs crawled like ants on an antheap. From there we were sent to the settlement Jeglec, Rovdinskiy region and Arkhangielsk oblast, which was 125 kilometers away from Vyelsk. We rode day and night giving the horses only a short rest. A few children died on the way, and many got frostbite on their ears, hands, or legs. On March 1 we were already at the settlement, and on March 3 we were chased out to work. Every day we were chased to work at 6 in the morning, and released from work often even at 10 at night. For breakfast there was "kipyatok" [boiling water], for lunch— oats with bedbugs or roaches, of which there were plenty there, and on great occasions a rotten fish and for dinner also "kipyatok." We got bread like clay with chaff, and one could break a skull with a loaf. If not for berries and mushrooms, who knows who would have stayed alive. Anyway from a settlement of 450 people 150 stayed behind in graves. But never for a moment until the end of our stay at the settlement did we stop hearing that accursed "davay! davay!" [go on!] How many people had their pay reduced by ¼ for half a year for being a few minutes late for work. And after all, everyone had almost half their pay withheld for various purposes of "gosudarstvo" [the state]. Two men also went to jail, and after a year only one of them came back and barely alive, and the other one died in prison. In September 1941 the moments of which everyone dreamed took place: the amnesty was proclaimed. But it was difficult to break away from the hell, because the red devils having caught a man alive let only a corpse leave. So we only got documents on February 20, 1942, and we left for the South. But living in the back-woods and seeing only the partially visible sun, as well as trees and marshes without end and only sometimes feeling death of starvation look into our eyes we didn't know the "soviet paradise" well enough yet. So arriving in Vologda—the "city of death," in which people dropped of hunger like flies, it was hard to breathe. There was a smell of corpses in the air, worse than in a deadhouse. Corpses lay in the streets, in squares, and even on railroad tracks. The order-keeping force did not manage to pick them up. Sleighs with a crate on top were riding through the city, people who were still twitching were thrown atop of it and they were collected in a pit. After over two days we left there. We were also traveling in freight cars, but this time no one was watching us and the doors were open and one could freely leave at every station. to get water, etc. Bread, and other food products, were given to us on the way at Polish outposts. So it would have seemed that everything was going to be well if there wasn't an epidemic of typhus. More and more frequently some ill person would be carried out of the car onto a station, and sometimes even a corpse. Afterward the illness started in our car too. On April 12 we arrived in Dzalal-Abad and there we got off. A few days after our arrival I went to the hospital, and a few days later my sister came too also with typhus.

On May 8 dad died of typhus in the hospital. Mother's despair didn't help and the crying of the children didn't help, of my brother and of my sisters. A man is born only once and only dies once. And so it happened.

In June in Dzalal-Abad a Polish school was established, which I started attending. We studied at school for a few hours, during the break we were given lunch and then dinner. Afterward we received bread, marmalade, margarine, canned food, etc.

Because of mama's illness we left Dzalal-Abad only on August 20, 1940 [1942]. We rode the train for four days to Krasnovodsk. We had even too much food for the journey. In Krasnovodsk they added some more, so there was no way of taking all of it, even more so because mama's health began to fail again.

After arriving to the harbor we embarked on a ship which quickly started on its way. At the first moment I felt not quite myself on the ship, but soon I got used to the rocking of the ship and it seemed to me that I could go on like this to any place at all. People hardly thought about food on the ship, but we were very thirsty, so we had to stand on a gigantic line to get it. When we were approaching Pahlevi we were moved to a smaller ship on which we arrived to the coast. When I stood on firm ground I didn't know what to do in my joy that I am no longer in "paradise." Afterward we went to the camp by cars. At first we registered, and then went to the tents. There is no point talking about food anymore, everyone is full and hunger is forgotten.

In the middle of September mama was taken to the hospital, because of weakening of the heart. Until September 22 we were still waiting for mama, but we had to go to Teheran by ourselves because mama didn't improve.

We arrived in Teheran on September 24. We were admiring beautiful views along the way.

After some time I started attending school here in Teheran studying in my native tongue.

The school year is over now and we received our report cards.

Here in a foreign land, under a foreign sky, we feel almost free and if it were not for the fact that our Motherland is captured and for the thought of brothers groaning in prisons and concentration camps under German occupation, we would need nothing more. Indeed the gates of our lives have reopened again for us. Because whoever wants to may work freely, may study in his native tongue, and may play in his free time.

For which praise and glory to Great Lord and the Polish Government.

DOCUMENT NO. 30

PGC/Box120

WŁADYSŁAW T.
Baranowicze county
Nowogród voivodeship

My Life in Russia

We were deported to Russia on February 10, 1940. When we arrived we were given very poor housing. There were many bedbugs, lice, and fleas. After a few days they sent the children to school and the older people to work. Children were forced to go to school, and whoever refused was imprisoned in the bathhouse and denied food. When we first got to school we were mocked and beaten—if a Pole said there was a God he was beaten up. Father had to work very hard to earn enough to support the whole family, and not only my father but so did all the Poles who were deported to Russia. For two years we lived in that awful, poor, stupid Russia. After two years the Poles started leaving Russia. Polish people had to get a pass to leave Russia. The trip South was awful. People died of hunger in the train cars and their corpses were thrown out the window along the way. We came to Vologda and were issued food ration cards and bread for the trip. My father was walking toward the car with his bread when a prisoner tried to steal his bread. Fortunately, the police arrested the prisoner and took him away. They would throw the corpses out of the cars and the train would grind the bodies apart on the tracks. From Vologda we left to Chkalov. There, the Polish outpost gave us food and we went all the way to the harbor in pahlevi. The end.

DOCUMENT NO. 31

PGC/Box 120

HENRYK S.
Baranowicze county
Nowogród voivodeship

It took place in February. The Russians came and did a house search. They were looking for weapons. They took us to the station in country wagons. There were very many people in our freight car. It was cramped and stuffy. When the train started we cried that we would never see our home again. We traveled for four days and nights. They didn't give food we used snow to make water. In Siberia the barracks were cramped again. I was going to school. They taught us that there was not God. Once I spoke up in Polish and our teacher sent me to the supervisor and he yelled at me. They drilled two holes in the ceiling. The commander would say into one: "Boh, Boh daj pieroh" [God, God, give a dumpling] and nothing would happen. To the other hole he said: Soviet, Soviet daj kanfiet [Soviet, Soviet, give a candy] and candies would fall down. He would laugh that God gave nothing. The Polish children ran away. Dad died of hunger. He swelled up. They wrapped him up in a sheet and threw him into the ground. My brother didn't have shoes and didn't go to work they took him to prison for two months. Over thirty people died at the settlement. We would stand on a line for bread from evening till morning. More than once we didn't have bread for two days in a row. We waited for our pay for a long time, because the paymaster wasn't there and there was nothing to buy bread with. At first we sold clothes in Russian villages to get bread, but then we ran out of clothes.

Grade 2B.
I am 13.

DOCUMENT NO. 32

PAC/Box 49

UNIDENTIFIED GIRL
Lida county
Nowogród voivodeship

My Biography

I was born August 18, 1925. In the Mikolsk colony, Lida county, Nowogród vojevodship. At seven I began going to school. My papa was an military colonist. We had 25 hectares of land. On which we worked jointly. In 1939 the Polish-German war broke out. Then I stopped going to school because it was terrible. The Germans bombarded towns, bridges, train tracks, and villages. There were very many spies at that time. Who listened to what people said. When the Soviets invaded us. They started to take stock and grain and generally whatever they liked. They closed the mills. They started to set up committees, and they ruled as they liked. In our community they shot the village head and his deputy. They shot priests and many other people innocently accused. By the committee members. They ordered teachers to teach in Russian. And the teacher who didn't know Russian they sent to a Russian course. There were compulsory elections. Actually I didn't have to go to the elections because I was too young. But papa and mama had to vote because they were taken by force. But they didn't know who they voted for. The Soviets wrote down all the people. On February 10, 1940, at one in the night somebody knocked on the door papa opened. 2 wagons came and two Russian soldiers with rifles and 4 of ours from the committee. One soldier stood at the door with a rifle. They ordered papa and mama and my brother to sit down on chairs. And they started looking for weapons. They looked everywhere in the whole house. And when they didn't find anything. Then they told us to get ready and said that we are going to another oblast in Russia. They didn't let us take anything away. only what we were wearing. After half an hour they deported us. It was very cold. It was 12 kilometers to the station. They took us to the station. And they locked us in truck cars. It was dark in the cars because there were no lights. Sometimes not often they gave candles. They gave very little bread and it was impossible to eat the soup. They didn't let us out of the cars nowhere. Only for cooking water and for soup. That's how we went for 3 weeks. We got to the place. They gave us wagons and we went 12 km. to the settlement. to the Irkutsk oblast, Tayshet region, Zlota Gora settlement. They took us to the barracks. We rested there for 3 days. And they sent us out to work in the forest. And to loading cars. It went to 60 degrees C. below it was very cold. We sawed wood and loaded thick wood on the platform. We worked hard a year and 10 months. At first they gave us about a kilogram of bread later 600 grams and still later 400 grams. In the mess hall they gave very poor soup. They paid very little for work. Not enough to survive. We had to sell what we had from Poland. Because it was not enough for bread. In September on September 18, 1941, we got departure certificates. And I beg pardon for going back to it. When we were in the settlement there was snow till May and later a short summer. In the summer there were little flies that bit horribly so that you couldn't go out without mosquito netting. On

December 13, 1941, we left the settlement at our own cost. Because there were no transports. Whoever had money he left at his own cost. And whoever did not have stayed in the settlement. We went away too. We went south 2 months. We arrived at Dzalal-Abad on February 13, 1942. There they took us to a kolkhoz. They took us 50 km. by wagons. They took us to big mountains in Kirghizia. We could not understand them. They didn't give us bread. nor wood to burn. They gave us houses forced to by the NKVD. They disliked us terribly. In one house three of us families lived. At the beginning they gave small children two hundred grams of wheat but later they didn't give anything at all. The elder of the kolkhoz ordered the children's heads to be cut off. It was terribly hard we cooked and ate grass. I did not work on the kolkhoz because I had typhus. Later when I got better I could not work because of the grass I ate. We were on the kolkhoz more than three months. Later we moved from the Karl Marx kolkhoz to the army and were fed by the army we got soup and a bit of bread and some victuals. We were very happy that we didn't eat grass. Later they registered us for departure. August 4, 1942, we left from Suzak for Iran. We came to Pahlevi. And from Pahlevi we came to Terhan and moved into camp third.

DOCUMENT NO. 33

PGC/Box 122

WŁADYSŁAW M.
Lida county
Nowogród voivodeship

Remembrance

In my settlement first lieutenant St. Kowalski was the head of the gmina. After taking over the village the Soviets burst into the gmina seat and four soldiers with bayonets led the head out. To this foursome a platoon was added and they led him in the direction of the nearest forest. People ran out of the roadside village. The people begged to let him go with great crying and lamentations. It didn't help. On the way they beat him, spit in his face, threatened that the good times of domination are over, now you'd want to work even if only as a streetworker, and not to collect money for nothing in the gmina, but it's too late. With just such threats they brought him to the edge of the forest. There they searched him, undressed down to his underwear in front of the crying people they still beat him with butts at the end until he had bruises, mistreated him, kicking him, threatening that he shouldn't expect that Poland will ever rise again. They shot him, powerless, in the chest with a revolver. They asked that someone knock out his golden teeth, because it's a pity to leave them behind. After everything they threw him into a hole under a fir tree and there they buried him.

At the settlement one couldn't sleep in the dark and cramped barracks. In each crack plenty of bedbugs hid. One couldn't escape from these bedbugs which were multiplying at "Zlota Gora."* And lice, fleas crawled on everyone. Lice and fleas everyone killed during a free hour, although there weren't many such hours, because on almost every Sunday train cars arrived to be loaded with wood logs of over one meter in diameter. Naturally they were loaded on with the help of our hands and ropes. On Easter and other holidays many more of them came.

I went to school in Russia. The teacher Aleksandra Pavlovna always used to say: you forget about Poland, you will never go back, only in Poland you were well but in the country you don't know, you were taught wrongly (we were almost all from the countryside or from settlements like me) there is no God, we bolsheviks live without god and nobody took our country away from us as they did to you Poles. Sign up to be soviet citizens and you will be better off, because only soviet planes, tanks, locomotives, ships are strong and one should never even have the thought that enemy should come close to the frontiers.

---

*Zlota Gora, the name of the settlement [author's note].

DOCUMENT NO. 34

PGC/Box 117

WŁADYSŁAW P.
Born 1928
Nieśwież county
Nowogród voivodeship

During the first days after the Bolshevik invasion, some Ukrainians and some Jews were threatening the Poles, and even assaults and robberies took place. After two weeks the Bolsheviks started deporting the Poles cleverly and in secret.

On 2.10.1940 at daybreak a country wagon arrived at our home with two bolshevik soldiers and two Byelorussians. We were all still asleep except for Mama. Russians did not let us to leave the house. They kept asking where is dad. They threated that if we don't tell, they'll shoot us dead. We kept replying that we didn't know anything about dad. since the time of the Polish-German war. Afterward they searched us in search of gold or weapons. I saw how some precious jewels were taken by the Bolshevik soldiers. We were given an hour and a half to pack up our things. They stepped on our most precious religious feelings by taking holy pictures off the walls and throwing curses at them. There was a crowd of Byelorussians present at our departure who bid us farewell crying.

In the frost of 39 degrees Celsius they drove us to the Rejtanowo train station. They locked us up in a freight car which was devoid of light and heat. In one car there were 40 persons. On the road for a number of days. They didn't give us food—which we took from home but we were missing water. There I worked during the summers at chopping wood. In the winter because of lack of clothing and poor clamate conditions I had to stay in the Barracks which required constant heating. It was hard for mother to support four children by herself, so I had to work to support a family consisting of 5 persons. Me, Mama, and three little sisters who were younger than I.

Because of lack of nourishment and clothing illnesses prevailed at the settlement, such as for instance typhus, frostbite of hands or legs, and "Cynga" [scurvy]. They would give each worker half a kilogram of bread which was unbaked and soup with added water. And for children 300 grams of bread each and the same soup. Because of this dysentery illness started. I was sick with "cynga," Typhus, and dysentery. But I managed to regain sound health after these illnesses thanks to God. In the face of such terrible illnesses prevailing, cases of death often occurred.

In the neighboring barracks at Mr. Duda's a child died. According to Polish custom we arranged for a funeral procession for the burial it was in the winter of 1940. Mostly women and children were walking in it. When the Bolsheviks saw the procession, they came with revorvels to disperse us. But the women weren't giving in they kept walking as they looked at the blasphemies of the bolsheviks. At that time the bolshevik militiaman named Koshelev jumped in front of the coffin pushed the women aside, took away the cross and tramped it with his feet. Behind him the militia commander by the name of Shpunov jumped in and started kicking and trampling the women who wanted to get the cross back. Other Bolshevkiks were dispersing the crowd.

When we were liberated We decided to leave for the south of USSR. Passing through Vologda the Russians robbed us. We had a very hard journey for a week we didn't get any food it's simply impossible to describe how we suffered.

DOCUMENT NO. 35

ZYGMUNT C.
Nowogródek
Nowogród voivodeship

I was walking for bilberries and I was falling in the mud there was still snow and I had to go for bilberries to trade for bread for a whole half pood [1 pood equals about 36 pounds] basket we getted a kilo of bread. But mama worked hard mama was still sick she had to worked. We had such misery that lice were biting.

DOCUMENT NO. 36

PGC/Box 118

SERGIUSZ M.
Born 1927
Nowogródek
Nowogród voivodeship

Right after the Soviet army invaded our town everything got scarce: salt, flour, bread, sugar, cloth, shoes, etc. The Soviets began treating us wickedly. They took my papa away every few days to the police, they frightened him, searched him, and demanded various declarations. In the first days of 1940 they arrested my father. They searched our house, they destroyed all our documents and photographs of my papa, so as not to leave any trace of him behind. Several months later they also deported us: i.e., mama, my brother, and me. They gave us ½ hour to pack our things on condition that you could take 60 kilograms per each person, and that we not take any sharp objects with us.

They loaded us on dark freight cars and deported us to the depths of Russia. During the journey they didn't give us either water or anything to eat for several days. They unloaded us at the "Achinsk" station. From there we walked 60 km. to the kolkhoz where they assigned us. There were 5 Polish families at that kolkhoz. There were not any men older than me. The residents there called us prisoners from the first time they met us. I went to the forest every day to chop wood. I worked up to my knees in mud. For that I got 300 grams of bread a day and with that I had to live through the whole day. There were days I didn't get anything neither me, nor my mama, nor my brother, then we collapsed with

Document #36   93

hunger. We had no medical aid at all. We got sick with typhus, fatigue, malaria, pneumonia, etc. We lived in mud huts.

After the amnesty the Soviet authorities did not want to let us leave the kolkhoz. We ran away from the kolkhoz at night, to the Polish agency, which was about 40 km. away from us. There my brother and I joined the Junaks and mama joined the army. We left Russia for Persia with the army, where our life got much better and slowly we got our health back.

DOCUMENT NO. 37

PGC/Box 120

STANISŁAW W.
Słonim county
Nowogród voivodeship

My Life in Russia

We arrived at the settlement and my mother went to the commander for bread. The commander told her to go to the kitchen and get some soup because there was no bread at the time, and bread would be there in three hours. Mother went to the kitchen and the cook said that it was five rubles and Mama only had one ruble. On the second day father went to work and me and my brother went to get bread. On the third day our teachers came. All young boys and girls were sent to school. We got to school and our teacher asked if there was God and we said there was God. When we were hungry we went to steal potatoes in the mounds outside the village. In the Fall we went to the village to work, then in the Fall I would cart potatoes to potato mounds. When winter came there was nothing to eat and father was sick. We went to steal potatoes from the mounds where I carted them. At twelve o'clock we took sleighs to carry potatoes on, mama climbed into the mound and I crawled in to help mama. After five days we went to get potatoes again, we got to the mounds and there was a man standing there with a rifle. The kolkhoz man said "ruki vyerch" [hands up] to mama and dad walked up from behind him with a knife and got him in the head, that kolkhoz man. Then we took the potatoes. Father got sick in his legs and he couldn't go to work. Then my brother my sister and I went to work in the forest. There was a lot of snow in the forest. When I walked into the forest I had snow up to my head. I got 13 rubles for ten days. Then summer came and father went to the brickyards to work. We left for Uzbekistan, where again we started working very hard and living in poverty. The end.

War Through Children's Eyes

DOCUMENT NO. 38

PGC/Box 124

KAZIMIERZ S.
Stołpce county
Nowogród voivodeship

One Day at Voluntary Deportation

In syberia we worked in the woods. The day started with the bell. In the morning at 5 they rang the rouse. After the rouse work about the barracks and meager breakfast. After that work the bell for work in the woods is heard at 6:30. Work is very hard. and cheap. It lasted until 12, and at 12 they rang the bell for lunch. Lunch was very meager, so we boiled water and a tiny morsel of bread bought the previous evening. One could buy some soup, which was meager but expensive. After such lunch at 1 PM they rang for wood work.

After the afternoon work they rang for dinner at 4 PM. After the bell, when everyone is returning from work, they order one to work around the barracks. At 6 PM the shop is opened, then everyone races to get there and line up in a so-called "Ocheradj" [line]. After bread is bought a new line is formed around the kitchen, for poor soup. After dinner at 10 PM there is a bell, after the bell no one was allowed to walk around the settlement, everyone was bedding down. Nights were restless. after fighting the bedbugs and fleas everyone fell into deep sleep, and was woken up by the morning bell.

Polesie Voivodeship

DOCUMENT NO. 39

PGC/Box 117

RYSZARD S.
Born 1928
Brześć county
Polesie voivodeship

When the bolsheviks entered Poland people in the village were very saddened many people were crying because the bolsheviks were coming. For a few days they were good to the people but afterward they took away cows horses grains eggs they allowed prisoners to murder people for the smallest offense. They did searches after searches they were looking for weapons and they took away any valuable thing they found golden rings, watches, bicycles, etc. They took my father to prison because he was the gamekeeper and oppressed the people because he was a big master. When father returned after two months the bolsheviks said that there are no gamekeepers anymore and they allowed those who welcomed the bolsheviks to destroy the woods and to build decent houses for themselves and they also took the wood away to Russia.

On February 10 on Saturday the bolshevik NKVD came in and ordered us to get ready it was impossible for father to move because there was a man with a gun they didn't let us take many things because it would only be a nuisance during the trip and when you get there you will get everything there is plenty of everything over in our country, they drove us to the station put us in a freight car they drove us for a whole week they didn't give food then they gave a little bread and soup which nobody wanted to eat, the toilet was a hole in the middle of the car without any walls around it where both men and women went. When we got there they took us by sleigh to the barracks in the settlement. After a few days they rushed us to work because if you didn't go you wouldn't get bread they didn't care if you were sick they only cared if you had fever, so many people died I was then 13 I did very heavy work I was carting water for people they gave me a horse that kicked me many times so I would make a somersault, and I had to work like that because there was nothing to live on in the winter when the frost was 60 degrees in torn leather shoes and gloves torn during my work because there was no place to buy new ones and this is how we lived the whole time in Russia until the amnesty took place at that time they allowed us to go where we wanted to go me and my entire family went to Uzbekistan during the journey we suffered terrible hunger because we often went for a few days without a morsel of bread in our stomachs very many people were dying

of hunger they would then ride with sleighs through the streets and pick
up the corpses they would pick them up with a pitchfork and throw them
on the sleighs and drive outside the city of Taskent and throw them on a
pile pour crude oil over it and burn it down.

then I joined "Junacy" 3.24.1942 then we were very well because we
had clothes to wear and we had enough to eat and until now it is still
very good.

DOCUMENT NO. 40

PGC/Box 122

WITOLD S.
Brześć county
Polesie voivodeship

1. What changed in our home life after the invasion of the Soviet
occupiers on our country?

When the soviet occupiers entered Poland, conditions started
changing. Shops and warehouses were closed. Nothing could be bought
in the village. Sometimes there was not even any bread for a few days. In
the morning one runs to the line to get a morsel of bread for breakfast, if
one gets it that's good and if not then one eats without bread. Various
offices were established. Homes were taken away from Poles. In other
villages they even closed down churches. In our village they imposed
taxes on the church 1750 rubles a month and even more. All the inhabitants put in a few dozen rubles and that's how it was paid. Various
organizations were created. A few byelorussians even joined the pioneers. At that time kolkhozes were being organized. The byelorussians
volunteered to go to these kolkhozes because they thought it would be
better there. But when they started taking livestock away to those
kolkhozes Then the population started rebelling. Because the entire
harvest would be taken away and the farmer only got the assigned
portion. A cooperative was established in which there was nothing
except for vodka and cologne water. And when they delivered a sack of
sugar then the line was half a kilometer long. Sawmills were closed
down. Peasants were employed at pulling down trees and the pay for
that was very small. Very many were arrested without any reason i.e.
because one was a mailman during the Polish times. It was prohibited to
hang up any holy paintings at home. It was forbidden to ring the bells for
a mass, because one communist when they rang for Christmas Midnight
Mass at night he ran to the N.K.V.D. that he can not sleep because the

bells are disturbing him. One was not allowed to utilize Polish language in the streets only soviet. There were no clothes. There was no petrol at all, we were even without petrol. The glassworks was demolished and clubs were built with that material. The library was inactivated the Polish books were burnt. "Zags" were created. One was not allowed to be married in a church only one had to go to the "zags" and registered. At the very beginning when the soviets were entering one Jew Bańszczyk became the militia commander. He was very sadistic and cruel towards the Poles. When they were deporting to Russia he was then walking around and saying that one could only take 100 kilograms and he took everything away: furniture clothes food and other things. Taxes were collected on livestock products, i.e., leather, or this much and that much milk, meat, etc. Russian schools were created, religion classes were abrogated. The cross and the portraits were taken down and in their place they put a red flag and Lenin, Stalin. There were no books. Afterward they organized a school in which classes were taught in Polish language, for instance, geography, history, botany, mathematics there was Polish Language but there were no books. After 8 in the evening it was not allowed to walk around in the streets.

DOCUMENT NO. 41

PGC/Box 120

STANISŁAW K.
Drohiczyn county
Polesie voivodeship

I was taken to the USSR with my family, to the village Tiogry in the Arkhangelsk oblast.

We arrived in Russia they gave us a lodging without beds and without a stove. We slept on the bare ground and on the second day the Russians right away ordered us to go to work and my brother and daddy went to work. And when they worked for a month and were supposed to get paid the two of them got 200 rubles. But one could not buy anything because there was nothing but bread with half of bran and there was little of this bread because they gave every worker 400 grams and for the children 200 grams and we were very hungry. And soon mommy fell sick with pneumonia because she caught a cold and didn't have warm clothing. And when we left the village we loaded into the rail cars and went south. On the way people were dying of hunger and cold and then the train stopped at a station and they threw the corpses into the ditches because the Russians didn't let them be buried and on the third station mommy died like this and they took mommy out from the train.

When we arrived in Uzbekstan lice came upon us and I and daddy fell sick with typhus I was a month in the hospital and was about to go out from the hospital and daddy died at night and I started to cry that I was left without parents.

And there was nobody at the funeral because the Russians took the corpse and they threw it into the mortuary. And when I got out of the hospital on the second day I was very sad that I came into the hospital with daddy and got out without daddy. After some time I joined the junaks and now I am with the junaks.

Grade 3A.

DOCUMENT NO. 42

PGC/Box 120

JERZY W.
Drohiczyn county
Polesie voivodeship

Feb. 10, 1940. Deportation to Russia

In the morning when it was still dark Russian soldiers came to our house armed with rifles and revolvers. One soldier with a rifle stood at the door so nobody fleed and the others searched around. After the search one of the soldiers yelled at my father to take a little of everything and later the rest and that we will go nearby to a town and then we'll return. Father took a little bit of everything and we loaded it up on sleds. Meanwhile they didn't take us to town but to cold freight cars at the station. It was very cold in the car, I cried because my feet were frozen. All the people had it hard because they didn't have anything to eat and it was very jammed. It was only three days later that they brought us a little bit to eat. When we reached the place they ordered us out of the freight cars and go to the barracks. In the barracks it was cold, little kids cried from the cold and from hunger. The next day the commandant came and said father had to go to work loading freight cars that he will earn a lot 300 rubles every ten days. But when it came to paying it wasn't 300 rubles but 40 rubles. And 60 already the most you could get. And they didn't want to change father from such heavy work. Father worked two years loading freight cars. There were three of us in the family: father me and my older brother. They gave 200 grams of bread for one person and if you worked 500 grams. And in the mess hall soup as thin as water. They made me and my brother go to school, in the Russian school I heard for the first time that there is no God and we started arguing that God exists and always will. The teacher wanted to take us to the commandant. Afterwards the teacher never argued with us that there is no God. People suffered a lot because people died every day from hunger and cold. If we stayed in Russia two more years nobody would ever have returned to Poland.

Two years later news came whoever wanted to go south to Tashkent. Then we loaded our bags onto a wagon and the next day we left. It was even worse on the road because people didn't eat anything for three or four days. And there was nothing else to do but steal. Otherwise everybody would have died from hunger. On the way people began to die of hunger and cold. Once my father went for bread and got a bad cold. When he came back he got so sick that his arms and legs were twisted up. After a while he died and he didn't say anything. I started to cry and didn't know what to do. When we stopped I went to the police and asked them to take my father. I still don't know if they buried my father or not and I don't know where. When we got to a town and there we got off. My brother Stefan joined the Junaks. And I went to the Polish orphanage. It was bad there too because there was nothing to eat. But it was still a little better. A couple of weeks later they took the orphanage abroad. And I joined the Junaks too and now things are very good.

DOCUMENT NO. 43

PGC/Box 122

JULIAN M.
Kamień Koszyrski county
Polesie voivodeship

Since September 25, 1939, the period of interregnum started, the Poles retreated, the Soviets did not invade yet. Gangs consisting of young boys, mostly thieves released from prisons, prowled around. I lived in the country. My father was the owner of the estate Czarucze [?] in Kamień-Koszyrski county in Polesie. The local populace for the most part awaited the arrival of soviet authorities, they supposed that they will be given the land confiscated from the owners, that there will be no taxes, etc. They were disillusioned soon after. Father was arrested on October 1, 1939. He was arrested by a group which robbed the house under the pretense of a search and walked away along with my father.

My family was led outside to the front of the house and was kept there at gunpoint until the plundering was over. On October third we arrived in Kamień-Koszyrski we barely managed to pick up the most necessary things. The furniture of the house was taken away to Russia a few days later. 80 thoroughbred heifers were marked out for slaughter. In spite of repressions against them the local people helped us as best they could. A month after the invasion of the Russians one of the local communists came to me saying how "silly we are." Bolsheviks generally felt insecure, there were few of them. In prison my father was continuously promised that he will be released any day (he was released after 2 years in Bukhty Nakhodki beyond Vladivostock, as a result of the amnesty.) Schools and courses were opened up again. Anyone who had completed 7 years of elementary school and a 6-week teachers course could become a teacher. Religion classes were abrogated and antireligious talks were introduced. Polish libraries were closed. The library of Macierz Szkolna was carried away to a factory as wastepaper. Everything Polish was repressed at every step, by words and deeds. There were plenty of antireligious and anticapitalist posters everywhere. They organized parades of children with small red flags, the children hid the flags as best they could, holding them downward. Shops were partially requisitioned, partially the merchandise was bought out by the bolsheviks for zloties, which stopped circulating a few days later. Lines of cars loaded with furniture, wood, merchandise, and even some old, plundered childrens toys headed toward the station. The bolsheviks came shabby, dirty, and ragged. The examining magistrate lieutenant Gushchyn had one set of linen and one uniform, only here he started acquiring, or "receiving" from no one knows where. In February 1940 they deported the prisoners among them my father from a makeshift prison in Kamień-Koszyrski to Kovel. It was in the evening the street lights were turned off by the bolsheviks. Everywhere foot and horse militia patrols circled around. The column of prisoners was surrounded by machine guns and rushed to run along slippery streets. 2 kilometers to the station. The wife of the arrested police commander ran towards them, closer, to see if her husband was also being deported. A militiaman broke her two ribs by striking her with the butt. Militiamen on horses galloped in front of the column and behind it trampling people. This deportation made an enormous impression even on the most pro-communist groups. They started expressing their dislike of bolshevism openly, in spite of repressions. There was no way of getting a job. Lack of salt, petroleum, sugar, soap, etc. was being felt. Lines were formed, because there was only one shop active in the city. People would faint while waiting all day for a bar of soap, people would break each other's ribs in the squeeze, fingers were cut off with doors. On the other hand the army and N.K.V.D. had free access to everything, without lines. One day when our friends, at whose place a Soviet captain was staying, turned to him regarding my father, they were answered by the question: "What had he been." When he found out that he was an owner of an estate, he replied: "There is nothing I can do if he killed someone or stole something, all this could be taken care of, but he is a "pomeshchik" [landlord], I can do nothing.

On 4.13.1940 we were deported to North Kazakhstan. It is hard to describe what went on during the journey. Cramped cars, lack of water, of food, cries of children, the sick, and the hungry. After two weeks they threw us out at the station at Taincha [?] beyond Petropavlovsk. All belongings were thrown on one pile, many things were lost. They distributed us to settlements in trucks. We got off in an area in front of the "Village Council" building: do what you please, you will live here and you will die here. With great difficulties, we managed to earn money by selling our things and to build a hut of clay and straw with our own hands. There was no wood in the steppes. Being 14 years old I started working to support the family consisting of 6 persons. I worked in the brickyard, at digging wells, at building in the kolkhoz, in the fields, I did what could be done. For two months of work I got 27 kilograms of wheat and 16 rubles. My clothes and shoes wore out quickly and there were never any new ones. The mill didn't work, one had to grind wheat on a handmill, often I was so hungry that I ate raw flour. My cousin got ill, there was no medical care. He was cured by a miracle and by nature. With lack of soap, one washed with white clay. The population did not know anything about what was going on abroad. Soviet propaganda convinced the Russians that in England, America, etc., it was even worse, that people there have no freedom, living conditions, and food at all. Each Russian or Pole was watched, if anything was said it was only in a close circle. The custom of informing flourished. I remember the statement of the school director, J. Glushchenko, that England is a prostitute, that she does everything for profit. For arriving to work 10 minutes late one was threatened with prison for 6 weeks, etc. In the brickyard I earned 200 rubles a month, or 30 kilograms of flour for 6 persons, And the work was beyond one's strength. Dysentery ran riot. Religion was persecuted at every step in school, at meetings, in offices. For any imprudent word one was threatened with prison or a labor camp. Work was compulsory from 16 years up. No one is sure of his position, for instance: One day the director of the brickyard is arrested, the next day the driver of that very brickyard becomes the director. Children work, drink, and smoke from the earliest age, from hunger, they have no principles, either moral or ethical. The stations are crowded, people wait for trains for a few days. Such is Russia. I did not even write 1/100 of what I saw.

DOCUMENT NO. 44

PAC/Box 49

JAN S.
Born 1927
Kobryń county
Polesie voivodeship

After the invasion by the licentious Soviet government I was living in Szemiotówka it was a settlement for colonists. At that time we were persecuted a lot by the soviet authorities and by the ukrainians. Every day the ukrainians would come in riding bicycles with small red flags. Soviet armed cars with the commissar brought over by one ukrainian Prokop from the village of Nowosiołki would come in every day, so we would give up our weapons. He had a terrible vengeance on us, and all the time gave us grief and took a young mare away from us and said that he would send us to labor at Syberia forever. Ukrainian bands kept raiding us and breaking paintings from the walls they took our Polish books away from us. One evening a Polish woman came over to us and told us to hide because they wanted to murder us. We left our house and went to the woods after some time we heard only our dogs were barking again and again. We spent three days in the woods without food.

The Soviets ordered us to give fife poods [1 pood equals about 36 pounds] of rye for the defense of the Soviet state so when we didn't give they came with the troops and ordered us to give rye because if we don't give they will shoot us. After some time, from Saturday to Sunday it was on February 10 a Soviet army car with the commissar came and we were arrested when we were still in our beds. They wouldn't even let us dress they only told us to put all our belongings in the middle of the house and they did a search, they moved little rags and scraps of paper from place to place, checking if something written against them was not written on them. After the search they read the sentence to us in the sentence *it said that we are Soviet citizens* and they are resettling us into another county. They ordered us to take 100 kilograms worth of things per person. Ukrainian sleighs came to fetch us to go to the station. The Soviets loaded us into the sleighs and drove us to the station for two days. The frost in the courtyard reached 50 degrees. At the station they loaded us into a train car at gunpoint and our things were loaded on by Ukrainians and better things they stole, like Kozak Jan and Gryć Stanisław not even half of our things brought to the car. The cars *had bars* on them they looked like a coffin. In addition as they were driving us the locomotive would pull so that we couldn't cook anything or eat something warm. Every two days in the cars they gave us four hundred grams of bread in the cars and every two days for dinner lenten kasha or lenten cabbage soup with corncobs, they would give water once a day and sometimes they would let us go out to get water once every three days. Once every twenty-four hours people would be let out to relieve their needs but at gunpoint. there was *not enough drinking water* and there was no way *to wash* oneself in the cars. people looked like negroes they were so dirty. After our two-week trial in the cars we arrived at the station where we were supposed to get off. The name of the station was Jemca, a 10 "kvartal" [territorial forest unit] settlement in voivodeship Arkhangielsk, Plesiec county. We came to the settlement which was surrounded by woods on four sides. We lived in wooden barracks. As soon as we arrived our commander told us that we were sent here not by Soviet government but by the people with whom we lived in Poland.

At first they searched us to see if we didn't bring weapons by any chance. The commander would check the barracks up to three times a day to see if anybody ran away. A few days after our arrival they ordered us to go to work in the woods. Because anyone who doesn't go to work or misses days and does not fulfill his quota will be tried and put in a lagier [camp]. Men were ordered to work in the woods chopping down trees and women to work on "birzha" [barge]. I worked in the woods gathering branches and burning them, in the woods there were about two meters of snow, so sometimes I fell in and would climb out my whole will to live would leave me. I caught a cold working in the woods and I was sick for nearly a month. When I came back from work there wasn't even a place to fall asleep because there were such bedbugs in the barracks and so many of them that at night if you strike a match your *body was black* and on the *walls were grey* with bedbugs. Every week the commander would call meetings to have people fulfill their quota so they would fulfill their designated plan. When you went to a meeting you had to cover your ears because the commander yelled so that you could go deaf. When I see that the commander goes to the barracks I ran away to the john not to see him in his komsomol [Soviet youth organization] hat. The commander's assistant always ran around to have people clean floors, and when someone mentioned bedbugs to him he wouldn't come for a few days because he was ashamed. When time came to get dinner you had to stand in the line for half a day to get bread you had to stand at least since five in the morning until two in the afternoon. When they bring a pair of *paper shoes* or fabric thin like gauze then people would smell it out and stand there from two in the morning until eleven. But by the time the salesman supplies the commander and the wood foreman and the Russians not even a meter would be left for us Poles, and sometimes fights break out because of this in the line. When I go to pick up the pay I often have to stand there for five days before I get a few rubles. At work they said we have to work eight hours but *when I don't fulfill the quota I can work even fifteen hours.* When I came back from work I had to sit by the fire for an hour to warm up. When I rubbed my ears or nose at work the foreman yelled why I wasn't working. They brought lunch to the wood at three in the afternoon the lunch was cold almost ice cold and a hundred grams of bread. When I come back from work I wouldn't find supper and if I don't go to work then they write up a progul [vagrancy]. We had to walk nine kilometers to work in the woods. We went to work in postoly [bast shoes] because we could never earn enough money for shoes. A pair of postoly cost two rubles, and a *pair of shoes* at least *eight hundred rubles.* Only the wood foreman and the commander were able to buy shoes. After some time of living at the settlement they read the amnesty aloud. We got very happy at that meeting. It was not to the commander's liking. Nobody from the settlement went to work and the commander called a voluntary meeting to have people go to work. The commander of the settlement said that they will raise the pay and will give more bread. But we left for the station not to be under the commander's authority. I went to work to get a little more bread. Because they gave 600 grams of bread to workers and 400 grams to those who didn't work and nothing more. I worked in the woods on a tractor, I worked in the cold and hungry. Because I didn't even have clothes and the frost was about 60 degrees. After a few days I got sick in the lungs and stayed in bed at the hospital. Mama sold our last things to survive. Things were very *cheap*, and *bread cost up to 80 rubles a kilogram.* After leaving the hospital I didn't go to work only I intended to leave. I went with some people from the settlement to the stationmaster to ask for a train car. They gave us a car and we and with 7 other families loaded ourselves onto it and after 5 days started on a trip to Tashkent. During the journey they didn't give us *wood or bread or nothing warm.* After a few days of the journey we met a transport of Polish soldiers. When they saw us they gave us some produce some money and that's how we fed ourselves. After a few more days we again met 2 transports of Polish soldiers at the Ural. Again we were given some money and some produce. An officer of the soldiers provided us with food cards for bread and dinner. We arrived at Chenkient and they wanted to throw us out of the car. But we went to the stationmaster to assign us somewhere to some kolkhoz. They drove us to the station Stalinkient and assigned us to the Mankient kolkhoz. They unloaded us from the car and we sat there for two nights cold and hungry. The uzbeks came and took us to the kolkhoz and there we were given 200 grams of bread. We went to work and there they also gave us *200 grams* of bread each and a serving of soup *for money*. My older brother Stanisław S——. couldn't survive there and he went to join the army at Czakpak. There was a Polish delegation in our kolkhoz. They gave us relief 4 kilos of flour and some clothes. After a few days my brother sent us a letter to leave for Yangyul because transports of soldiers' families are leaving. It was *hard for us because the militia watched our every step*. But we sold the rest of our things and we *bribed a car from "rem-zavod"* [repair shop] of one *Japanese choffeur*. One night on October 20 we took our things out into the corn and at 12 at night the car came and we loaded ourselves into it and left for Yangyul.

We paid 900 rubles for two persons. At Yangyul there was a Polish outpost. We were given a tent and we spent a few days there, they gave us bread and dinners.

Afterward we registered and on October 27 we left for a journey to Krasnovodsk. On the way we were given dry produce so that we wouldn't be hungry. In Krasnovodsk they took our Soviet money from us. After 2 days we left by ship for Pahlevi. We came to Pahlevi on October 30.

DOCUMENT NO. 45

PGC/Box 120

JÓZEF S.
Kosów county
Polesie voivodeship

Life in Russia

On February 10, 1940, we were taken to Russia. This trip was difficult and terrible. They took everything away from us and said that when we arrive they will give everything back to us. They took us to Siberia, to the middle of a forest where there were a few barracks and around them the snow and woods. In two days they sent my father, mother, and sisters to work in the forest. Only after a few weeks they started to sell us bread: for a worker 1 kilogram for children and old people ½. At the canteen they sold a plate of soup for 3 rubles and a good worker earned 3 rubles a day. After such a diet and work my father and brother and generally all the people began to get sick and die. My father and brother were a little more healthy but they had to go for hard work. Then my brother caught cold and began to be sick. If it had been possible to take care of him he could have gotten better but he had nothing to eat and he died. He was 17 years old at that time. Then my father got sick and there was not even enough money to buy bread, then my mother had to sell clothing and shoes she had brought from Poland. Then there was nothing to sell so I went with mommy to cut wood. It was very hard work. Often we had to cry and get mad a lot. Then the portions of bread were cut down they began to give workers 600 grams and the others 200 grams. After a few weeks my father died if he had something to eat he surely would have lived. During his illness he thought about his farm and his belongings and was very sad that he had worked so hard to have something and now he was dying of hunger. He cried all the time before he died. After my father's death things were very bad for us. We had to walk 2 to 9 kilometers to pick cranberries so we could sell them and have something to live on. But this living was very meager. We thought that we would all die. Finally after the amnesty we received passports and left the settlement. Next to the settlement there remained a whole mountain covered with Polish graves. From the settlement they took us to a tractor road and we waited for a tractor. We were very hungry we were very cold because we rode all night. Very many people died during this trip. Then they threw us out into the snow and ordered us to wait until the railway cars come and did not give us anything to eat. They loaded 97 of us into the train and 78 of us remained the rest died on the way. When we reached the Polish outposts we got food and left Russia. We will certainly never forget this life.

DOCUMENT NO. 46

PGC/Box 117

ANTONI D.
Born 1927
Łuniniec county
Polesie voivodeship

My experiences in Russia

In September 1939 when the Soviet army crossed the Polish border a great uneasiness settled over the Polish people at the sight of the things that were going on. And what went on I will tell you. The soldiers ran in town from shop to shop bought up whatever they could and mostly watches, rolls, sausages, dress fabrics, and bicycles. Two Soviets went into a shop and ask the shopkeeper how much this watch costs one hundred zlotys, I have no zlotys, well then in rubles all right he asks the prices of other watches—until finally he says to the other soldier "znaish Kola vezmiom wsije ruchne chasy" [you know, Kola, we'll take all the watches] They took twenty watches paid and went to the next shop where they took dress material in whole rolls. they could barely carry it, but they saw sausage, Kola let's go and buy the sausage now, and surely there is no sausage there only there is a wooden one on display in the window like at home in Moscow. All the same let's go and look. they go into the store and ask if it is possible to get at least 100 grams of sausage, why not, and can we get half a kilo, you can even get five kilograms. So give us 10 kilograms each of sausage and put it around their necks because they were already loaded with rolls even their hats. because they bought rolls by the hundreds and then when he got tired and they became heavy he threw out a few. Two months after the Soviets came to Poland there was an election. And how it was I will tell you. They chased everybody into one large hall. There one of the ruling NKVD men got up and said that no one should dare to cross off his vote because this will mean that he is going against the "Sovietska vlast" [Soviet authority] The election did not take place in the way that they said it would, because they chose for themselves a certain prisoner who had been in prison in Polish times for crimes he had committed. But some almost half crossed off and so did what they wanted to do. A few weeks later they wrote down what everyone owned and no one was allowed to sell anything or kill anything. Until February tenth at 1 o'clock there was crying all around We heard knocking on the door but so strong that the windowpanes shook. Soviet soldiers were banging with the butts of their rifles. Father opened the door 5 jumped in and right away shouted hands up. They searched us and then ordered us to dress and rush out to the sleighs. we were only allowed to take 20 poods with us. Outside we could only hear crying, the howling of dogs and here and there shots. We got on the sleigh they took us to the station there they loaded 50 people into one freight car. They closed up the cars there were bars on the windows. when we went 7 days without water and food only what people took with them from home when the Soviets weren't looking. The children lay down near the door licked the hoar frost off the nails but there was not much of this hoar frost. After those seven days we ripped the bars off the windows and scooped the snow off the train. We went another 7 days, until finally we arrived at the settlement. The settlement was composed of 6 low barracks with very small windows stuffed up with rags because there were no windowpanes and propped up by stakes. We got out of the train they brought us to those barracks. In these barracks there were wooden benches instead of beds. The walls were all red from bedbugs and cockroaches, lice marched in crowds over those benches on which they ordered us to put our things. They did not give us bread because where there was a canteen it was only for workers, for coupons. And since we had just arrived they didn't give us any. The next day the NKVD came to chase us out to work, we went to the forest from the age 13 to 60 everyone because if someone didn't go they put him in the clink, didn't give him bread and he had a progu [vagrancy] and whoever got a progu had his bread ration reduced to 200 grams and they deducted 50% of his pay for 10 months. We worked for 12 hours because it was impossible to earn for this $\frac{1}{2}$ kilogram of bread because a kilogram of bread cost 2 rubles, a portion of soup a few groats boiled in plain water cost 3 rubles. because this was a private canteen And daily a worker could earn 2 rubles at most. They didn't take illness into account at all when someone did not have a fever they said he was healthy. Children under 13 went to school. At school they wanted to turn them into communists and tried various methods as for instance they ordered the children to ask God to give them candy and then Stalin. and then they made candy fall from the ceiling If one of the older prisoners got sick the doctor gave him a pill, about 30 minutes after taking this pill he gave up his life. So during one year half of the people died. Finally when we got our papers we left for the south the way was again difficult because we traveled for a month and a half and during the whole trip we only got two kilograms of bread each from four Polish outposts. and I joined the Junaks.

DOCUMENT NO. 47

PGC/Box 119

ANDRZEJ W.
Born 1929
Łuniniec county
Polesie voivodeship

My experiences in Russia

On February 10 I was deported from Poland to Russia. They brought us to a settlement and ordered us to get off. They gave us a so-called barracks which had holes in it. Almost all Poles could not bear this homesickness and despair. On the second day they gave us bread and some sugar. They gave us three days of rest, after resting father and brother went to work. The first job was very hard, because we were not used to this work. Afterward I went to work I worked together with my sister, work went very well for me I was earning five rubles a day, I was able to buy a serving of soup and a piece of bread. I worked at that railroad for two weeks, work was very hard. After two weeks I got ill with a very severe and dangerous illness which is called "plevrit" [pleurisy]. At first I had a stitch in the side, and afterward I could neither sit nor lie down I simply couldn't breathe air. On the second day I get up look and there is a big swelling on the side. Then father went and asked for a wagon from a horsekeeper and they drove me to the hospital, I was admitted to the hospital. There they cut my hair gave hospital clothes. On the second day a doctor examined me and ordered to take me to the surgery chamber. They were performing surgeries without even putting any ointment on they took a knife and started cutting it was very painful. A liter and a half of pus then poured forth from my side. The food was very poor and the same for everyone, whether someone was there with dysentery or "plevrit," or even typhus, the food was all the same. I was in bed at that settlement for 7 months, afterward the doctor ordered to have me signed out, with the note that the illness was not cured. I arrived at the settlement I was very weak. My brother was making every effort to have me cured I was sent to Arkhangielsk when I arrived there they immediately took me to the dressing station, they took off the bandage and there was plenty of pus they washed me and put me in bed to rest. Afterward they took me for X-rays and it turned out that my lungs almost completely rotted. Then the doctors started making great efforts. In a few days they performed another surgery on my back. In two months I was completely recovered. I was ill for nine months. Then my brother came took me home father and mother greeted me with great joy. Afterward it was very bad because all the products were sold for food coupons and only workers got half a kilogram and I was given 200 grams. There was great oppression. Afterward an order came to leave Russia. All the Poles received passports for leaving. We left when it was already the Winter season. The journey was very hard. 95 persons were stuck in one car. We were traveling for 2 months so we bred many different insects and lice. We arrived at Vozb Station. There soon my parents died and I joined junaks. It wasn't bad in the junaks because we had enough food to eat. Afterward we came to Pahlevi!

MIECZYSŁAW B.
Pińsk county
Polesie voivodeship

My Recollections from Russia

We were in Russia for three years. I was very sad when I was leaving my home. Mommy and daddy went to work at a brick factory. My little brother and I also went to work, our commandant who was in charge of the whole settlement of Polish families repeated these words to us all the time if you don't earn you will not eat. and my little sister who was only 2½ cried all the time because she did not have enough to eat. And the cursed Russians all the time tried to talk us out of Polish prayers and hymns, but it's all right the good Lord will pay them back for this and we will also repay them. And most often they said that they had freed us from the masters' hands and as they say od iha panskiego [from the master's yoke]. We didn't answer them anything to that we only said and asked them why did you come to get us in Poland? And they didn't answer anything to that. My uncle was in a camp where he worked very hard. When we had to go into the forest to pick berries or mushrooms we had to get a pass, and sometimes they didn't give it. My daddy still stayed in Russia in prison as punishment for not going to work for two days. After a few months I was going to school where I only learned math and the rest did not enter my head. I went to school so there they persuaded us not to believe in anything except for their red star because they said that this was their God the Soviets did not want to believe in the living God at all and they also wanted to train us young ones to forget about everything because they would never let us out to be free of their yoke. Thanks to God and England that she took us in and now we are in the half free Fatherland. Maybe the Good Lord and the Most Holy Virgin Mary will pay them back for all our terrible suffering. Later also my younger brother went to school as a second grade pupil and one time he asked the lady teacher such a question, where does the first man come from if there is no God? And she says that to such a question she had no answer. We were laughing that without God you can't even get to the front step. The teacher got all red and went to the director. We always told her to let us out early because we had to hunt down some doggie with a noose. And she was very mean and evil and sometimes I was hit on the head with a thick huge stick.

Stanisławów Voivodeship

DOCUMENT NO. 49

PGC/Box 120

STANISŁAW J.
Stanisławów voivodeship

From where we lived they took me to Russia with the whole family. On 10th of February, 1940. In the cars it was very cramped people lay on bare boards like cattle. In Russia my sister died. Mommy didn't know that she would die and gave her to the hospital. The nurses did not take care of the children but went to older men and talked with them and the children cried and my sister 3 times fell on the floor and killed herself because the bed was very high and she had high fever and was only 5 years old. In Russia I was starving a lot there was nothing to eat and I gathered grass in Russia and mommy cooked soup from it. And then when we left the settlement we got on the train and went all the way to Volga and then we sailed on the river. We sailed on the deck of a barge and as it approached the shore people fell into the water and were drowning and nobody dared to try and rescue him.

Pupil Stanislaw J. grade I

DOCUMENT NO. 50

PGC/Box 117

STANISŁAW SKWIRZYŃSKI
Born 1928
Dolina county
Stanisławów voivodeship

I remember the day October 3 like today, when the NKVD came and began searching. They were looking for weapons and we didn't have any so they left. But the next night they came again and they started an interrogation and we shook with fear like in a fever. In the end they took papa to Dolina as if for questioning. The next day mama went to Dolina to find out something about papa. When she got there the militiamen didn't let anyone inside the prison gates. But Mama wanted absolutely to see papa but she didn't take another step when she got such a strong blow of a gun butt in her stomach that she fell down and lost consciousness and fainted. They carried mama back home and only after a long while she regained consciousness. One day we got news that papa is in the hospital so without thinking long we went there. I didn't recognize my own papa because he had his whole face wrapped round with bandages and only made signs with his eyes and head that he can't speak. It turned out that papa was kept in a cement cell and got abscesses but that wasn't enough, the NKVD accused papa of belonging to secret organizations and hiding weapons which papa never had then they beat papa so that he fainted. His face and back were black and blue, papa could not take it and they took him to the hospital where he stayed 2 months. And in January they deported him to the depths of Russia and since that time we never had any news of him.

DOCUMENT NO. 51

PAC/Box 49

JANUSZ K.
Born 1930
Kałusz county
Stanisławów voivodeship

I was not under German occupation.

I was in the country in Mysłów in the Stanisławów voivodeship at my grandparents; after the invasion of the Soviet forces we were thrown out of our estate and completely robbed. We moved in with a peasant in the village, where on the night of April 12–13 1940 my grandparents and 11-year-old sister were taken away by force. The people of the village (Ukrainians) attacked the car and a struggle with rifle butts began. They did not want to let us go, they snatched me away by force and hid me in the attic, a few days later in the night they took me to Lwów where I found my mommy. We were in hiding until June 29 1940 using false names. On that day they took us away in the night, packed us into a freight car filled with 59 people. The trip was horrible. They didn't give us water, every 48 hours some soup. It was not allowed to open the door or the barred little window. At the stations when he asked for water, the soldiers shouted "skatina" [you pig]. After a 4-week trip we arrived at Joshkar-Ota, from where we went 100 kilometers to forest center 31. Nurumbal Forest. After 3 days they chased mommy out to work, she was a lesorob [forestry worker] she felled huge trees, took them to the landing, and in the spring she floated them down the river, standing in the water up to her knees. I chopped wood for heating the barracks, I carried water, prepared tea for my mother. I was very much afraid that a tree might kill mommy (there were many accidents) so after work I went out to meet her but not far, because there were wolves and bears. After the amnesty we went to my granny in Kazakhstan. After three days we arrived at the railway station, and after 3 weeks of very tiresome journey—we could not buy anything other than ice cream, we arrived at granny's. Grandpa was already dead, he died of hunger. Granny, with my sister, lived in great poverty. Mommy and my sister went to work, to the combine, and I went with granny into the distant steppes to gather wormwood for heating. We cooked soup in the evening. After a few months we went to the south of Russia. We traveled for 4 weeks, they didn't want to accept us anywhere, hunger, lice, and typhus went with us. They unloaded us in Dzalal-Abad at the Frunze kolkhoz, in a stable, without windows or a door, and with mud up to our ankles. We were perishing from hunger. We became sick with spotted fever. Despite our efforts, we were not given any help. During this time the Polish army, 5th division came to Dzalal-Abad. officers of the 5th p.a.l. [artillery regiment] spirited us away during the night, put us in town, in a rented hut. After a long illness, with the help of the army, we regained our health and with the first transport, in a passenger train, comfortably, went to Krasnovodzk, from where we sailed by ship over the Caspian Sea to Iran. It was very crowded and cold on the ship, but the thought that we were leaving the "paradise" gave us strength. From Pahlevi we went in clean cars, under the escort of our soldiers to Terhan to Camp No. 2 From the moment of our landing, our lives changed, we have good care and a good school, if it were not for missing Poland, it would be quite good for us.

I cannot answer the 6th question, because as a minor I did not vote.

DOCUMENT NO. 52

PGC/Box 120

ALFRED P.
Kałusz county
Stanisławów voivodeship

I remember as if it were today Saturday February 10, 1940, Russian soldiers came to our village with horses and wagons and trampled the grain and after a while they appeared in our yard, they started knocking to open the door, they wanted to kill my father, they didn't let us take anything from our house just what we had on us and bedding, they said everything we needed would be there, and after a while we were already in the freight cars, I was very hungry during the journey, I had nothing to drink, I was so thirsty I scraped snow from the iron, it froze there from the cold, it was bitter but I sucked it anyhow. We got very good soup, so good that for supper there was one grain of semolina in every pot of water.

In Russia I had very much trouble and suffering, my father and mother went to work, and I had to look after my two little sisters, but at the time I was still small myself, they liked me a lot, and before they died they called for me, I played and walked around with them, but for a very short period, I got up, looked after them, and put them to bed at night. Once I had fun playing with my little sisters all day, and we waited till father and mother came and brought a bit of bread, and when father and mother came and gave us a little bread we went to bed and began to sleep, but my sister whose name was Hania wouldn't leave us in peace, and we made so much noise that the whole room rumbled, and after we made a lot of noise we went to sleep. The next morning I got up and my sister Hania whom I loved very much was barely alive, when my mother saw her she cried when she went to her, and then she took her in her arms, but my sister started trembling right away, and people started shouting at once at my mother to put her down, then my mother started crying again and complaining about her fate, she went to the doctor and told him to come look after my sister, because my sister was very sick, and he said: let the lady bring her here because I haven't got time, I can't waste time for free, and he didn't have any work to do except lie on his bed and drink vodka. My mother went to the barracks and started dressing my sister, and my sister started shaking again, and my mother went back to the doctor, and finally the doctor came to our barracks, he looked around the walls to see if there were any [religious] pictures and he saw that they were full of pictures, and then frowned and muttered something, he examined and examined and when he finished examining he told my mother to go with him to the clinic and he would give her some powder and my mother went. My mother went to the clinic and he gave her some powder and he told her to give the powder to my sister three times a day, but my sister took the powder only once, and when she took it she died, because the doctor gave her a different powder and she got poisoned.

We buried my sister in the woods by four spruce trees, and we planted the biggest rose growing near her grave on her grave, and my sister Andzia and I often went to her grave to pray and to pick roses.

In the second settlement

When the amnesty came they moved us to another settlement. It was better in this settlement but it was still poor. My sister got sick, the doctor came, and when he examined her he said to take her to the hospital right away. The commandant took my sister by car to the hospital. My mother went with my sister because she knew that the sisters [i.e., nurses] there didn't look after the sick so she went. Once the commandant said to my father, Mr. P [——] go to the station with the bricks and go see your daughter on the way, fine, said my father, so get ready for tomorrow, fine.

The next day my father drove the tractor to the station, which was in Kirov. My father was on his way and my mother telephoned the settlement so father would come, because my sister was already dead and she had to be buried. When my father got to the hospital he found my mother standing by the telephone and calling father about burying her. Father hadn't buried my sister yet when they called him to the telephone. The commandant is telephoning to tell father to come because I was sick, but I got better in two months.

I didn't learn anything good from this trouble except stealing.

Grade 3 C.

DOCUMENT NO. 53

PGC/Box 120

EUGIENIUSZ P.
Kałusz county
Stanisławów voivodeship

On February 10, 1940, we were loaded into a freight car. There were many persons in the car. We got one bucket of soup in ten days. At the settlement my brother and mother worked hard. On Sundays when there was nothing to eat I felt very sad. I was going to school. They laughed and said that God is made of birch wood.

DOCUMENT NO. 54

PGC/Box 119

JAN M.
Born 1928
Rohatyn county
Stanisławów voivodeship

On the Way to Russia

It was a cold night, the snow fell and the wind blew. It was on February 10 at three in the morning, when everyone slept soundly.

Suddenly there was a loud knocking. I jumped up from my bed it frightened me very much and also my mommy. Daddy got up put on the light and opened the door, four Russians rush into the apartment and two Ukrainians with rifles drawn, at this sight I became even more frightened and rushed out from bed got dressed and sat down. After a moment they gathered the whole family into one room daddy, mommy, my brother, sister, and me. They asked daddy where we want to go to Russia or to Germany, daddy said to America. Then they became very angry and ordered us to dress well because we were going to Germany. My brother and I began to pack our things. A few minutes later we put a few of our things on the sleigh and we went to the station on foot, other people were also coming from other parts. When we got to the station it was already getting light, we waited at the station for 3 hours and then we were ordered to get into freight cars. It was very cold in them, there was a stove but nothing to heat with. My brother was not there for a long time suddenly we hear that someone is opening the car and my brother enters.

We stood at that station for two days, there was nothing hot to eat because there was no coal or wood. Before our departure one of our friends came to say goodbye so we asked him to bring some coal and he brought some coal right away we lit the stove, in a few hours we set off on our way. When the train started the women began to cry, and the men began to sing the Polish national anthem.

DOCUMENT NO. 55

PGC/Box 120

Józef M.
Rohatyn county
Stanisławów voivodeship

My Worst Experiences in Russia

When we came to Russia to the settlement there wasn't money to buy bread, and there was no place to sell any of our things because the Soviets didn't let nobody into our barracks. If you had something of your own you cooked it for yourself, and if you didn't you died of hunger, and when we'd already gone out to work they walked around the barracks and if somebody was praying the punishment was they didn't give you bread. When we went to work a lot of people froze something and didn't go to work, then they punished you by not giving you bread. When somebody died you had to pay a lot for planks for a coffin and they didn't even give you a fit place for a grave only in the valley, and when spring came all the coffins floated up to the surface. Then the coffins had to be hauled out of the water again and buried in a proper place.

DOCUMENT NO. 56

PGC/Box 117

CZESŁAW S.
Born 1927
Stanisławów county
Stanisławów voivodeship

When the soviet troops entered, on the first day, right away they started operations in the area of plunder. Before they entered the village in which we lived at that time, their troops surrounded the village and started disarming persons possessing weapons. My father was a policeman and he had had weapons which he turned in in the morning and he didn't get a receipt. Further plunder took place in the village, grain, radios, and a great number of clocks and watches, which were taken away under threats or stolen, were taken away from the population. My father was dressed in civilian clothes and the uniform was hidden because policemen were persecuted. On that day it was 9.19.1939 at 3 in the afternoon and father was asleep because he was tired after an entire night without sleep. He had spent the previous night in the forest because he was chased by a patrol. At that time 4 soldiers on horses burst in they surrounded the house and two came into the house, where father slept. Their end was to rob us. They started searching they found the uniform of my father's. One woke father up and asked whose uniform it was. Father had to confess because in our house there was no young man, then they demanded that father turn in his weapons and father replied to this "I returned it in the morning" the soldier demanded a receipt which was not given to anyone. They ordered father to get dressed in his uniform and go with them to their command post, naturally father did as they requested. Mother wanted to go with father, but a soldier nudged mother and me not to bid father goodbye. Father left the house behind him walked two soldiers, then they mounted their horses and they ordered father to walk ahead to the nearby farm. One stood outside the house and watched that nobody left the house. After 5 minutes the older one appeared and sent him back. Himself he walked into the house and, threatening that father would never come back, and ordered to give him jewelry which I had hidden away and I had to give it away and he left. Mother and her father got dressed and went to the farm. There was plenty of russian troops there, who didn't allow mother anywhere, when mother resisted the commander said that father was deported to russia. Mother had to walk away. In some 45 minutes we heard a few shots on the farm. On 9.20.1939 the russian troops left. and servants who were staying at the time on the farm let us know that my father is lying in the farm cellar shot to death. Men went there they brought back father robbed of his shoes, his money, jewelry, and the top part of his uniform. We buried father at the nearby cemetery. The burial took place without a priest because the russians did not allow priests. My father was put to cruel tortures, he had eight holes in his head and was pierced with a bayonet. Our family had consisted of my father, mother, and me. I was left only with my mother, we were persecuted all the time because they claimed that we were the family of a "bourgeois" (master, whom they don't recognize). They persecuted us until 2.10.1942 [the correct year is 1940] and on that day they deported us to russia for hard labor, to destroy Polish masters. At the settlement where we worked mother made efforts to get lighter work than in the copper or sulfur mines. So the director of the mines said: "There is no lighter work for masters and you will be working in the mines until death." They persecuted us like this all the time throughout our stay in russia. My mother got seriously ill after a year of work in the mines, but they didn't want to release her from the mines. If someone didn't go to work they imprisoned you, so mother, ill, had to continue working under the surface of earth, where even the healthiest man died after 4 years of work or he was not able to work. When mother got ill for the second time with appendicitis after long investigations mother was released and I was taken to work.

The death of my father and further persecution against me and my mother.

DOCUMENT NO. 57

PGC/Box 119

STANISŁAW K.
Born 1928
Stryj county
Stanisławów voivodeship

The Russians invaded on September 17 1939. When the Russians came to our village they told all the families to give them grain if someone does not give they will burn the whole village they gave one day for this. Later they said that every family should hang out a Russian flag if someone does not do it they will execute the whole family or throw them into prison from our village they took a few peasants for work and they kept them at gunpoint these peasants worked at gunpoint they gave food not bread but oats After a week they woke us up at night at 12 o'clock they held my whole family at gunpoint they gave us 1 hour to get ready so we didn't even have time to get dressed or eat because right away they chased us outdoors into the snow and they did not let us take food they said that they would give us much food they took on the sleigh and took us to town to the station and then before dawn there was a great frost so some of the children froze and when we arrived at the station they ordered us to get into the railway cars and and locked us in and kept us like that for two days and we were so cold that we could not stand it and on the third day they gave us two kilograms of bread for the whole day for the nine of us the whole time they drove us through the Polish forests they kept us in the darkness they closed the windows and closed the doors it was dark for us all the time we traveled for a day and at nine in the evening we left Poland so already on the Russian side they opened the windows and gave us oat soup and 200 grams of flour per person the further they took us into the interior of Russia the less food they gave us and so they drove us for two months and when they brought us to the Ural they said that "budit vam kharasho budietie mieli vsiho mnoha (I translate into Polish that everything will be fine for you you will have a lot of everything) the next day they took my mother, brother, and sister to work and I went to work I was then eleven years old and the work they gave me was carrying boards from the sawmill a hundred meters but the boards were not so small more or less 12 meters long and five centimeters thick so I carried them all the time after a month my mother got sick with typhus. My sister and brother got sick because there was hunger and cold and she had very difficult work the boards fell from above and mother had to carry them to the wagon it sometimes happened many times that a board would fall on the hands on the head my mother was very sick she went to the doctor so the doctor said that she could still stand it so finally my mother got so sick that she could not stand on her feet they took my mother to the hospital, my sister and brother my brother was 8 year old it was cold in the hospital my mother was covered with only one blanket and in 1940 my mother died of her illness and from hunger four days later my sister died and my brother somehow survived but they took him right away to the orphanage after a month they took me and my two younger sisters and brought us to another locality they kept us all the time for two days they gave us a soup that was just like water they kept us in the hospital for 15 days took blood from us drew it out of our arms pushed a needle into our veins and pumped it like water from a well then they assigned us to orphanages they ordered us not to believe in God and not to pray one time I put out the light so that I could pray and when the Russians saw it they locked me in an old toilet for two days and they didn't give me any food so I wasted away so much that later I escaped to my older brother I ran all the time and it was far to my brother's eight kilometers I was with my brother for two days and again I went to work so whoever carried only a few boards did not get any money sometimes I earned 80 rubles for 10 days so again there was nothing to buy sometimes it was possible to push one's way into the shop because there were about two thousand people so they pushed so that the shop squeaked so that they had to repair it every day the people were so hungry that they grabbed dogs and killed them they ate the meat and used the skin to cover themselves with so that it would not be so cold very many people died especially children, I still remember well when we went from Siberia to the Uzbeks it was even worse there it was 12 kilometers from the station so we traveled by camel but only the little children when we arrived the Uzbeks kept us on a bare field for two days and two nights when the rain began to fall it became very cold and there was no food later they put two families in one kibitka [clay hut] so one family was very unfortunate there were twelve of them ten children and when their father got sick and there was no one to work for those children so they wasted away they didn't have anything to eat and there was little water and one day the father got sick and at night he died and he lay at home for three days so that these children from all this hunger and cold got sick and three got spotted fever so before they got them to the hospital on those camels they died during the trip one day I got sick too I got a cold as I worked in the field picking cotton and I fell where I stood and could not get up, a comrade and my bother came over right away picked me up and carried me home I lay there for five days and again they called me to work and I was not well yet, one day the Polish army was forming and they were collecting boys for the junaks when we found out we walked those 12 kilometers to the town and it was very cold then I signed up for the Junaks so I said goodbye to my father and went to the station and there they kept us for 10 days and when we got on the train we traveled for one day to Vrevsk there I was in quarantine for 15 days and it was so cold there as in a dog house I could not stand it and I went to a Polish doctor and they took me to the hospital I stayed there until February 10 1941 and right after I left the hospital they gave us our uniforms and at six in the morning we got on a train and they took us to a port and there we boarded a ship we settled down to sleep on the deck and when the ship got to the open sea it began to roll and water splashed onto the deck then we got so cold and there was no food they only gave us a little fish each and a bisquit we traveled for 24 hours when we got out on land began to look around we thought that we were in another world right away we ate our fill and went to the baths washed in hot water and went to sleep and on the next day they took us to Terhan.

DOCUMENT NO. 58

PGC/Box 120

PIOTR N.
Tłumacz county
Stanisławów voivodeship

Under the occupation of the Red Army

10.2.1940, at 3 AM, Russian NKVD men came to our house, saying that father was to raise his hands up and looked for weapons. They ordered us to dress and pack our things. They took us by sleigh to the train. They packed us into the railway cars like swine, if you'll excuse the expression. The train stood there for quite a while, until there was the sound of a whistle and we were off. We were very sad and we cried all the time. They didn't feed us at all and they continued faster and faster into the interior of Russia. We arrived in Murasha, where they unloaded us from the railway cars and put us into cars. We went by car to Koma ASSR, which was more than 500 km. There they unloaded us from the cars and led us, like a flock of sheep to barracks, which were like a stable. They did not feed us, but pushed us to work. We spent the entire time hungry and cold. Until finally after two years there came the amnesty. To announce this amnesty already? But no, the Russians pushed us to work even harder. We escaped from the settlement, because the Russians did not let us go, we got into the train and went to Kotlas. There were many Poles in Kotlas. After a long time we left Kotlas hungry and cold. There were Polish outposts there, where they gave a little bread and even soup. We traveled for a whole month to Guzar. In Guzar, things were already good, the Poles took care of us, gave us bread, rice[,] cereal[,] and soup. The Polish Army took care of us, and advised us to join the Polish Army.

When we were at the settlement, the Russians did not give us anything to eat, and from the age of 14 to 70 they drove us to work, put us in the clink when we didn't want to work. There was a rebellion, because we didn't want to go to school, and our parents didn't want to let us go. If our parents had let us go to school, we would have learned that: there is no God, we should not believe in Our Lord God. In the kolkhozes we ate dogs, because there was nothing to eat. My family when we were at the settlement, during the whole time we ate two dead horses. And no sickness came to us because of the dead horses. Our Poles threw themselves under the train because there was nothing to eat. Whole families died at the settlements. And the whole of Siberia was a cemetery of Polish families. And this is how the Red Army tormented us.

Tarnopol Voivodeship

JAN K.
Tarnopol voivodeship

One day in Russia I hadn't eaten for 3 or four days. And we walked to work and we only got two hundred grams of bread a day it was little we walked and cried. We had to sell our clothes. My mother worked very hard and my little brother and I didn't have boots we had to walk to work barefoot and mama got typhus there was nothing to eat. Mama had to work because if she didn't go to work she didn't get anything to eat, and she died. My little brother and I cried and the Soviets laughed at us and we went looking for planks for a coffin and we didn't find any planks and we buried Mama without a coffin and they laughed at us because we cried. There was no money and no wood and we had to strip bark and we didn't have soap. We had to stand in line and we stood in line from five till six at night and didn't get anything. The Soviets pushed to the head of the line and we were in line first and the man who sold bread gave it to the soviets without them waiting in line and they shoved ahead so hard that sometimes somebody broke his leg. We had to work hard for a piece of bread and it was very cold in the hut and there wasn't a stove just a little tinplate heater. It was sad and lice bit and a lot of Poles were sick.

K. Jan pupil in Grade 3 a.

DOCUMENT NO. 60

TADEUSZ M.
Born 1928
Borczów county
Tarnopol voivodeship

My Departure to the U.S.S.R. Without My Parents

When the Bolsheviks came at 2 o'clock at night they took us away without our parents. They took me and my brother and my sister and my aunt. My brother and sister were about 5 years old. My father was a prisoner in Germany, and my mother went to grandmother's, and they took us at night and loaded us on a freight car. When we had crossed the border into the U.S.S.R. mother came. They didn't want to let her into the car and we went off alone. They didn't let us take anything from home, because the Russians immediately took everything for them-selves and carried it off to the Ukrainian district. The Russians took us to "siberia" for 2 months in closed cars. On the way we were very hungry, because now and then they only gave us thin soup. We reached "siberia" at the end of April, and the next day they made me and my aunt go to work, there was a lot of snow and we went to work hungry. We worked all year, the Russian commandants would come and say if the quotas were filled we'd be all right. And how were things all right with them when they gave a working man 600 grams of bread and if you didn't work 300 grams, and that's how we lived without our parents. We went into the woods to pick mushrooms, and that's how we nourished ourselves. The second year the commandant of the barracks was so wicked, he told my aunt to send me to Russian school, and my brother and sister who were 6 years old to the Russian nursery. The com-mandant told my aunt you can fill the quota by yourself and you will be all right, you'll be working just for yourself. But we didn't want to send my brother and sister to the nursery at all. He came every day and bothered us about the nursery, that they will be all right there. He took me by force to the Russian school It was 40 kilometers to the village of Zakajnova. I stayed there 5 days in that school, but I didn't learn nothing at all. It was just for appearance' sake that I was there. After 5 days one morning I set out to run away from the school to my family so I could help my brother and sister. I got to the barracks in the evening and the commandant asks me how are you studying there, but he didn't know that I had run away. What are the names of the teachers, and I said I don't know. And when the commandant found out I had run away from school, he wanted to lock me up in jail. I ran away to the forest so as not to go to school, and he ran hard to try to catch me. I helped my aunt work in the forest, and I slept in the forest and they brought me what they could to eat. Then the commandant didn't give us any bread. And he kept wanting to take my brother and sister to the nursery, where it would be all right. The Russians wanted to turn them into Bolsheviks. But we wouldn't let them go, we said let them die with us, and we won't let them to speak Russian. The commandant always said that we would die and never see poland and poland won't exist no more. He always wanted to take me to Russian school, that you will learn Russian there and there is no God there and you won't believe in God anymore and you will be all right there. I hid in the forest and I never went to the Russian school. In our barracks they took 3 to prison and left 3 sisters all alone, and their Father died in prison. Then we went to the Uzbeks here we were in a kolkhoz for half a year, it was a little better there because they didn't say to send my brother and sister to the nursery. Then the amnesty came and we were free. And the commandant kept saying that

War Through Children's Eyes

you won't see Poland again. And this is what I thought when he talked like that: a time came when poland exists.

DOCUMENT NO. 61

PGC/Box 120

ADOLF N.
Brody county
Tarnopol voivodeship

They deported us to Russia on February 10, 1940. It was very cold. In our transport at the station there were one hundred freight cars 3 locomotives pulled the train. They didn't give us water on the way. Lice bit us. I chopped wood in the settlement but often I was hungry. I never got meat at all. At school they said there was no Lord God and to throw religious medallions in the stove. I didn't. The clothes we had from Poland we traded for flour. One whole family of 9 people died of hunger. I got typhus and my father died of hunger.

It was good in the Polish army

Many Polish children died in the settlement, about forty.

Grade 2 B.
I am 12.

DOCUMENT NO. 62

PGC/Box 120

CZESŁAW K.
Brody county
Tarnopol voivodeship

My father worked in the forest he made three or four rubles a day and he had to work very hard and they didn't even allow rest on a holiday. They had to go to their jobs in torn cloth shoes because there was no money for new ones, and even at home there was nothing to buy bread with so mother had to sell clothing and only for that we bought bread and if there wasn't anything to sell then we had to sit at home hungry and it was very cold. From frost and hunger people died. Afterward they chased me out to work I had to walk 15 kilometers to the forest. Before I got to the forest I'd be so tired that I had to sit in the snow and when the evening came then I had to walk back home. When I got home then right away the desatnik [work supervisor] arrived and called to kantora [office] and they didn't let one buy bread or sleep only they would chase us to the forest out in the snow and there had to work and they watched so one wouldn't run away from work but I didn't have strength because I was hungry. In addition lice bit because there was no soap and there was no place and mother cried all day long because she had nothing to eat and there was no one to earn money for bread and it was very cold and they got cold and now mother and father died. Father died in a train car in Russia from hunger and mama in Teheran in a hospital.

DOCUMENT NO. 63

PAC/Box 50

URSZULA B.
Born 1931
Czortków
Tarnopol voivodeship

September 1, 1939, war broke out. A terrible gun battle took place. The air raids bothered us. We had to hide in the shelter, but it was terrible there. A lot of people fell. It was like that for several days. When it quieted down, the morning of Sept. 19, 1939, the Bolsheviks invaded. And again a new yoke begins. Right away they started arresting people. They robbed all the stores. They threw people out of their homes onto the street and lived there themselves. I saw many people complaining that they don't have anywhere to live and are hungry. After all this I went to my aunt's. Because we didn't have anything to eat. Mama stayed because they didn't let her go. But my two brothers and I were at my aunt's, then they deported my older brother, they said he might be a partisan. The Polish people were forced to vote. The first election took place Nov. 1, 1939 [the correct date is October 22]. They led people at rifle point. There was hunger in Poland. The Soviets stole everything that came their way. The Soviets treated us like animals. July 22, 1941 [probably June 22]. On Friday at seven o'clock in the morning, when the Bolsheviks took us. It was despair. They led us at rifle point. They put us into coal cars, together with our things. They closed the doors on the world. There were guards in the cars. They only opened one window. It was suffocating they gave us water once a day. At the stations they gave us water mixed with flour. That was soup. And very little. They didn't let you go to the bathroom when you wanted, only when they wanted. They took us to Abakan Krasnojarsk and then to a settlement. They gave children 400 grams of bread and grown-ups 600 grams. And they order you to go to work in the mine. Sick or not sick. They didn't care. We suffered like that a long time. Aug. 12, 1942 [the correct year is 1941]

Great joy came and the Poles were freed. Thanks to Gen. Sikorski. We were called to go south. When I left Russia it was Feb. 3, 1942. I came south to Samarkand. People were dying in the streets. Our young people. They were dying of hunger.

I have a great grievance against the Soviets through them I lost a beloved Uncle. After the death of my Uncle I went with my aunt to our cousin in Shakhryshab, she was in the army. From there I went with the army to hospitable Iran!

If I were ordered back to Russia I would take my own life!

Dear God, send me back as soon as possible to the bosom of my homeland!!

DOCUMENT NO. 64

PGC/Box 117

MARIA W.
Born 1925
Kamionka Strumiłowa county
Tarnopol voivodeship

From the moment the war broke out, great changes took place that were most unpleasant for the Poles. When, as everyone knows, Russia occupied Polish territory, it seemed that she was coming to the assistance of the Poles. In the first days they treated the Poles very gently and protected them from attacks by the local Ukrainians. But soon the Ukrainians bribed the Soviet authorities and then they attacked the Polish communities together, robbing and pillaging, taking men into prison In the settlement where I lived the Ukrainians began to torment us badly. They attacked at night, killing farmers. In the settlement neighboring ours it happened that in the evening the farmers were sitting down to dinner when a whole bunch of armed Ukrainians attacked and killed one of the men through the window and in many other houses, wounding others, robbed the more valuable belongings, leaving behind abandoned houses. On another evening they attacked a certain farm, where they completely destroyed the house and practically killed the people, ripping the clothes off them and everything that had been in the house only rubble remained and in it those who had been seriously wounded and left naked. They broke all their kitchenware over the people's heads and as they were leaving they threatened that if they reported them to the authorities they would come back and finish them off and would destroy the whole settlement. They tormented us dreadfully. But there were also quite a few Ukrainians who reported to the Poles about the crimes of the others. Then also in our settlement there were robberies in broad daylight. Not only clothing, but all home and household implements. And they even took all the cows, horses, and pigs. They left only one cow for each household and broke into the stores of potatoes and beets. They also took everything from the barns. There was emptiness everywhere. Russian soldiers stood with rifles and watched that the Poles should not resist these robberies. A man from our settlement who was on the side of the Ukrainians reported on all the secret plans made for our deportation and always warned the Poles. On December 24, 1939, on Christmas Eve, the men found out that they are to be arrested in the night and at 7 that evening they left their homes. They remained in hiding in Lwów for quite a long time without getting any word back to their families. When things calmed down a little they came back to our village but they did not show themselves to anyone. During this time the Ukrainians and the Soviets made population lists several times although we did not know what they needed it for. Finally one day, a few days before our departure, they came to search for weapons and looked everywhere. The search went on all through the settlement. No weapons were found anywhere. And constantly they asked even little children where they fathers were but they never found out anything. Then they ordered us to notify our fathers that they should return to their farms since nothing bad would happen to them. Only they should return to their children. But our men hesitated and were afraid. On Friday, February 9, news came again that we could be expected to be deported from our farms. They were to deport us to Germany and they lied to us that we would be happy there. The Poles believed it and at the same time did not believe it. The next day before dawn many empty sleighs prepared for our deportation drew up and were loaded with whole families, including the fathers who had returned believing their lies, thinking that they would remain peacefully on their farms.

DOCUMENT NO. 65

PGC/Box 117

JÓZEF C.
Born 1927
Kamionka Strumiłowa county
Tarnopol voivodeship

1939. The Bolsheviks invaded on September seventeenth. Three days after the invasion we saw red army men in our colony. There was commotion in the colony. Several red army men came in automobiles an older lieutenant ordered them to take down holy pictures in the school and when nobody wanted to they took them down themselves and broke them. They burned the library, so that you couldn't read Polish books. Near the main road was a figure of the Mother of God which the colony bought before the war. One day a car came with red army men and stopped in front of the statue. The Soviets wrote down something and went on. A little later an order came that the colony demolish the statue, but nobody had the courage to demolish it. So two days later some older man with several soldiers came, called a meeting of the whole colony, started to tell us to comply with their orders, and to take down holy pictures in homes. And that statue if you don't remove it by noon, you'll see. He said I advise you to comply with authority, it will be better for you, you will have everything. Noon came he gave the order to his soldiers to demolish the figure so the soldiers demolished it. He said since you don't want to demolish it yourselves, from tomorrow there will be a militia here to watch over you. The next morning that same commandant came, and 12 civilians with him who had rifles and arm bands, and they had a hammer and sickle on their caps. They rented the house. They were like militia, they had to see that no [unofficial] meetings happened, they searched whether anybody didn't have weapons and on that occasion they took expensive things. They reported everything that someone did. They said, you oppressed us, now we will oppress you. We will oppress you and soon we will deport you. That was in the month of February, at 10 in the morning, the army surrounded the colony, so that nobody ran away. An auto came to every house and they took the whole family letting you take 50 kilos per person.

It was a very sad time when everybody said goodbye to their native home and native land.

DOCUMENT NO. 66

PGC/Box 120

Józef J.
Kopyczyńce county
Tarnopol voivodeship

From where I lived they took me to Russia with the whole family. On 10th of February 1940. In the rail car it was very bad because there was nothing to eat only stale bread. It was very cramped. In our car it stunk very bad because there was a privy in the car. On the way they did not give water or bread. When they gave water it spilled because the train rode unevenly. When we arrived in the settlement Daddy was there only a week and died and on the second day my brother Tadek died. Daddy was 40 and Tadek 21 years old. Mommy cried a lot because Daddy could have lived a long time but died from hunger and caught a cold and there was no medicine or a doctor. When Daddy died it was very hard because there was nobody who could work. I gathered grass and mommy cooked soup. Mommy was very sick when Daddy died. When I was hungry because there was nothing to eat at home I went on the fields to look for potatoes. I went with my brother to the forest to gather wood.

Grade I A.

DOCUMENT NO. 67

PGC/Box 117

BOLESŁAW S.
Kopyczyńce county
Tarnopol voivodeship

The Polish nation groans in captivity

When the Soviets invaded our land. They began to buy up the goods in stores for rubles Soviet soldiers started to break into the lines and climbed over people and they bought up the merchandise. Dec. 31, 1939, when Polish money stopped being valid they went to private stores and loaded goods on their cars and took them to the depths of their country they paid the owners with Polish money and the next day the money stopped circulating, mothers went out to the market to shop for food for their children and nobody wants to take Polish money, poor mothers who had zlotys yesterday for several weeks supplies and today die of hunger. If there was someone to look after them they stayed alive, others went to the hamlets to beg, wealthy fathers were deported to lagers [camps].

In the hamlets they appropriated grain from the peasants by area depending how they were rich. We had 26 morgs [1 morg equals 0.6 hectares] of land, they assigned us to give 90 hundredweights of grain, and they paid 25 zlotys per hundredweight. They loaded it on wagons and sent it to Germany.

Feb. 10, 1940, two soldiers came at 4 in the morning they woke us and told us to wait until 6 o'clock, at 6 o'clock the commander came and read us that (za prikazom verkhovno soveta Z.S.S.R. perecelajem vtoraju oblast [on the order of the Supreme Soviet, you are resettled into another region]) because you are not trusted in this land, they took us to the station the trip lasted one and a half months they gave us very little bread and other food, they didn't open the cars, they didn't provide water, we had to ask laborers working at the stations to give us snow through a small window and the Soviet soldiers drove them away.

For one and a half months we didn't wash lice bit without mercy. They took us to the heart of the forest 70 km. from the railway they ordered us to work at cutting down the forest and rafting on the river. The work was hard they made us work from dawn to night. The mess was thin cabbage soup without any fat, and sometimes grits and it was hard to get. There were 7 of us in the house my father and 17-year-old brother went to work my father was already old he was 50 so he couldn't earn enough for all of us he earned 4 rubles a day and my brother wasn't strong enough yet and couldn't earn enough to keep the family. One winter day my brother went to work, through the carelessness of workers near him the top of a pine tree got him and broke an arm and he was hurt almost all over and he went around the hospitals for 7 months.

One Sunday they forced all the people to work to meet their work plans. At work they cut off my father's finger and father went to the hospital it was hard they didn't give us any relief we had to sell the last pillow out from under the children for the price of a 400 gram loaf of bread. Women who had small children the settlement commandant went around the houses and made them go to his office when he got them all there he called a militiaman and they began to drive all the women into a small tiurma [prison] and the women protested that they have small children at home and they didn't want to go, the commandant beat them and drove them all into tiurma he only let them out in the evening, the little children cried at home because they didn't eat at noon it was cold at home because outside it was more than 50°C. below.

People froze their hands, feet, ears, noses. They didn't see drippings for two years. I went to the soviet 6th grade where they taught about all the countries of the world in geography. They taught us that the English are keeping half the world oppressed the African, Indian, Australian, and Canadian nations, that they take everything away from these countries and everything into their own pockets, that not only do they, one, flay off people's skin but, two, that the suffering people in India die by the millions and all the nations are oppressed in the colony at hard labor and the English are the overseers and that they give very hard sentences for offenses. They say that there is no developed culture in England and in the mines they still haul coal with horses. They say that the English in Ireland took more than 2 million people from their homeland.

DOCUMENT NO. 68

PGC/Box 117

KAZIMIERZ F.
Born 1927
Kopyczyńce county
Tarnopol voivodeship

My experiences in Russia

In 1939 Moskale [a derogatory word for Russians] overran our Country. When they entered, they started robbing and arresting us. They were closing churches, demolishing Polish schools, establishing kolkhozes, and instilled us with communism. Everyone was hiding in cellars and different secluded places. These days became for us threatening with death. When Moskale entered the store they would stuff themselves with yeast and with everything their eyes saw, and they stuffed their pockets with sausages and when they didn't have a place to stuff them they would put them in their bootlegs and on their shoulders, so they couldn't move when they left the store. Day after day passed with such robbery and assaults, until a time came of even worse lives and misery. I remember as if it were today, in 1940 on January 10 [correct date is February 10] at night Moskale attacked our house. They surrounded the house all around so that no one escapes from the house and started knocking on the door until they knocked it down and burst inside. We all sprang up from beds and were standing there as if grown into the ground. And here we see three Moskale come in and scream "rooki vyerh" [hands up]. Dad put his hands up, and they started up towards him and led him to the other room at gunpoint. The others started searching for weapons. But they couldn't find any weapons. Mama started crying and we all did too. And they started talking. We give you two hours to pack up and we are leaving in two hours. When mama heard these words she fainted immediately and me and Sister started packing what we could. After two hours they loaded us by force at gunpoint into the sleighs. We were all bidding goodbye to our family house. When we were riding we were watching our house until it disappeared from view. When we arrived at the station we saw transports of passenger trains locked up with padlocks. A soldier with a gun stood next to each car watching that nobody escapes. When we entered the car we found only plank beds on which we were supposed to sleep. Each car was stuffed with 50 persons in each together with the luggage. All of us started crying in despair not knowing what to do. Each one of us knew that we were going to be deported deep into Russia to Siberia. Some started running away through the windows and hiding in the forests. During these escapes of people, Russian soldiers shot to kill. The evening came, some spread themselves on the plank beds, and others had no place so they were sitting on the floor. In all cars there were no toilets only a hole in the floor. Those who went there we covered up with blankets. The train was supposed to start the next night. Before leaving came the moment of separation from fatherland. We all started crying and bidding farewell one more time to our beloved Fatherland, we knew that we were going to our doom and that we will never return to It again. The train started right away and we left for the russian hell. Along the way they didn't give us any food or water. We had nothing to drink so from thirst we sucked on frozen screws in the car. The trip was very terrible, hungry and cold. The trip lasted a whole month. Until one day we were unloaded on the side. At the side there were sleighs and they rode with us to the barracks. There they distributed us throughout the entire barracks. After a few hours the evening came and we lay down to sleep. On the second day in the morning we had not gotten up yet and we already heard the N.K.V.D. run into the barracks and they started driving us out to work. Each one of us from the age of 15 up had to go to work, because if he didn't go they would put him in jail for a few months. My Mama was very ill and she couldn't go to work so they forced her to because they locked her up in jail for three weeks. In jail Mama almost died of hunger, because for the whole day they gave 20 grams of bread and one liter of water. When Mama left the jail she had to go to work. At work Mama cried from pain and despair. When Mama came back from work she was barely alive. Dad too worked at "grushchiki," that is he was loading train cars with wood. There Dad exerted all his strength, because he worked day and night. As soon as the cars arrived, Dad had to go even at night. At night they woke Dad up and chased him to work. At work Dad froze his legs and hands. The frost was very great, it reached over 50 degrees. At work people died of hunger cold and frost. Food was given only so one could have a bite to eat. During the war they gave 700 grams of bread for each worker and those who didn't work got 300 grams. There was a mess hall in which they cooked soup and one could buy it one liter each for a person per day. We called this soup caudle because a few groats were swimming on top of it. Hunger prevailed in all the barracks even at the Moskale because they too didn't get any more than we did. They got the same as we did. They told us fulfill the norm and when we fulfill it we will get more money. None of us could fulfill that norm, because even the Moskale themselves couldn't fulfill it, even though they work all their lives. In the entire settlement there was only one store in which one could buy bread but only in exchange for food coupons and the merchandise was there once a month, shoes, coats, and cloth. We didn't buy that merchandise because we had nothing to buy bread with. And even if we wanted to one day, it ran out, because Moskale, when they found out that merchandise was delivered, would secure their places in the line at night, on the so-called ocherit in Russian. There was also a school in which they taught communism. They signed us up at that school and instilled communism into us. They said that God was stalin and that stalin gives everything. We weren't listening to that because we knew well who God was. In that school they wanted to break our spirit and turn us into communists. But they couldn't do anything with us because we were persevering and we didn't lose our spirit, and Our Lord seeing our agony freed us from that russian yoke. And so in 1942 on July 30 we were liberated.

DOCUMENT NO. 69

PGC/Box 117

MARIAN H.
Born 1927
Przemyślany county
Tarnopol voivodeship

A few weeks after the coming of the Bolsheviks, they took my paternal uncle to the school building in Mazów and began to beat him, to give up the weapon he didn't have, after beating him for half an hour they led Uncle H[——] out to the pond and ordered him to chop the ice, because they thought he had thrown the gun in the pond. When they were convinced that there was nothing there they put him into the well to see if it wasn't there, but they didn't find anything there. They went back to the school and beat him again. After beating him for an hour they let him go all black and blue and splattered with blood. The next day my father took a cart to my grandfather's and fled to Lwów with my very sick and beaten uncle.

Feb. 5, 1940. The Bolsheviks came and surrounded us with the local militia, they got to robbing at once. They took grain, wood, and things. They took all the wood for building a house and carpenter's tools. They took all our clothing, they only left us about two shirts. We ran away to the town of Gliniany and we came back home from there after a week but there was no reason to. The doors and windows were pulled out, the stove smashed, and the pictures ripped apart. Our house looked as if nobody had lived in it for 10 years, but we hadn't been away only 4 days.

DOCUMENT NO. 70

PGC/Box 117

ANTONI P.
Born 1927
Radziechów county
Tarnopol voivodeship

I am gripped by fear when I remember the time the Bolsheviks entered our village. There were two Polish officers on the road going home to their wives and children. Some Ukrainians and Bolsheviks grabbed them. After three days of real murder they were shot, and the Ukrainians took their shoes and clothing. Before he died one said to tell his wife he was alive no more.

DOCUMENT NO. 71

PGC/Box 119

K.S.
Born 1927
Radziechów county
Tarnopol voivodeship

My recollections of USSS occupation

February 10 1940 in the night already before dawn the whole family still slept I was already awake And suddenly someone is banging on the door with the butt of a rifle I jumped to open the door but my father did not let me Daddy got up took a revolver and went to open the door and see who it was and what he wants. At first I thought it was the Ukrainians. I look and here they are leading daddy in at the point of a gun daddy is going first and after daddy two soldiers with rifles pointing at daddy when they sat daddy down on a stool they read out an order that we are to leave They did not allow us to take anything But mommy figured out a way and brought up from the cellar a 5 liter bottle of vodka and asked the soldiers to drink because anyway it will have to be poured out. At first they didn't want to drink. one of the soldiers said that mommy should give the first glass to daddy when daddy drank a glass of vodka then they sat down at the table and in 10 minutes the whole bottle was empty the Bolsheviks got so drunk that they threw down their rifles and began to curse Stalin. And we taking advantage of the situation took all our things and wanted to escape but the village was surrounded with troops so we had to leave for the station in Radziechów.

DOCUMENT NO. 72

PGC/Box 124

MIECZYSŁAW P.
Skałat county
Tarnopol voivodeship

An Orphaned Pole

On February 10 when heating fuel had not been delivered to school, there were no lessons and when I was going home I was picked up and driven home wher my father stood under the gun even when my father went to the toilet the NKVD went with him they did not let us take any food products, later for 2 days they did not give us anything to eat on the way until on the 3rd day they gave us soup and 200 grams of bread per person. It was the worst for little children who cried for milk but for 2 weeks they did not see any. When we arrived at our destination, my father, mother, and older brother went to the forest to chop wood according to quotas and I as a 14-year-old boy had to bring the timber in from the woods for heating in the village although I fell into the snow up to my shoulders I was not allowed to get into the sleigh. in the spring when the snow melted I picked frozen berries and only on the sly. I went to the field where they cooked potatoes for pigs filled my pockets and brought them home. then I was taken with my family to the forest where there was nothing but three barracks for a few days we got nothing to eat and they chased us to work in the field we picked sorrel and ate it like cattle let out of the barn they let us clear a piece of the forest with a tractor we planted potatoes which later the pigs of one of the khaziay [farmer] dug up in the fall they gave us 10 rubles for 10 days which were spent in 3 days in school we learned Russian German and other subjects at the geography lesson professor Lavrenty Pavlovich told us what benefits we derive from the golstrom [i.e., Gulfstream] current which makes it possible for us to catch fish in the winter. And that in 1937 the Americans wanted to block off the curent, but they were not successful because the curent was so strong that it broke the dam and then they gave it up. without interruption they told us how strong they are that they are not afraid of anyone that Poland would never rise again and when the amnesty came and one of the Polish boys asked whether his words had come true he said that it was only temporary.

DOCUMENT NO. 73

PGC/Box 117

FRANCISZEK S.
Tarnopol county
Tarnopol voivodeship

On September 17, 1939, at 3 o'clock in the afternoon the soviets entered Tarnopol and said that they are coming to aid us.

On September 18 they started robbing stores and breaking up our troops.

Us Poles did not want to surrender without a struggle. The soviets won because their forces were much bigger.

On October 9th the Ukrainians together with the soviets burned us down.

They couldn't burn down our house because it was covered with a tiled roof. So they broke our windows and promised to kill us.

On June 9 the soviets arrived and took us away. On the way they told us that they are moving us to another village. When they were taking us my Mother took with her the painting of Our Lady, when the soviet saw it in mother's hand he snatched it away from her hands and threw it against the ground with all his might the frame broke my mother wanted to pick it up from the ground but the evil soviet again is pushing mother away. When he walked away mother picked up the painting with sorrow.

They drove us to the station and loaded into freight cars of 18 ton capacity, 55 persons in each: men, women, and children together.

They drove us to russia at gunpoint, to a settlement in siberia.

After four days we were signed up for soviet school. At school they taught us that there is no God.

We were irritated by such a school where they don't allow us to praise the Lord.

But then also it was not for long.

Afterward they chased us out to work.

They didn't care that we were minors. In the winter the frost 48 degrees they chased us to work. The holidays are coming parents went to the commander to ask his permission to arrange the holidays.

But the commander fiercely asks parents to go away and says there is no God and there is no need for holidays. On Christmas holidays day in the morning the commander arrives and chases us out to work, he threatens that if someone doesn't go out to work they will be tried.

Easter holidays I also spent this way.

During the month of September I worked at cleaning up a narrow track. At the station I walked into a booth in which there was a radio. As I was sitting I listened with fear to the soviet news during which general Anders spoke—All of you Poles are free from this moment on.

I ran to my parents with great joy and I tell them this, they don't want to believe me. But after three days the commander says to us that we are free.

We turn to him to ask for travel documents. They issued them to us with difficulty and vexation. From siberia we were transported to Central Asia. To Uzbekistan. There I worked in a kolkhoz, very hard, and there is nothing to eat.

So I picked whatever grass there was, my mother cooked it for me and I ate it without great eagerness but I had to because there was nothing else.

Finally I joined junaks.

DOCUMENT NO. 74

PGC/Box 117

JANUSZ N.
Born 1927
Tarnopol
Tarnopol voivodeship

One of the moving facts that has stayed in my memory: I lived with my Mother and brother as a military family in the Military House in Tarnopol. A group of Polish officers also lived there. From the moment the news spread that the Russians had crossed our border the officers living next door to us began to prepare for receiving them in a fitting way thinking that they are cultured civilized people. But this was not so, after the entry of the Russian forces into Tarnopol they began to conduct searches looking for Polish officers. Our officers found out about this and made hurried plans to leave. At the moment when they were to enter their car the Russians rushed in and began to ask whether there were

·any Polish officers here. My Mother said that there were no officers but they did not believe her and began to search, and noticed the officers going into their car right away they began to shoot at them, our men got out of the car and surrendered seeing that there was no other way out. The Russian officer ordered them to turn around and a moment later a salvo rang out as one they fell dead and those cadavers lay out in the courtyard for several days and another thing also moved me that the wife of one of the officers found her husband among the dead. With a rending cry she threw herself at his corpse shouting Bolshevik dogs!! the Russians heard this and locked her up in prison. Then followed persecution of the Poles and they began to lock people up in prison, for any word that they did not like they conducted an investigation. From one factory they removed the machines saying that they had to fix them, but they took them to Russia. I went to the grocery store and saw a Russian who was buying food supplies for 500 rubles. The grocer asked him politely why he was buying so much and the officer answered that he had to send them to his wife because she had not seen such delicacies there as for instance bisquits for a sick stomach.

My impressions of the Russian occupation.

DOCUMENT NO. 75

PGC/Box 117

STANISŁAW B.
Trembowla county
Tarnopol voivodeship

"Exemplary Economy"

When the Soviets entered Poland, they immediately started organizing meetings and forcing the populace to renounce the Christian faith. When people didn't want to attend the meetings, the NKVD would go from house to house, and whoever was caught had to pay fines in grain. In our village of Boryczówka they did not allow us to study in Polish: only one subject was taught in Polish, we were allowed to read and speak in Polish, but other languages were taught in Russian. We couldn't pray at school, they would close down the churches and wanted us to pay them for the church. We couldn't buy anything at one store. They would confiscate anything they found and ship it to their own country. They would take away our potatoes by planes, and then they would drop them from planes as if we didn't have any potatoes in our village. They took away our machines for threshing grain and carried them away in the direction of Russia. They prohibited us from having a radio in the common house, they closed down the library and kept carrying things away. On July 13, 1940, the Soviets came to our house, to the courtyard, my cousin was standing in the doorway and baitzy [soldiers] threw their guns down at her and yelled where was her simja [family]. My cousin got frightened and fainted, and baitzy sat down in the doorway and kept laughing. No one else was at home and when the neighbours saw my sister on the ground they thought she was dead and wanted to run into the courtyard but the baitzy didn't let them and said they would shoot prjamo w lop [right in the head]. Finally they pleaded with them and recovered my sister from fainting. Me, father, brother, and sister ran off into the wheat field, when we found out what was going on in our house we had to go back because the Soviets said that if we are not there then they will take away our old granny who lived on another street, was sick and eighty-five years old. When we got to the courtyard the Russians asked if it was the khadziej [farmer] of that farm and father said yes, and they ordered us to pack in half an hour and take with us at most fifty kilograms, what one had on and what one could carry by hand. They took us to the county seat Trembowla to the militia station and there they conducted an interrogation with us for thirteen days, they asked father who he was and what he was doing and if he fought against the Soviets during the World War, and what his military rank was. Everybody knows they found out nothing. There were many of us there, they always did everything at night. After thirteen days, at night, they drove us by cars to a station to go to Tarnopol, by freight cars with sixty persons in each 18-ton car. They put bars on doors and windows, we were driven without food or drink to where baitzy said everything bude kharasho [will be all right], lice bit us without mercy. We rode like this for two months, didn't leave the cars, mothers would throw dead children through the bars, they died of hunger, and be left along the way and no one would ever see them again. We got to the settlement of Viettki and went to the barracks, there we had not only lice but bedbugs too, so many of them that we couldn't see the walls. On the second day people had to go to work because there was nothing to eat, every weak one had to saw wood to earn 200 grams of bread and adin rub [one ruble]. Soup at the mess cost one ruble and 80 kopecks, two people had to work to buy one serving of soup which consisted of a small piece of fish and a few groats.

Only those who had fever were permitted to visit the doctor, and each cripple had to work. If someone was late for work they would be tried, one man at our settlement was late for work so he went to be tried and was sentenced to 8 years in prison, his wife in despair went out of her mind and they took her away someplace, nobody knows where.

When somebody died they didn't even want to give planks for the coffin. A child of one forester Heler died so they had to steal planks to make a coffin.

We had to keep asking for a long time to get a horse and a wagon to take the body to the cemetery, because the cemetery was over a dozen kilometers away and crosses were there at each grave and a stone with the date engraved on it. Those were graves of Polish soldiers buried during the world war. In the winter the frost reached 45 degrees Celsius and still we had to work in the woods chopping down trees, up to our waists in snow. We had to go to the baths together with Soviet women, even if someone didn't want to they had to, lice and dirt hurt in the baths, Soviet women acted brazenly towards the Poles. After long and hard work they announced that amnesty for the Poles had been discussed, and before the amnesty they had been telling us that we would never see Poland again. The commander of the settlement, Porshniov, said that there would be a Poland only if he grows hair on his hand. He said that Poles shouldn't think that if there is an amnesty we won't have to work but that ishcho bolshe bidety robotati [there will be even more work]. Poles absolutely wanted to leave that settlement because the German-Soviet front lines were close, only 40 kilometers away but the soviets wouldn't let us go.

Finally we broke away, they gave us a barge which was so broken down that it came apart on the Volga river, everyone was saved because there were many small ships on the Volga. We traveled for two months from Vologda to Tashkent, we were hungry and lice bit us because we went on our own. We learned to steal because we had to survive from that. We got as far as Kazakhstan and there they drove us to kolkhozes a few persons in each, we couldn't get clothing or bread we walked around naked and hungry.

DOCUMENT NO. 76

PGC/Box 124

Józef N.
Born 1926
Trembowla county
Tarnopol voivodeship

My most difficult moment during my Mother's arrest in Russia

They deported me, with my whole family on February 10, '40 to Russia, they closed us in a railway car. After a long trip we arrived to

Kami oblast. At first things were good for us we still had some provisions from Poland we brought a home orchestra from Poland in which I also played. After a long stay in Russia my father sold his instrument and the others also sold theirs but I held on to my trumpet despite all the hunger I underwent I did not sell it. One time the commandant chose my mommy to go for two months of timber floating my mommy went with my older sister. I stayed behind with two sisters and a brother at home. Mommy left us a few rubles and I also went to work. I hauled timber, later when I strained myself I could not haul timber, then the commandant did not let me rest and get cured but chased me in the morning to burn tree branches and I could not walk because it hurt me inside but I had to. My younger sister ran the house. After their return after two months mommy and my sister came back to us mommy told her impressions of death on the water, expecting to receive her pay. As her pay mommy got 30 rubles. Mommy went to the commandant and asks him for a pass to check the receipts. The commandant did not give the pass and told mommy to go hang herself. I and my older sister did not know anything. Mommy came to the barracks took a rope a little bread and went into the woods. I held my mommy back in her grief she hit me with the rope and went away. A few hours later they found mommy on a spruce tree mommy had a rope around her neck. Under the tree stood some girls mommy thought it was my sisters and wanted to say something but the girls raised up a rumpus to the commandant who had an ax in his belt and he chopped down the spruce and mommy was taken to the kantor [office]. Mommy already crazy grabbed the commandant's ax and struck him in the back the commandant fell to the floor. At that moment I wanted to go into the kantor unfortunately the door was locked. I took a piece of wood broke the window and smashed through the bars wanting to free mommy. Unconscious mommy lay on the commandant's kajka [bunk]. I crawled in through the window take mommy's hand suddenly a militiaman rushed in and chased me away he put handcuffs on mommy and led her to the bania [bath]. Mommy got the handcuffs off with a nail and wanted to escape but she was not successful because a Polish man was watching her. On the next day they took mommy to a jail 300 kilometers away from me. I understood that I had to work and I continued to haul timber. I had a horse that was falling over together with me. I hauled timber for one month and then I got sick and could not work. The commandant notified the seller that he should not give us bread but the seller had an understanding for children and he gave us bread secretly. One time the commandant rushes into the barracks and ask why I did not go to work, I say that I am sick, and he says to that and what about an excuse from the doctor. I did

War Through Children's Eyes

not have an excuse because he did not understand my illness because it was a rupture of a person the commandant took me to the kantor and asks will you not malinger and go to work and I say no because I am sick. He wrote down an official record and read it to me and says: ty podchyniajsia [obey] I remained silent he grabs me by the head and to the bania. I stuck my head out and say to my younger sister bring me a little bread and this Pole who betrayed my mother said to the commandant that I had broken the window and am sticking out my head. The commandant rushed into the bania kicked me and I only licked myself after three days he let me out soon mommy came from jail her feet frozen her face wrinkled. Later mommy rested my sister and I went to work later mommy. ' finally the happy moment came we went to the south. There I joined the junaks mommy went to Africa with my sisters and brother. My father is in the army.

DOCUMENT NO. 77

PGC/Box 117

HENRYK N.
Zaleszczyki
Tarnopol voivodeship

Sept. 17, 1939, a line of cars with refugees stretching from the bridge separating Romania from Poland, to the neighboring villages, notwithstanding the objection of the Romanian frontier authorities broke through and reached the land of Romania. Panic reigned in the town: Terrible rumors went around, like the Germans were reaching the Bug line, the Polish army was in a terrible retreat, and like the red flag was flying on the castle in Warsaw because a new government had been elected which decided to defend Warsaw, and a new rumor that the Russians had crossed the border. Some said that they were coming to help us to form a united front against the Germans, others said that they were against Poland and united with Germany. Because of that rumor and as a result of the accounts of refugees about the killing of the Polish people by the Germans, people started leaving town quickly. Mostly everybody fled, without regard to nationality and wealth. But after the air raid which fell on Zaleszczyki when the refugees were on the Romanian side and massed together and surrounded by an army cordon, frightened by planes of unknown nationality circling overhead they began to leave inhospitable Romania and come back again. People preferred to die, however, on the land of their homeland.

A strange coincidence, the day the Bolsheviks entered our town, i.e., Sept. 18, 1939, was the day the golden Polish autumn weather ended. That same morning it began to rain and it fell incessantly. In the quiet of the morning, there suddenly was an unpleasant whirring sound. After a while two Soviet tanks came around the corner going in the direction of Romania. The tanks crossed the bridge and entered Romanian territory and after a short time came back. The tanks stopped at the customs office and human heads emerged that looked rather like devils they were so sooty. After a while an auto came with Soviet soldiers and it seemed to me with "siberia" blowing from them. In our boarding house which stood right on the river the artillery billeted. The local people started to approach the soldiers. They conducted the conversation in Ukrainian. At the beginning the soldiers did not want to talk but later however they loosened their tongues. The main theme on their side was that in the U.S.S.R. matches cost only two kopecks. The whole day they didn't send them provisions. When towards evening they feasted them with supplies from the boarding house they loosened their tongues. We learned that they never saw milk or eggs in the army and they continually asked that we give them "honey" which is what they called jam.

During the summer season we lived in the boarding house but in the winter in town. Because of such close contact with the army we decided to move to town. But here we met with the objection of the landlord who said: "Your Polish times have come to an end, now our times begin." However with the help of friends we forced our way into our apartment but we moved very soon. In town there were columns of the army surrounded by people and they told each other the reply to the question whether there are oranges in Russia, one of the soldiers replied that there are very many factories in Russia which manufacture oranges. At that answer somebody in the crowd asked: "maybe you manufacture Greta Garbo too?", the answer was that "hundreds a day are produced." To the bakeries which stopped baking bread they brought flour, but from a Polish mill. Several houses in town were demolished by the "bright tankmen." The main street which led through Zaleszczyki was totally ploughed up, because the Russians wanted to show that they had tractors. The dry goods stores were full of soldiers buying. The day after the Bolsheviks entered, I was walking through town, when several autos full of soldiers caught my attention and they were rushing in the direction of Tarnopol. Going on I heard shouts calling out and after a while I saw women with children fleeing in panic from the neighboring village, a whole crowd of Ukrainians with bundles rushing along to town shouting: "They're beating our people from Romania, some unknown army is on the way and they beat and kill our men." I ran home with this news to my mother who locked me in my room. The next day we found out. The Ukrainians attacked the Polish colony of Śmigłowo with the object of robbing and murdering the colonists, but it wasn't all that easy. When the colonists saw the other colonists [Ukrainians] approaching they pulled out who knows where from rifles going back to the [1863] uprising and even a machine gun and they started peppering the Ukrainians and they occupied their village and only surrendered when the Bolshevik army came the next day. They organized a school system. I started going to school. But what kind of a school could it be without religion and later without the Polish language. Teachers we didn't know continually tried to convince us that Polish teachers taught us badly, that the history they taught us was false and that there is no God and they took down the crosses and in their place hung portraits of Bolshevik leaders. They organized meetings where they forced us to belong to Bolshevik youth associations.

In town it got worse and worse with food. Dry goods and food stores the owners closed. Instead they opened "cooperatives" where there were only advertising packages. There were only a few bakeries in town. By 6 o'clock in the morning I was standing in line to buy a piece of bread. From time to time a few articles of food appeared in the stores and lines formed at once usually several people went out of them with broken ribs.

At school we ran away from lessons more and more because you had to fight for provisions and heat. At the school meetings after the "agitator" made a long speech about the "Bolshevik pioneers" he asked if anyone had any conclusions to draw and people answered, less and less bread! There is no kerosene! There is no sugar! There is no wood! They whistled and shouted. It got to the point that they wanted to close our school. Polish soldiers came back from fighting the Germans but how they came back. Ukrainian bands attacked the returning Polish soldiers and robbed them of their clothes and let them go home beaten and naked. In the building where the judiciary was housed they took officers who had struggled across the German-Soviet border to get home and the Bolsheviks caught them and deported them to Russia. The whole Dniester from the shore was fenced with barbed wire. But that did not help and all through the night there was the sound of shots fired at young people and men of draft age who were running away. At the beginning the Ukrainian population was favorably inclined to the Bolsheviks and also to the first elections. After the first elections, after voting for the annexation of "Western Ukrainia" to the USSR, they began to arrest Ukrainian leaders. You no longer saw hordes of Ukrainians with red bands on their arm and rifles and proudly and haughtily strutting around town. They didn't spit any more when they saw a Pole and with pity they nodded their heads in mutual understanding. But they began to lock up and deport Poles too. At night you could hear the hard steps of the NKVD leading away people they arrested. Everybody waited for his turn and the judgment of God.

Wilno Voivodeship

NIKODEM U.
Born 1927
Dzisna county
Wilno voivodeship

My Experiences in Russia

In 1939 when the flood swept across the borders of Poland, the way of life changed all through the eastern part. In my family home you couldn't sleep through a whole night in peace. I had to hide in safe places: in clumps of bushes, up trees, in haystacks standing in the fields, under bridges, wherever I could.

And that's how it was when that horde fell on town and country. You knew at once that they had never seen anything in Russia. I saw myself a political officer who went into a store with his wife and she didn't know what to buy. First she bought 8 kilograms of sausage. So, how was it? When they first came in, they both couldn't get their fill of the smell, like dogs on the track of a hare the two of them kept smelling that sausage. He couldn't control his appetite for that sausage very long, he totally lost patience and broke off half for himself and gave half to his wife. As soon as he bit into it his eyes lit up and he said: vkusnaja kelbasa [delicious sausage]. But his wife didn't say anything because the sausage made her eyes bulge as she stuffed it down and she only nodded her head three times yes. Not half a minute went by and he ate half the sausage and asked for another one. "Please if I could have another one," and the lady who was selling it said "Why not, you can have more than two" then both of them jumped with joy and she said: "Eight kilos please." The saleswoman gave it and he put it anywhere he had room, even inside the top of his boots. She bought calves' feet too, which she carried in her hands because she had no place to put it and maybe just because she wanted to show off.

In October an election was announced for a representative to a committee, who was fixed in advance. Everybody had to go anyhow. Old people who couldn't walk they took on wagons. For appearance' sake a room was prepared with a screen, but who ever went behind it was taken to jail that night, so almost nobody went there.

The town horde (Byelorussian herdsmen) took their prewar guns (slung on rope) and went around the colony taking the colonists' weapons and the woodsmens' and went around at night and didn't let people sleep. Why was that? Because they had all been sitting in prison and now they wanted to take revenge. They also persuaded others to make raids at night and rob. There were only a few of them because many didn't want to obey that damned government because they knew what soviet Russia means. The Byelorussians and the boorish militia (the ones who carried their weapons on rope slings) fought among themselves. The Byelorussians wanted the Polish government and didn't want to obey the local militia, and the militia resisted, but a lot perished on both sides.

Then the year 1940 came when many Poles were deported to the depths of Russia.

On the morning of February 10, when it was still gray outside, a wild swarm attacked our colony together with the NKVD. It was so hard to live through that time, when as many of them as possibly could, crowded into my family home and at their head was a NKVD man with a pistol pointed at my father, who stood calmly like an old soldier. Then the NKVD man said: obyskat dom [search the house] they all rushed around like they were hungry for food, and they didn't inspect but every one of them wanted to steal something. That ruffian, that thief (that's what my father called him) put dad behind a table and didn't let him move an inch, but he let me and my younger brother go out and get our things to pack. I ran to the granary and took some meat from the barrel. One of the village boors comes up to me and says: polovinu ostav [leave half of it] and I hit him with a stick on his noodle. Then some soldier heard us, and he came with the NKVD man and took me by the nape of the neck and dragged me to that same ruffian and reported that I had beaten a nineteen-year-old comrade. He shook his head and said da eto patsan [he's still a child] he let me go, and my younger brother had already broken the barrel open and packed the meat in his bag.

Within 15 minutes we had already got to the schoolhouse. We spent the whole day there.

At night when the sun went down the temp. was about −40°C. the caravan stretched 1-1/2 km. in the direction of the train station We passed by a church. The bells began to rattle as if to sound the alarm and we went farther, farther, and farther. We went through the village to the station, when they ordered us to get on. The next day the enormous transport moved towards the eastern border. In the hog cars it was packed They couldn't have stuffed as many pigs in as there were people. The doors were closed with a thick bar and eight locks and they were tied by rope.

That day we crossed the border (Zachacie). The whole transport roared when it heard that we are crossing the border. Singing broke out you could hear from the front to the back end of the train the national anthem.

Many days of monotonous life ensued.

We kept on traveling closed in by that bar and the locks. They took us to a silent wild place to transport us to the Krest settlement on the northern Dvina River in the wild forest.

At the beginning life was not hard because everybody had their food supplies and things to wear, but after a few months when things ran out a lot of people died. The NKVD was very fierce there. It was forbidden to go 100 meters away from the settlement. They only gave out 300 grams of bread per person. We didn't see anything sweet (sugar etc.) for 1/2 year.

It was horribly cold, it got down to 45–50° below C. They started forcing us out to work and talked to us like this u nas kto ne rabotaet tot i ne kushaet [here, if you don't work, you don't eat] and they robbed people because they didn't want to work themselves. My mama was unfit for heavy work. So she didn't go to work either. They took my dad, my sister, and my older brother 40 km. away from our settlement.

Two of us were left with mama. At the beginning I went to work because there was no bread. They put me to work hauling bread. At first I worked peacefully, until they got me. One morning when I was hauling bread, the settlement commandant noticed me. He came up and asked me: "Whose son are you, a colonist's or a forester's?" I said a colonist's. His hair stood up when he heard. He ordered me off the wagon and told me to go to the barracks where I lived. I got off and said: "I hope the snow runners break. He thought I had so little spirit that when he said to give the reins I would just give them to him. But I spoke up to him: "Vy govorite zhe u vas panov net, tak vozni sam" [you say there are no masters in Russia, so take them yourself]. He took them and as soon he started to go he upset the breadbasket. I laughed and ran away with the horse whip and left that boor all by himself. He went two kilometers in four hours. Since the horse was lazy he beat it so hard that he had no more strength to beat with.

All year he kept an eye on me and I kept both eyes on him.

Then came the time of hunger and cold and what was worse, death. Three hundred sq. meters were covered with corpses. Nobody could do anything about it. All you could do was trust in God.

The NKVD attitude toward us was very bad and sneering.

Our young people laid ambushes for the NKVD men (in which I took part too).

They came after us with pistols and we came at them with sling-shots. If we saw some boor taking a Polish girl to the commandant we got them apart and it was always the Russian who lost.

More and more people began to die of hunger and cold. A hundred went to work (every day) and 96 (average) came back.

Until happier times came.

On July 30 our premier of the Polish Republic signed an agreement with Stalin (who had been oppressing us till then) to free the Poles from the Russian yoke.

DOCUMENT NO. 79

PAC/Box 50

ANDRZEJ K.
Born 1932
Dzisna county
Wilno voivodeship

On September 17th 1939 the bolsheviks crossed the Polish border. Some peasants, and Jews most of all greeted the bolsheviks with flowers, because they thought that the bolsheviks would give them a lot of land and the riches stolen from institutions and estates. When the Soviet troops came to our town they immediately arrested the policemen and the military personnel who did not escape in time. The bolsheviks established 'selsovety' [village soviets], 'raikomy' [regional (county) committees] and other committees which the Jews, local communists, and those who arrived from Russia joined. The first founder of militia was a Jew Srol Zelikman, a local citizen. The regional chief of NKVD was Sapiehin, and they delegated from the 'raion' to our 'selsovet' the militiaman Fiedura. The bolsheviks appointed local authorities and Fiedura dropped by them night and day for conferences and then one of the suspects would disappear. In November [the correct date is October] the bolsheviks made an election and they chose deputies to local authorities. But they knew well that everybody had enough of them and would vote against. People didn't want to go to vote so the bolsheviks led them with drawn guns and if somebody protested he would not be there the next day because they arrested him. For the election they gave slips of paper which one supposedly could look at in a separate booth and if he didn't like the candidate he could cross him out and write in another. But it didn't happen this way because there was an armed soldier in the booth and if anybody would just glance at the ballot he would be in jail right away.

After the vote the bolsheviks boasted that the Polish population voted for them. The bolsheviks persecuted the Poles a lot in prisons. In Wilejka where the prison was one could hear shouts and moans, so in order for people not to hear them the bolsheviks started up engines, to drown out the moans.

When daddy came back from the war Srol immediately arrested him but when the servants from the estate pleaded with them they let daddy out. Mommy lay paralyzed for a few weeks but a soviet doctor cured her, and later he got friendly with us and warned daddy 2 days before his arrest and daddy ran away to Lithuania. The second election took place in the spring and they chased people forcibly, like during the first vote, and they brought the ballot box to the sick people so they should cast their ballots. After the vote the bolsheviks started their rule: they collected enormous taxes, took away cattle, horses, pigs and started to take away farming machines, furniture, etc. After daddy's running away NKVD came in March to take us, and my little brother was very sick with pneumonia, and mommy cried a lot, schoolchildren cried, village women came running, they brought in the selsovet secretary who lived in our village and who defended us against the bolsheviks because mommy took care of his children before the war. They did not take us then. But there was no calm day or night. Some militiamen came, agitators—they investigated, spied, and searched for something all the time. They took us on June 20, 1941, because they found White Eagle [the Polish national emblem] and some letters. We traveled 27 days to Siberia. There were 95 people in the rail car. They locked us in. Heat, stink and the lice were killing people—especially because they gave us only 2, rarely 3 pails of water, and most often it was taken from puddles. The illnesses started: dysentery and typhus, and in the end measles. They brought us on a ship to the Kalmanka port, and then by car to the distant farm. We fell very sick with diarrhea and measles, and mommy had to go work hard far from the home: she dug ditches, carried manure, scythed. They paid very little for it and gave only 400 grams of bread. During work 'polevod' [supervisor] cursed our people with dirty words. A few times they made a search and always took away something. Then came amnesty. We left Siberia on March 20, 1942, to Uzbekistan, and in August we left for Iran.

DOCUMENT NO. 80

PGC/Box 120

ADAM P.
Dzisna county
Wilno voivodeship

My Experiences During the Soviet Occupation

When my father woke up on the morning of September 17 he heard shots. Something is happening my father told my mother? My father and mother went to church. When they got onto the main road, they saw crowds of people already coming back from the church. You couldn't go any farther because the crowds were coming from the church they were all very worried. What is it? What is it? my father asked a neighbor. Oh neighbor, the Soviets came they burned the blockhouse and a lot of the Soviet army is already here. What will we do? Run away! And the children? We won't leave them behind. All the Byelorussians were glad. A few days later the Soviets began to take everything and carry it across the border. They had various elections, where they didn't admit my father or the others.

When the 10th of February came they took our neighbors and deported them. We thought maybe we would stay. A few minutes after our conversation we saw soldiers standing in our yard. They open the door and shout ruki v goru [hands up]. We were so frightened to see all those soldiers that my father and all of us put our hands up. They rushed into the house and searched it. They didn't find anything. They said they would take us to another oblast. They made my father sit on a chair and two soldiers guarded him. They told us to pack our stuff. When we started to take good things away and things to eat they didn't let us. They say everything will follow. They only let us take a little meat and pots and what we were wearing. They took us to the station from both sides and also in front and behind the soldiers marched. They brought us to the station, and put about 50 people in a freight car that wasn't very big. The cars were locked. On the way they let us out for water, wood, boiling water, and for a bit of bread. Everything was checked. We rode for a week on the train and the next week on sledges. It was worse traveling by sledge than in the freight car, first because it was very cold and second because we traveled day and night. Three days after our arrival in the settlement they forced us out to work. They also made all the small children work. When they made a school in our settlement, they sent all the children to school. They also sent me to school. I go to the soviet school, better than going to work. I work hard because they shout to meet the norms. They gave us little to eat. 300 grams of bread if you don't work, 700 grams if you do. In the mess hall they also cooked a kind of bran flour soup and that cost 25 kopecks. People died. The cemetery was big more than 300 tombs. When we were waiting for spring to come they took all the men, boys, and girls to work on the so-called raftings. Work on the raftings is very dangerous because you can get drowned. You have to get across the river from bank to bank. There were no planks or bridges. And it was all done through a floating forest. The forest floats. You jump on a trunk and run. When you jump you can't go back because the forest is no longer behind you. It flowed farther on. So you stay on two logs and float with the tree. When the tree floats to the bank you jump as fast as you can on the bank. I was often in the water up to my neck and even over my head. One time I heard a shout, a young girl drowned. Oh, how unlucky! That was work on the raftings. I got a cold and go back to the settlement to my family. I was sick for a whole month with pneumonia. It's a bit better with food they give workers a kilogram and more [of bread] and half a kilogram to nonworkers. At night lice, bedbugs, and hunger bothered us, and by day work again. In the summer I caught fish in the river and also worked in the forest. I worked up to the norm. I never see the money for the norm because they cheated. In the office they cheated on the money every way they could. They took the money for themselves and forged various kinds of signatures for others. One time I'm coming to the office for money, they don't give it to me, they say I took it already and show me a signature. Just like mine. So I sadly went back to my barracks. I tell my father that I won't go to work, think what they will, I'll only go out looking for mushrooms and berries. I walked for a long time until they took me back again to heavy work at the base. The Soviet-German War began and so did the Polish-Soviet treaty. They declared an amnesty for us, in the mess hall on August 15, 1941. After reading out the amnesty we all got together and sang hymns to God and Poland, national anthem.

The commandant wanted to leave the mess hall but he couldn't because we didn't let him. So he went back and listened unwillingly to our songs. They started to give us departure documents but only for your own region. We and everybody took the documents even though we had no money. A few days later people started leaving. Everybody who had documents left and they also had little money. We leave too. We waited 5 days for the boat. When we got on the boat we traveled happily because things might get better for us. Maybe we will work and earn money. They wanted us to go back to our home. Everybody objected and didn't get off the boat, they took us farther on. We got to the train station. We waited a month for the train. When we got in the train car we were also very happy when we set out in the direction of Chkalov. We were on the train for three months. People died. There wasn't a day that they didn't take a few or even many dead people off the train. There was no water or food so people went around begging. Everybody was hungry, weak, and tired, they got off the train when our train was unloaded. We were unloaded and they took us again to a kolkhoz. Life was better there. But we were sad when our father died. My mother and sister made stockings, socks, gloves, mittens, etc. I went for wood, chopped wood, and laid the fire in the stove when my mother cooked. In April they told us that a Polish army and Junak groups were being set up. So we left for Dzalal

Abad because Junaks were there. On April 12 I joined the Junaks! I was very happy because I won't work so hard and I won't be hungry.

DOCUMENT NO. 81

PGC/Box 117

WACŁAW K.
Born 1928
Oszmiana county
Wilno voivodeship

In 1939 on September 17 when the russians invaded then all the poles started worrying that the russians invaded.

After two months at 3 o'clock at night when everyone was asleep they arrived they started knocking at the windows and breaking the windows and through the windows they came into the house and ordered dad to lift his hands up, and to me to return the weapons because he will shoot and dad didn't have weapons so they killed him. At 6 in the morning he told mama to pack up to leave and they took me away and started beating me up so I would return the weapons. and he ordered me to drink the water from the well because he thought that the water was poisoned and I drank 13 liters of water. And they packed us up 32 families for one car (this is 125 persons) and we rode all day in the winter to the station nobody wanted to get off so they stuck with bayonets and threw people down from the car and then said that they froze and in this way threw them on the ground and then would ride over them. We traveled to Russia for 4 months. Who had bread ate that bread and who didn't have died of hunger. and they threw him out while the train was in motion the train was going so they threw him out alive and he killed himself. in the train there were 70 persons so cramped that there was no room, and who didn't listen they would heat up the stoves red hot and tie him to the stove and he died there and if he still lived a little they threw him out When we came to russia the frost was 60 degrees 80 degrees. When we got to russia at 1 in the morning and they unloaded us onto the Field on which there was nothing in the morning N.K.V.D. men came and started distributing us to settlements and to work right away and who didn't go they didn't give bread and money. We worked felling trees in the woods and they rushed young children to cart manure and I worked with the horses, and when they taught horses to ride then they ordered me to train them to ride and I would sit and teach him for 3 weeks and for this they gave 20 kopecks. After 2 years they gave passports and deported us to Uzbech and sailed on the river mulderia and whoever was ill they threw out into the river we rode for 1 month so on the following day 12 persons died in one day from hunger and those who were ill they would finish off with a bayonet.

DOCUMENT NO. 82

PGC/Box 120

MIECZYSŁAW K.
Oszmiana county
Wilno voivodeship

They deported me to Russia with mama and the five of us. On the day of February 10 1940.

When they brought us to the settlement then there was nothing to eat. Everyone was chased to work and all Polish children to a soviet school. Mama was ill so one day she didn't go to work. So commander of the settlement said he will give no bread. Mama said she will go when she recovers. So he gave bread. The next day mama went to cart trees so a tree fell on her leg and hurt mama's leg and she couldn't work. So I went to the forest and picked mushrooms. And I cooked supper with them and brought to the barracks I put it on the table crooked and the soup spilled on my chest and I got burned. In Russia I was oblast Arkhangielsk Toporek settlement.

Grade I.

DOCUMENT NO. 83

PAC/Box 50

IRENA Ł.
Born 1930
Mołodeczno county
Wilno voivodeship

I was not under the German occupation.

I lived in the Wilno area. Sept. 17 the Bolsheviks invaded. We were told that they will help us, but real Poles met them with a heavy heart.

We lived on the Izabelin estate, papa was the estate manager of Count Tyszkiewicz. One morning we got a telephone call that the Soviet army was coming. The owner of the estate fled to Wilno by car. Mama and I also left, but papa stayed to settle things and said he will make us go. We fled from the estate to Wilno where Count Tyszkiewicz was to wait for us. We were driven by a man we didn't trust and had to avoid and sidestep any conversation. But fortunately halfway there he abandoned us because he was afraid they would pillage the estate without his presence. We were left alone, with us there was a serving women who also abandoned us because she had relatives not far away. We were alone and we drove slowly and stopped for long times because we thought that papa would catch up with us, but our waits were in vain, instead of papa we saw Bolshevik tanks coming over the hill. We were stricken with great fear and everybody on the road began to flee, and in front of us the Polish police tearing down bridges. Our horses ran like mad, shells whistled over our heads, and we couldn't find the road to Wilno.

But fortunately in that turmoil two policemen jumped onto the wagon who before that had been hiding in the field behind the bushes.

Finally we reached the outskirts of Wilno and we were safer on the streets of Wilno but we also had a lot of difficulties, they set up barricades to stop the Bolshevik tanks.

But we soon get to no. 35 Wielkapohulanka Street, where Count Tyszkiewicz was to wait for us. But we didn't find him because he crossed the border to Lithuania. After our arrival there we had to bury our weapons that very night because we were afraid of being searched. We ended up in an apartment where we couldn't sleep on the bed but only hide in the corners and even in the bathroom. Since Wilno was terribly shot up by the Bolsheviks.

In such a marvelous city where nothing ever was scarce there were soon long lines for bread and other products and the flour storehouse was pillaged. They began to rob stores, hotels, and factories and they took various small trifles and they loaded them on automobiles and railway cars and they covered it with tarpaulin and they sent it to the depths of Russia.

But all the time what bothered us was the thought of what happened to papa, so we decided to go back to the estate. On the way we heard rumors that papa was murdered.

But it turned out that papa was alive. When the Soviet authorities learned that we came back they came at once and they set up around our house with machine guns and mama and papa were taken for questioning and they tormented them from 3 o'clock in the afternoon to 11 at night. The next day they came by auto and took my papa away. They said he will come back soon, but we had to wait a long long time for papa's return.

They searched our place and mama was taken to the militia where they did an interrogation. In the evening mama came back terribly frightened and every minute expected to be arrested but very happily they didn't come back for us again.

All our things were taken even the nails were torn out of the walls. We were thrown out of the palace and into a lodging where potatoes used to be kept. We were not given food and the same for heating. We suffered a long time until finally we were allowed to go to the nearby town of Małodeczno. In town it was also hard for bread, I had to get up at 4 in the morning and go stand in a line almost till noon in order to get a piece of bread.

When there were the elections we were all forced to go vote and vote for who the Soviet authority picked.

Older women who could not walk to the elections or were sick then they came and took them by car. The elections were compulsory and you could go to jail etc.

Later came deportation, with the first transport mostly they took non-Jews and colonists. It made a horrible impression when they took people at night and they gave them no things or food and it was cold at night because it was February and they took them to the station and loaded them in dark cold and dirty freight cars and locked them in a fast like some kind of bandits they sent them far north into the depths of Russia.

A few months after this it was April 13 they took us just like our fellow countrymen for deportation to Russia and they didn't give us our things and they packed us like herrings into disgusting wagons where pigs had been before us and they locked us in and we traveled by road across our Polish border. Across the border you could already see misery and miserable shacks and clay huts with smoke coming out. At the station there were railway employees wearing leggings and shabby galoshes on their feet and they were ragged and dirty and they asked for a piece of bread and soap. Conditions on the journey were awful. We rode in dirty dark cars. A guard with bayonets watched us and the cars were locked and they didn't let us out. For such a long time on the journey we got dinner only twice, which was given to us at night, and it was thin sour soup. After such a long and wearisome journey, which lasted 14 days, we got to the place. They unloaded us at the Sherbakt station. We were in Kazakhstan. At the new place where they unloaded us we had to wait a long time for dispositions. Then they came with autos which transported us to kolkhozes which were scattered around the steppe far from the station. Thirteen families of us were taken to the Emilyanovka kolkhoz, the kolkhoz was small, it had barely 40 huts, we were 25 kilometers from the station. In the kolkhoz far-flung from the station, among foreign people we felt lonely and out of place. They gave us

War Through Children's Eyes

lodgings where three families were living, it was a small and dirty little room where the Russian landlady had kept chickens and we paid 50 rubles per person for the place.

The climate was ghastly, hot in the summer and everything smothered in sand and it was hard to get water there were no lakes or rivers to be found anywhere and there were no stones anywhere and trees and bushes didn't exist at all. In the winter there were terrible snowstorms called "buran" so that all the cottages were buried and the temperature reached -70 C. degrees. A lot of people perished in the winter during these snowstorms and for the most part Poles, those snowstorms sometimes lasted more than a week. In the dark and cold lodgings we suffered a lot and there was no fire and also no food. During those snowstorms mama had to go to report to the kolkhoz chief.

They didn't give us any work and they considered us great delinquents and we did not have the right to go to the place where the cattle were. All year we had to live selling off our own rags. Only after a year did our countrymen get work for which they were not paid, only they wrote down your "workdays" and they only had to pay after a year. They paid with rotten wheat, which we had trouble carrying to the mill etc. but when it was milled we had barely a third per kilogram. When papa came back from the lagers [camps] we were happy. But papa wasn't with us long because he went to the army. Papa was taken into the army but he still got a month's leave, so papa came back to us. After papa's return we decided to go south. We left the steppe and "siberia" with great difficulties. On the way we suffered hunger and thirst. The trip lasted a whole month and finally we got to the place. After his sufferings in prison and the lagers papa came back swollen and sick and after five days in the new place papa died. We moved to the Molotov koklhoz where we just starved and we had to eat the roots of plants. After great suffering and trouble we got across the border. Under the protection of the Polish authorities we felt happy.

We are very happy to be on Iranian soil and for that we can be grateful to the Polish Government.

DOCUMENT NO. 84

PGC/Box 120

Stanisław C.
Wilejka county
Wilno voivodeship

In our car there were 40 people. We didn't have anything to drink or anything to eat. We traveled hungry. Lice bothered us. I worked in the settlement. I peeled bark off the trees. I hurt my foot at work and was sick for a month I didn't do anything. In school they laughed at the Lord God. The teacher ordered us to call out to God. Russian children called out and nothing happened but when Russian children called out to Stalin candy poured out but the Polish children didn't eat it. They fought with me that Poland was finished. I was saying that Poland exists and always will. For that they wanted to take papa. In the settlement a lot of people died. I got typhus.

12 years old

DOCUMENT NO. 85

PGC/Box 121

FRANCISZEK K.
Wilejka county
Wilno voivodeship

On the first day when the soviets entered Poland, everywhere in cities and villages pamphlets were distributed in which it said: beat Poles, Polish clerks, murder wealthy people, take away their possessions. Policemen were shot dead. Inhabitants of cities were exiled and their wealth was carried away to russia. Tile stoves were taken apart and carried away to russia. Polish soldiers were captured and executed. The forester was led to the forest at 12 midnight and shot dead. For absence at gatherings so-called meetings one was punished with prison. A colonist and his family were murdered at night and thrown into the cellar. In stores they bought everything in sight. Paintings and holy sculptures were destroyed. Our keeper's house was surrounded by 8 "boytzy" [soldiers] my father was ordered to put his hands up a search was made and we were ordered to pack up. We were taken to the station at gunpoint. At the station they loaded into dirty cars. 4 machine guns stood at the rear of the transport. There was stink in the cars one couldn't leave the car. Small children and even adults took care of their needs in the cars. There was no water people fainted of thirst. Typhus started spreading. People were dying. Cars were unlocked once every few days. One could always hear from the soviets that there will be no Poland. When we arrived they ordered men to bathe together with women. They took us to dirty houses where lice and bedbugs drank our blood without mercy. Every time we were late for work we were punished with jail. People were ordered to push dumpcarts in the mines

40 per one and for not fulfilling a norm they wouldn't get a worker's share of bread. Punishment for leaving an assigned area was exile to a labor camp. Mama who had a small child was ordered to go to work after the mother and the child were exhausted the child died. In an apartment 5 by 10 meters large lived 80 people. Lines thousand of persons long formed at day and at night around stores and mess halls. At night they controlled and did searches whether anyone had weapons or Polish papers. Jan Świstak who left for another settlement to visit his daughter, when N.K.V.D. caught him the commander himself was riding a horse with a revolver in his hand, in sprint, and he had to run ahead of him for eight kilometers. Mama sold father's army coat so for Easter she bought one egg for each one of us, and for father a packet of makhorka [tobacco]. Next to Polish housing manure picked out of toilets was spread. In the forest I used to saw wood for fuel where I worked very hard because I had to fulfill a norm of 6 cubic meters per person. I also learned to steal there because I had to live. To smoke, to use dirty words. One day when we were working I saw an old man carrying bread, we jumped up to him and took a loaf of bread from him because we were hungry.

DOCUMENT NO. 86

PGC/Box 120

Leon K.
Wilejka county
Wilno voivodeship

I. My experiences during the Soviet occupation. September 17, 1939, when enemies attacked our Country from the East and the West. The place I lived was occupied by the Bolsheviks. In the first days of the seizure of our land, the Soviets began arresting our more important people and deporting them to the distant east. All this Soviet behavior got more and more so. They imposed large contributions and tributes on the agricultural population, and they took grain and cattle. They grabbed whatever they could, and they devastated town and country. They took the spoils to the depths of russia. They tore down Polish eagles and flags in offices and schools. They defaced important postal and communal signs. They set up their own laws and offices.

II. February 10. On the night between Friday and Saturday when we were sound asleep, six Soviets and the predsedatel [village head] appeared under our windows armed with rifles and bayonets. One yelled otviraj dvery [open the door]. My father went down and opened the door, 4 soviets leaped into the room they yelled hands up, they searched the house, they took important documents from my father and mother. Then they said to take good clothes and food for several days. A few minutes later we mounted our horses and they took us to the station.

There they loaded us onto a freight car where there were more than 60 people. 6 transports left the station. On the way they only gave us a pail of cold water a day. The cars were padlocked, and there was an armed Soviet in every car.

After two weeks of traveling we ended up in the Urals. At one station we waited for sleighs with horses, which were to take us more than 150 kilometers. It was almost 60 degrees below.

III. Work in the settlement. After two days rest we went to work in the woods, we walked more than 10–15 km. to work. Every day without rest though it was 50 degrees C below. People unaccustomed to those conditions got frozen feet, hands, and ears. Typhus and other plagues reigned. People died like flies in hospitals and barracks, they were buried three and four in a grave. A lot were murdered by the Soviet commandants. The norms required 4 to 6 meters of wood a day.

They forced you to work from the age of 14 to 70. At first they gave a worker a kilogram of bread but later three hundred grams. Aside from bread they sold herring.

Occasionally they gave us half a kilo of oatmeal grits for a worker's ration book.

They forced us to go to Soviet schools and learn to read and write in Soviet. It was forbidden to pray and believe in the Lord God. After two years in captivity everybody went around like corpses from hunger and cold. Almost everybody went around showing naked body through his clothes. We lived thirty families in the barracks, we slept on beds made of boards, straw under us, and a blanket. Bedbugs and other bugs nested in the walls and spread diseases and other plagues. Everybody had ants under his collar because of the misery and hunger.

From the Urals we went to Kazakhstan. It was 100 km. from the settlement to the station, we went by foot in the winter, the snow was over our knees. And everybody had a sack on his back with the things he had kept. At the station we loaded onto a car that was going to Tashkent. A lot of people were left behind by the trains and perished. People got sick from not enough food and swelled up from hunger. Little children perished like flies and were thrown out of the car windows.

IV. In the kolkhoz. In the kolkhoz we worked in the fields.

TADEUSZ S.
Born 1927
Wilejka county
Wilno voivodeship

When the Soviets invaded us Mommy became frightened daddy was taken into captivity after a sickness lasting a month my mother died When they had made themselves at home in Poland they began to destroy statues crosses and they ordered the people to pray to the rifle because that is also a tool of death. on February 10 1940 at 2 in the morning they came to our apartment and they took us at the point of a rifle they took us without any reason and took us to Russia in the train it was crowded cold people were dying from hunger and cold. at the settlement we worked in the mines 12 hours a day at the mines there was water the clothes we had all rotted in a week after a 12-hour workday we had to stand in line another 12 barefoot in the cold. in the barracks there were bedbugs cockroaches and vermin of all sorts the stoves were busted. After such work people turned into skeletons and when we got the amnesty the people scattered to various places and I with my family went to a kolkhoz at the kolkhoz we worked day and night because it was very hot they gave us practically no food only what we could gather in the fields. with such a diet my brother died with no one to bury him so I buried him myself without a coffin even without a suit because we had only one for the two of us. after such suffering we escaped with my sister because daddy went into the Polish army which was forming then we walked for 200 kilometers on foot through the mountains of course barefoot over sharp stones in 40 degree heat and without water. At the station as we waited for a train we were robbed of everything so that all we had left was a can where there had been milk which we found in the garbage and which we used as a drinking cup.

Wołyń Voivodeship

PGC/Box 119

TADEUSZ L.
Born 1927
Dubno county
Wołyń voivodeship

In 1939 the Polish-German war broke out, and then the Soviet army marched into Poland. When the Ukrainians heard that the Soviet army was coming they began to revenge themselves on the Poles. They were very happy and for whole nights and days they stood by the roadside waiting for the arrival of the Soviets. One beautiful evening the Ukrainians came to us and took us and said come with us. They did not order us to take anything with us and with rifles pointed at us they lead away the whole family. They led us to a gate through which the army was to march and ordered us to lie down in the road and lie there without moving. On the sides of the road stood Ukrainians with rifles. At last we heard the noise of tanks when they arrived there was a lot of yelling. The women and children cried and prayed begging God to save us. The senior Soviet stopped the tanks and ordered us to get up and asked who had done this and he arrested the "presedolet" [village head] and told us to go home. The next evening the Ukrainians came and took away our cows, horses pigs etc. and even small things even my rabbits. And so they came every evening to revenge themselves on the people. And so we somehow survived until February 10 '40, in the morning we were still sleeping, suddenly we heard a knocking. Daddy got up opened the door and I saw NKVD. One of them shouted hands up they rushed us out of our beds in our underwear and lined us up in front of the window. One of them took out a paper and read that they are sending us to another locality. In 10 minutes they loaded us on sleighs. The way was difficult and cold. They led us like that for 6 kilometers with rifles pointed, and loaded us into railway cars as if we were some sort of animals. We stood at the station for 6 days from where we started away from the Polish land. In the cars they fed us once a day and then some kind of moldy bread and water. On Polish territory they did not give us anything, they said that when we cross the border there will be plenty of everything and on Russian territory they did not even give us water. And so we suffered through 21 days hungry and cold. It was lucky that we had a little of our own food. They train was surrounded by troops. Finally we reached Kotlas where we stayed for 4 days outside in 60 degree below weather. On the fifth day they took us to the settlement. We worked cutting down trees. On the second day they chased us out to work. We earned 2 rubles a day. We got bread with coupons only those who worked got 80 [800?] grams and those who could not work died from hunger. And so somehow luckily I survived the Russian captivity.

DOCUMENT NO. 89

PGC/Box 123

ROMAN J.
Born 1929
Dubno county
Wołyń voivodeship

Points.
1) Occupation of Poland by the USSR.
2) Packing us into railway cars.
3) The transport was buried under snow.
4) Taking us to our destination in the USSR.
5) Chasing us to work, and to school.

1) The Russians invaded us on September 21, when they drove into the places of several colonists, they drove into the grain so that they would not be seen, and they crushed the grain so that not one ear of grain stood up, they began to grab everything, they burst into the barn and began to take the hay, chaff, horses cows they slaughtered for food they took the pigs and took them to the station and sent them to the USSR. And when they invaded the town they caused waiting in line for buying things they bought up everything and to some shopkeepers they burst in beat them up and took everything. And when they found out that one guy was in jail they smashed up the jail and let him out and he showed them all the colonists who had done something to him and he also indicated to them the innocent and they put them in jail.

2) It was Sunday, early in the morning we were still sleeping and they began to knock on the door to be let in daddy got up opened the door, and they pointed a rifle and daddy raised his hands right away they searched but they did not find anything and they ordered us to pack and wrote down what we were taking and what we were leaving behind a horse and cart drew up and took us to the station and they began to search again and where they found a hatchet they took the people and put them in jail.

3) We stood at the station for a few days and they attached two locomotives and we set off on our way and we traveled for a week and we

War Through Children's Eyes

stood in a field and could not continue because there was a large snow-drift we stayed in the field for a few days and the snow covered our train up to the windows and it was not even possible to go out, later two more locomotives came and began to pull us out of this snow but they could not manage it and they began to dig out the doors and chased us out of the cars to dig out the transport but it was hard to do but slowly we did it and started on our way.

4) When we arrived at our destination at the old barracks it was cold and there was no stove the windows were broken and when you hung something on the wall right away it froze to the wall. For a few days we suffered a lot later when we became a little accustomed to it we began to make beds for ourselves we built a stove and it was already a little better.

5) After we had rested and eaten a little on the second day they chased daddy and mommy to work and the younger ones to work, even on a Sunday or holiday they did not let us rest and in the day we worked from 7 to 7 and we had to go to school because if someone did not go they fined the family 25 rubles and they taught that there is no God that man is descended from the ape and they did not let us pray before the lessons or after the lessons.

DOCUMENT NO. 90

PGC/Box 120

LEON M.
Born 1929
Horochów county
Wołyń voivodeship

On February 10 the Soviets came into the room when we were all asleep and started looking for weapons. They stood father in the corner at riflepoint. They didn't let us take anything because they said we'd be back home again in two days. Then they took us to freight cars thirteen or fourteen families in one car. It was cramped and dirty in the freight cars. There was no water on the way. People fainted without water. There were nine people in my family. Only father worked. He earned fifty or sixty rubles every ten days but they held back half of that for weapons for the Russian army. Father worked and got four hundred grams of bread, and people who didn't work got two hundred grams of bread. The bread was undercooked so that it was more by weight. For nine people we got two kilograms of bread. My mother died of hunger.

She gave everything what she got to the children and she got weaker and weaker and in the end she had to die. There was nothing at all to eat, and you had to go out at night to get something to eat. There were times you had to go and steal. They forced us to go to school, but they didn't teach Polish. They didn't allow you to profess religion either. The soup in the kitchen when they sold it was just water. And a third of it was worms. You went into the woods so as not to be so hungry. It was forbidden even to go to the woods without permission of the settlement commandant. Then we got passports and we went to Tashkent. While we were on the way my father and I lost the train in Kirov. Since then I haven't seen my family. Father went into the army and I went with my father. We came to Pahlevi and I got pneumonia. I stayed in the hospital in Pahlevi. The next day I came to Terhan. I am very happy I got away from that hell of Russia.

DOCUMENT NO. 91

LUDWIK K.
Horochów county
Wołyń voivodeship

A Pole in Exile

On the day the Bolsheviks crossed the Polish border the first political officers came to all the colonies they took the colonists loaded them on buses and said they would take them to be shot, a day went by then two and on the third day they came back from the questioning. Each one was given a good beating and then they were sent to the NKVD commissar and he decided whether to sent him to prison or whether to report every day at 6 o'clock for questioning.

In all the schools they broke the crosses smashed the portraits founded clubs closed churches, they said you shouldn't pray because there is no god, for us stalin is God. They stripped the soldiers returning from the German front and told them zabud' pro Polshchu [forget about Poland] it will never come back nasha krasna armia zavsigda vperod a v zad nikagda [our Red Army always goes forward and never retreats]. We will beat finland and lithuania, and then we'll get to England we'll drive out the bourgeoisie and our communist army will traverse the whole world. On the night of February 10 the politruks [political commissars] came and surrounded the building, the door was locked shut they took and ripped it off, they barged into the apartment they stood by

172   *War Through Children's Eyes*

every bed and they shout soberajs' [get out] they take every piece of clothing and feel it first if maybe there isn't something and if there is some watch or money he takes it and says you don't need it you can buy it in russia, but in russia you can't find a good watch if you look high and low, they took what there was and didn't even let you make breakfast in the morning, at 9 o'clock on the tenth they came with the sled they ordered you to leave your houses, they loaded you on the sled frost and snow like the world has never seen before, they took you to the station, on the way how many times they dumped the whole family in the snow, the frozen children cried, the NKVD man shouts to stop crying. but finally they got to the station they ordered us into freight cars inside there was snow up to your knees we started throwing the snow out of the car when we threw out the snow they gave us an iron stove and closed the doors of the car they screwed them shut, when you had to tend to your needs there was a kind of hole and there you had to tend to your needs the car full of stink when you want to air out the car sometime you have to knock hard on the car door and if the NKVD man wants to he can open and the whole trip he opened only 2 times to get some water, they gave us wood and bread once every other day and if there wasn't any, then every three days. When they had taken us into the depths of Russia there was screaming poverty their people stand in line from midnight for bread. At night they finally brought us to the forest we rode through the forest for 3 days we reached the settlement there were few barracks, in one lodging which was 8 meters long and 6 wide they crammed 48 people it was very hot there was no place to move. We walked to work in the forest to saw pines we worked 12 hours, a month goes by you go to the office and he says you earned little, you have to work, if you don't work to z golodu pomrosh [you will die of hunger].

DOCUMENT NO. 92

PGC/Box 120

ZYGMUNT Z.
Kowel county
Wołyń voivodeship

At night the Russians came they packed us up onto cars, and drove us to the station. They packed us into a freight car where lice walked along the boards. They didn't give water, bread was eaten by those who brought it from home. At the settlement Mama was working on the railroad. She cleaned tracks. I was standing with mama at the station I was hungry. A shalon [transport] with our troops was passing. Mama asked the lieutenant and he took me along. I boarded the car even though it was sad to part with Mama. I often stole potatoes at the station.

Grade 2B.
I am 12.

DOCUMENT NO. 93

PAC/Box 50

ELŻBIETA P.
Born 1925
Krzemieniec county
Wołyń voivodeship

At 4:00 AM on the seventeenth of September, 1939, Soviet troops crossed the Polish border on the line between Podwołoczyska and Mołotków. The security guards and the KOP, who had increased their border alert, at first defended themselves doggedly. Bolshevik forces advanced incessantly. At the watchtowers at Mołotków and Brzezina the Bolsheviks used machine guns in a hard fought battle. Both watchtowers were burned down. A few soldiers were burnt to death. A few soldiers were killed, among them my father Marian P[——]. The rest escaped, saving their lives. With the invasion of Soviet troops, the Poles experienced a period of cruelty at the hands of the Ukrainians.

At once all colonists were arrested and imprisoned. The arrests were made by Ukrainian peasants and a few local Poles. These Poles, together with the Ukrainians, took from the colonists not only: cattle, horses, pigs, poultry, inventory of dry goods, furniture from homes, but one was not even allowed to keep for oneself the grain needed for bread. Each time it took a week of going to the committee and asking before they would come. And then, as if doing a great favor, they would dole out only a fraction of what one worked for by the sweat of his brow. At so-called "skhody" or meetings, which were held at the marketplace at Białozórka, and at which the Russian commissar was always present, they would tell untrue stories about the colonists and demand their death or exile. On November 1, 1939, the Bolsheviks registered colonists' families and office workers. On 11/11 all colonist families were driven from the settlement back to where they came from. Everybody came from the voivodeships of Warsaw, Kielce, or Cracow, so they had to journey past the Bug river to cross the border created there by the

Germans. A few families remained. Because mama was very sick we stayed too, but not for long. On 2/10 of 1940 we were exiled to the Ural. They allowed us to take twenty poods' worth of belongings.

They loaded us into freight cars, 35 persons in each. There was a small stove there, but there was so little coal that walls were covered by frost and everything would freeze. Throughout the ride, once every twenty-four hours, we got a bit of bread and some soup, which would cause stomach trouble, and a bucket of water per wagon. In Solikamsk all of us spent three days in prison, from where they drove us to a settlement 180 kilometers away. We traveled by sleds. A few older persons and children died on the way.

Labor was compulsory at the settlement. Everyone over 16 had to work on "lesovalka" [felling timber]. On the other hand, children between 9 and 16 years old had to work on "podgotovka" [preparing the forest for felling timber], i.e., building the road both in the winter and in the summer, clearing and cleaning the wood, haymaking, and other tasks. For so-called "progul" [vagrancy] one was liable to be imprisoned, while for being late they would deduct 25% of our pay for 6 months. Our family consisted of 9 persons. Mama of ill health could not even earn money for our bread. We suffered much hunger and cold. Two brothers died. The moment of deliverance came unexpectedly. One was allowed to leave, but at one's own expense. We sold everything we still had. I put in an application for admission to P.C.K. [Polish Red Cross]. I was admitted, on account of which I was to receive a free train ticket to as far as Kujbyshev. Mama and the rest of the family had to pay for their tickets. We escaped from the settlement, but not without difficulties.

We took a barge first, and then sailed on a ship. At Kamskoe-Uste some unknown gang of thieves robbed our people stealthily. Our last 100 rubles and the last of our linen was stolen. We remained wearing what we had on and without money. "Kipiatok" [boiling water] was our food for three days. Exhausted and completely weakened, we still did not for a second lose faith and hope in getting back to the Motherland. We arrived at Kujbyshev. Our beloved Polish soldiers waited for us at the harbor. They drove us in cars to school number 42, where we were fed at once. After a three day rest the local outpost supplied us with food for the journey and we left for the South as part of an organized transport. A young man named Józef Sokołowski was the commander of our group. He received food money for the people, but the people unfortunately did not receive much of it and they would give their last shirts in exchange for a morsel of bread. We disembarked at Kata-Kurnan, where we spent two weeks sitting at the station under the sky and got 40 dekagrams of bread per person. Water was available. After two weeks everyone was transported to different kolkhozes. We got along as best we could. The local people were favorably inclined towards us and helped a lot. We worked at picking cotton and received at least three meals a day. Not much of anything good. On 12/21, after two weeks of work, came an order to depart. The Uzbeks at once put their horses to carriages and took us to the station by "arby." We were sure that we would make a stop in Poland, or at least we were consoled that we would. We were deceiving ourselves in vain. On 1/8 1941 we stopped in Turkestan. We were ordered off the train. From there everyone was transported to nearby kolkhozes. We were assigned to kolkhoz Kalin Number 12 at Stary Ikan (Old Ikan), far away from Turkestan. At the beginning things were after a fashion. Every day we got a "lepioshka" [flat bread] and half a liter of soup per person, and we all lived together in a "chajnan" [i.e., chajkhana, a tearoom]. After a week we got "kibitki" [clay huts]. Seventeen of us lived in a tiny "kibitka" with holes in the ceiling, leaky doors, and little windows covered with glued-on paper. We slept on the floor next to one another. The kolkhoz gave each of us a bundle of straw to sleep on. We received 20 dekagrams of flour per child, and 40 dekagrams per adult and that was our constant nourishment. The spring arrived. Everyone had to work and fulfill a quota. They stopped giving flour for the children and the workers got payment according to their work quota.

The work quota was so large that it was impossible to complete even a half of it. For instance, hoeing 2500 square meters of cotton brought a worker 80 dekagrams of flour. One received the same for carrying it down from the hills for a distance of 500 meters. Here again began the days of hard work and hunger. People fed themselves on grass and strange roots picked from the fields. A terrible typhus epidemic broke out. Everyone who got sick was driven to the hospital. Except for three persons, everyone from our kibitka was taken to the hospital in Turkestan. The hospital was overcrowded. People lay on the floors and tables. Dirt. Lice walked on the floor. The doctors and staff treated our people very badly. At least eight persons died each day. The deputies in Turkestan [i.e., employees of the social service apparatus established by the Polish embassy after resumption of Polish-Soviet diplomatic relations in 1941] looked into this matter and started supplying food to sick Poles. Each day the deputies sent a slice of bread and ½ liter of cocoa or pudding per person. This lasted a very short time since mister deputy died suddenly. The second one was elected and this one did not care very much about the affairs of the general Polish population. In that hospital four persons from our kibitka died. My 15 year old sister died too. The rest of us returned to the kolkhoz. We worked with whatever strength we had, as best we could, on private jobs for the Uzbeks, to earn a morsel of bread. The deputies supplied aid, but exclusively to the Jews. Poles dispersed on kolkhozes had to labor very hard and knew little about how much was sent to them from abroad. Our elected delegations frequently spent as much as a week in Turkestan begging our deputy for help. This did not move him very much and he continued to do as he pleased. We had nothing at all left to wear. I was wearing out my last dress, me and my mother both. We found out a few days before that a freight car with clothing had come to the deputyship, so four of us got together and on the night of 7/10 we went to the mister deputy. In town, the Polish Jews, elegantly outfitted by mister deputy were promenading in the streets. At the deputyship they received bread and flour, and sugar and lard for the children. They didn't pay for shelter. They occupied themselves with profiteering and lived carefree. The Poles, on the other hand, suffered hunger and labored hard in the kolkhozes. We decided not to yield until we got something. We demanded help for three days, without yielding. We shed many tears in the process. In spite of this, that imperturbable man kept sending us to his secretary, and that one in turn back to the deputy and after three days, with his heart aching, he gave us a blouse each. He excused himself by saying he had nothing else, and that next time we would get clothing and shoes. That was an empty promise. Aside from that little blouse we also got 30 rubles for the whole family. That was the entire aid from the deputyship. We wrote a group complaint to Kuibyshev and Tashkent but it did not help any. In July a representative came to Turkestan from Jangi-Yul, and a Paderewski day nursery was established in Turkestan. Children orphans and half-orphans up to 14 years of age were admitted there. My younger brothers and sisters were also admitted. Me and mama stayed in the kolkhoz and continued working hard. Every time we went to work without breakfast and labored all day in the sweat of our brows under the blazing sun I would think of my dear father who, if he had only lived, would not have allowed that we should suffer such hardships. His Motherland was more precious to him and he gave his life to Her. We are also suffering for Her. We tried to withstand everything in peace, and we put our only hope in the Lord. We heard the news that from 14 and 16 years old up they were admitting children to the Junaks. The deputy in Turkestan was the admitting officer. Those admitted were to go abroad. Families of the Junaks would also be sent to the same site. Mama, who could not bear watching how hard I had to work, agreed that I should join the Junaks with the hope that, as I was promised, she would be able to leave the Kolkhoz and be together with us again. On 7/27 my dear Mama walked me a few kilometers from the kolkhoz, where we said goodbye. I was only admitted after two days. On 7/30 I left for Vrevsk. It was very good there and after a two-week stay at Vrevsk we left for Krasnovodsk from where we arrived at Pahlevi by ship.

DOCUMENT NO. 94

PAC/Box 50

Sław R.
Born 1930
Krzemieniec county
Wołyń voivodeship

When the Soviets entered our land we felt the lack of everything because the Soviets bought everything for rubles. The grocery stores, the mercers shops stores and others were empty. To buy bread you had to get up at night for the line. Sugar and fat were very hard to get and you paid enormous amounts. For fat and other products mama exchanged various things like: dresses and sheets. In the first days the Soviets arrested all the higher administrators, the police, village and hamlet heads. On February 10 they deported the military colonists and foresters with their households to the depths of Russia to work. Before that they took their horses, cows, and grain away from them. They abolished Polish offices and put Bolsheviks and Jews in place of Poles. The people were depressed and any minute they expected worse to come. The first deportation was in heavy winter. They took the sick, the crippled, and small children a lot died on the way. They also took horses, cows, and grain, and farm tools away from the bigger farmers. In the cities they took houses away from the citizens and various businesses for the benefit of the state. Before the elections in 1940 on Polish lands occupied by the Bolsheviks there were "meetings" where each time a militiaman came for those who didn't want to go to the gatherings and also for mama. Although mama didn't want to she had to go because any of the Poles who didn't go could expect to be arrested. The meetings were preparations for the elections. Before the voting itself they made lists of citizens who were entitled to the right to vote. The wife of the political director Pińczuk came to see mama, since Polish times they were in prison for eight years for communism. Mama insisted and didn't want to go, since papa was already in prison, arrested for being particularly suspicious and dangerous. Mama said that as the wife of a man who was arrested she shouldn't vote and simply didn't want to. They wrote her on the list. Election day fell on Easter Sunday. From six in the morning the militiamen went and forced people out to vote. Mama went to church when she returned a militiaman came and mama was forced to go. The voting looked like this: they led the people into the hall they gave them a card and ordered them to throw it in the urn. You couldn't do anything else because there were guards all around and militiamen with bayonets. Every person from fear of arrest or deportation put their card into the urn. I know that not only Poles didn't want to vote, but Ukrainians and Jews but they were forced to. People who were in the hospital the election committee took an urn and cards to the hospital and there this is the way the sick voted, that means they put the cards in the urn just as they were given to them. If they noticed that someone spoke up and demanded the freedom he was promised, that night that person was no more. Before the voting they arrested Mr. Berger, Basiński, Jagodziński, my papa, and many others. Every day they organized pre-election gatherings and completely openly they said that anyone who didn't vote, or spoke against it, or didn't want those candidates it means they are enemies of the Soviets and there are prisons, siberia, and shakhty [mines] for enemies. April 13, 1942 [the correct year is 1940], they deported all the arrested families to Russia. Our family to Northern Kazakhstan. They deported us from Krzemieniec at night under escort. Our journey to Kazakhstan lasted 14 days, we went by freight train; where we were very tightly packed, we were not allowed to get out of the cars at the stations. During the whole journey they gave us dinner 4 times, the conditions of the journey were terrible. After two weeks of traveling they let us off in a field and we went to the Mironowka settlement. The people there received us unfriendlily, they considered us Polish masters and that's what they called us. We lived with other people. We went to the fields to do farm work they only paid for work after the new year they paid us 1 ruble 8 kopecks per day, at the time a small loaf of bread cost 25 rubles. They didn't want to sell us anything in the cooperatives. We didn't see sugar or soap there, and there was even very little bread we lived mainly on boiled flour. Mama traded various things for flour, finally we ran out of things. When papa came we didn't have even a piece of bread or flour. Papa brought us bread, sugar, and fat. We stayed in Kazakhstan until April 16, 1942 that is until papa came, who was in the Polish army now and happily found us and took us south to Guzar. It was better for us in Guzar because we were under army care, but illness and heat bothered us there. We all got dysentery and malaria. August 13, 1943 [probably 1942] we went to Krasnovotsk and from there to Iran by boat. The trip to Iran was very hard because we were sick; we were packed in the train and uncomfortable it was worse on the boat. Living conditions changed in Iran. We didn't fight over a piece of bread—sweet tea and tidbits that we never saw in Russia!

PGC/Box 120

JAN M.
Krzemieniec county
Wołyń voivodeship

Eastern Polish Territories under Russian Occupation

The Soviet taking of power over Eastern Poland made a strange impression on me. As soon as Soviet troops invaded Poland the stores were emptied of all merchandise. Shortly afterwards, all stores were emptied and locked. Shortages of food and dry goods were experienced by all. During the first days a small part of the populace rejoiced, but after this experience any general contentment almost disappeared. Within the course of a month the area in which I lived was emptied of everything; everything was carried away. In school, religous lessons were forbidden. Crosses and paintings were removed and the Polish language was banned. After that I stopped going to school. With the course of time even worse things happened. Everything on our farm was carried away without a thought for our future livlihood. They confiscated all of our livestock and farming tools and assigned ½ hectare of land for our entire family (6 persons). I was seized with despair about how all these slogans and proclamations which theoretically seemed democratic had become so terrible and oppressive. Furniture was taken and distributed among the local Ruthenians who were in the committees. During the elections voters were forced to choose candidates picked beforehand. Whoever resisted was arrested. My most unpleasant moments occurred on 2.10.1940 when they started evicting us from our native settlements. This is a day which I shall remember for as long as I live. We were exiled to Soviet Russia. After a hard, three day journey we found ourselves in the North, at Archangielsk "oblast," amidst impassable forests and swamps. Here the Polish exiles experienced even worse days. In cold and hunger, a constant struggle for a morsel of bread was the order of the day. The pay we received was not even enough to feed ourselves with, so we helped ourselves by selling clothes and shoes and whatever we managed to keep with us. Under these conditions a great many people became sick and died. There was almost no medical care; an orderly would come to those who were dying, but he could not help in any way. We were forbidden to leave the settlement and forced to work. If someone missed work he would be tried. For being late for work my father was sentenced to three months, during which time they deducted 50% of the money he was earning. To deepen our suffering they would constantly tell us to forget our Fatherland for we would never return to it. We lived among a foreign populace which was doing *no better than we were.* Only a few high communist officials got on well. But during these two years I observed a great respect for labor present in the entire country. On the other hand, a worker was not respected, but only taken advantage of. Oftentimes labor went unrewarded, and a person requesting the money he earned only exposed himself to greater troubles, sometimes even prison. Older people and those unable to work came to a pitiful end if there was not one to care for them. Everyday they would carry away a few dead, among them were my brother and young sister. In addition, typhus was spreading and many people died from it. Still, thanks to Divine Providence and to a change in circumstances, Polish authorities managed to get us out of Russia.

DOCUMENT NO. 96

PGC/Box 117

PAWEŁ P.
Born 1927
Krzemieniec county
Wołyń voivodeship

My Experiences in Russia

I was born Jan. 25, 1927, in Veterans Colony. I lived there until the arrival of the Soviet army. One autumn night in 1939, Oct. 17, [the correct date is September 17] the Soviet army invaded Polish soil. I usually slept in the summer hut all summer, the hut was in the orchard. So when I heard the noise and gunfire I was the first to wake up and ran fast to tell my father. Before I reached the house a grenade exploded under my feet, at that moment I felt pain in my right leg and left hip. Slowly I reached my father's bedroom. I woke up the whole family. I ran like a madman and couldn't calm down. Morning came and units began to pass near the house through the gardens. It was daytime when an infantry unit entered our yard, they handcuffed my father and tied him to the well, then one of them ordered father to drink the water, then they let us all drink, they thought the well was poisoned. When the unit left they killed nine colonists in the village, and they even burned one colonist's whole farm. Two weeks later they tore down our chapel and deported the priest in handcuffs to Russia. They tortured and robbed the people in town. Then they killed a few people from the village and threw them under the Soviet tanks. A few days later they arrested us and deported us to Russia. They arrested us Feb. 10, 1940. In the settlement where they took us sickness reigned and hunger troubled us. When the amnesty came out in 1941 in the month of September, the Russians didn't want to let us leave the settlement, but they said to buy cows and build barracks. When we got certificates we went to Uzbekistan and there I went through great pains and misfortunes. In Uzbekistan my late mother died and my dear late sister died of hunger, then I took my dying brother to the hospital, he died the next day and finally my late father was drafted in the Polish army in Russia. Mother and sister died April 7, 1942, and my brother on April 21, 1942, and my late father was drafted in the army April 28, 1942. We were very sad and grieving my older sister and I to bury almost the whole family in the course of a month. Not long after, my late father died in the army. We were left two orphans, death by hunger looked us in the eyes, but I defended myself as best I could so I could stay alive, so someday I could tell how they mistreated us Poles in Russia. Not just my family died of hunger, but many others died whole families. I remember than in one kolkhoz in Uzbekistan there were 7 seven families that died of hunger, all that was left was one two-year-old child, the child cried when I went into the house and said to me "daddy doesn't want to get up, Zosia cries and cries." The child really was hungry, because it turned out the parents died the night before.

Not long after I went to Krasnovodsk. So ended my wanderings.

DOCUMENT NO. 97

PGC/Box 124

KAZIMIERZ ZOŁYNIAK
Krzemieniec county
Wołyń voivodeship

My Stay in Russia

Two weeks after my father was arrested April 13 we were deported to Russia. We went in freight cars where it was very cramped because of the large number of people (an average of some 50 people in a car). The doors were shut and we had the feeling that we were in a cellar or a tomb. I write in a tomb because the mood was truly tomblike with children crying and mothers sobbing. Truly I felt like crying but I gathered all my courage and wanted somehow to comfort the crying women (there were no men just a few boys of school age). One of the worst things was that the Russian soldiers didn't allow relatives or friends to come to see us. They didn't allow them to bring us anything or say goodbye to us we were outcasts of society because our fathers served Poland. But that didn't last long, because we set off fast and after thirteen days of wearisome travel we were at the place, that means in northern Kazakhstan in the village of "Starosukhotin." Right after we arrived we went to work in the kolkhoz because we didn't have so many things that we could live on them. I started to graze cows and my two brothers worked with the oxen. Mama stayed "home" and helped the Russian landlady because we lived with her. We didn't get anything for our work in the kolkhoz only the "workday" was written down for which we were to get paid in the future. We earned more than 600 workdays for pay and we never got anything at all because apparently there was no harvest. That was an irony of fate after so much work and wearing out our only clothes at work not to get anything. We lived through the winter with the greatest difficulty and we sold the rest of our clothing and waited to see what would happen. More and more often we heard about the death of our Poles either through hunger or freezing. We saw the people living there and I won't say that they were delighted with such living conditions. A constant struggle for existence for daily bread made them blind to everything else. I didn't like to seek their company because they curse and blaspheme God at every step. Every evening there were "meetings" at the "club" where people were encouraged to work. People on a low rung of civilization believed everything they were told. In the spring we went to work in the steppe only because they gave workers food. The work was very hard from morning till late evening you had to grind on like that ox. The food was simply for the dogs, in the morning water cooked with flour mostly bran, at lunch a kind of "soup" with a piece of meat as hard as shoe leather and in the evening salt water with barley bread like clay. When night came the wild orgies began. Women and men lived together and they made the most shameless scenes and paid no attention to us. At times like that I wanted to leave that barn and go sleep on the steppe. Although I was only 13 it seemed to me that they weren't people but wild animals with very low instincts.

DOCUMENT NO. 98

PGC/Box 120

ZDZISŁAW JAGODZIŃSKI
Born 1926
Krzemieniec county
Wołyń voivodeship

In the middle of September 1939, when there was still war with Germany, rumors spread that the bolsheviks were coming to aid Poland.

This seemed strange, but probable. Soviet troops entered Poland, but they did not enter Krzemieniec, fearing it was mined. Only after the bolsheviks had taken over the local settlements around our county did the first cavalry troops ride into the city.

When I went out on the streets that day, numerous patrol units, militiamen composed of Jews, were circling the streets. They walked about with red arm bands and guns, searching whoever they encountered. There were few Soviet troops. Only in the days that followed did the Soviet divisions march through the city. Marching columns of infantry, cannons, and constantly faltering tractors rumbled on.

We soon discovered that the rumors about bolsheviks coming to aid us were false. Even before entering the city the Soviet planes dropped leaflets (which I saw with my own eyes) calling on peasants to occupy the estates of landowners, to beat them up, etc. We stayed in our homes as the peasantry, agitated, went out looting. The bolsheviks established order as soon as they entered. They were rather tolerant at first, but gradually they started behaving more and more severely.

After the disarmament by the bolsheviks, father returned from the front and worked in the high school. He was dismissed from his job after the New Year. At that time, either bolsheviks or local communists, mostly Jews, were appointed to the higher offices in the city. Until New Year (1940) a Polish high school with old professors existed, and I attended it. There was no special campaign. Only religious lessons were canceled, and the Ukrainian language introduced. But there were many spies (among students) and they were mostly Jews. It is a significant fact that after the occupation the number of Jews in the high school grew considerably. For instance, in our class, which included about 30–40 pupils, there were 15 Jews.

Stores were locked up, but in some of them one could still purchase some items. One had to stand in long lines. Privately, one could secure produce and materials from older merchants. But shortly afterwards, Soviet authorities caught them and confiscated their supplies. Profiteering developed in this way. People would travel 10 kilometers to get something to eat. Peasants would trade by exchanging produce for other things. So there were no problems with food, one only needed to exchange things, clothes, etc. In the beginning there was a great demand for these things, both among the villagers and the Soviet "dignitaries" who hastily bought up clothing. Their wives, who arrived poorly dressed, brightened themselves up with red berets which were worn with pride. During the first weeks of occupation, Polish currency had the same buying power as Soviet currency.

There were tremendous campaigns. One went to meetings under

threat of punishment. The agitators constantly called to vote for annexation, or rather, for joining "Zapodnoy Ukraine and Zapodna Byelorussia" [Western Ukraine and Western Belorussia] to the USSR. Then they organized an election, or a so-called "plebiscite." Of course, the results of the election were determined in advance. Spies and confidence men would follow every step of the voters. Afterwards they announced the "rightful" annexation of occupied Polish lands to the USSR, of course at the "freely expressed demand of the population." Shortly thereafter began a period of interrogations, arrests, inquiries, and the imposition of taxes. A militia force was created. NKVD arrived.

In the New Year (1940) a Polish ten-year school was created. Pińczuk, a Jew and a communist, was appointed director. Some teachers were Polish, some Jewish. Then a propaganda campaign was started. They would teach the history of the USSR, its constitution, etc. A network of confidence men was created in the school, but we shunned them, guarding our speach. We constantly listened to the London radio station.

The outbreak of war with Finland was a great event. A meeting was called at which the bolsheviks threw thunderbolts at tiny Finland and its supporters, the "imperialist England and France." On February 10, 1940, an unusually frosty day (the winter of 1939–1940 was extremely severe), the first groups of Poles were exiled into the depths of Russia. This was brutally conducted, with children freezing to death in train cars. The rest of us who remained awaited our turn. A relaxation followed. After father was dismissed from his job they kept summoning him to NKVD for interrogations. They would call him in every few hours and interrogate him with a system of perpetual questions. Before Easter, between Good Friday and Holy Saturday, they unexpectedly conducted a house search on our home. Two militiamen watched father, who was sitting in a chair in only his underwear, while the NKVD man searched. Of course he found nothing. So he took only a photograph of two military attaché friends (he had a fancy for the gold watch, but was tamed by the presence of the militiamen) and they left with father, turning their heads at us suspiciously, and announcing that father would be returned the following day. Of course we did not believe it. On the same day they arrested a considerable number of local citizens—mostly Poles, most of the intelligentsia, and those who seemed uncertain to them or who were reported on by someone.

At Easter one could still bring something or another to the jail. Afterwards, father was moved to prison. Two weeks later an NKVD party appeared again at our door, and rumors spread that they were going to exile us. At the night of April 12–13, 1940, vehicles arrived, soldiers surrounded the house, and they ordered us to pack up our things. They took count of the furniture and they let us take a few packages. They told us that there was a long journey ahead of us, where one didn't know, and that father would join us at the train station. We didn't know whether or not to believe it.

One cart after another drove in the direction of the station, carrying the exiles. They loaded us into cattle freight cars. They locked up and bolted the doors. We lay down on floors made of planks. A primitive toilet was built there. Light came in through four tiny windows. Throughout the entire night of 14–15 of April they were bringing in deportees from the whole country. On Sunday crowds of our countrymen gathered to bid us goodbye. Soldiers dispersed them brutally. I saw a soldier hit our friend, Miss Nowicka, in the face as she tried to hand bread and milk to her acquaintances. We left Krzemieniec on April 15, and traveled for thirteen days on the route Zdołbunów, Shepetovka, Briansk, Penza, Kazan, Svierdlovsk, Pyetropavlosk. During the journey we received dinner five times, and it was so inedible that we got sick to our stomachs. Along the road, and especially before the Ural, we saw collapsing cottages, Orthodox churches converted into warehouses, and crowds of beggars asking for bread. The commander of the echelon told us that we were going to Tashkent. The train turned to different tracks all the time. So we couldn't orient ourselves as to where we were going. Finally, on April 26 they unloaded us in the Kazakhstan steppes in the Krasnoarmyesky region, on the North of Kazakhstan "oblast" and took us to the village of Chermoshnyanka, together with a group of exiles (here in Russia they called us "Pyeresyelentze"). There, they dropped us off and told us to look for housing. We were new, strange intruders from a hostile country. The populace, under Soviet domination for the past 20 years, was wasted away and poor. Although we were exiles, we had some clothing with us, although not all were allowed to bring some along. They would have only a cow or a small homestead (farm), and they had to pay high taxes—at every step they would squeeze their last juices from them, and it was very difficult to get clothing.

We lived in clay huts and had to pay for our housing mostly with our belongings. The local people were envious of these things and tried to take advantage of us in every possible way. They demanded our belongings in exchange for food products and housing. We also made some money selling our things. During the first months the demand was great. Afterwards, some fabrics and materials began coming into the cooperative store. Though one had to pay "payek" [bread ration] and stand in lines at the cooperative store, they preferred it anyway, having bought out enough of our things. In spite of this, we were selling our belongings for the entire duration of our exile, although in the last days we often sold it dirt-cheap.

After our arrival in Kazakhstan they issued us Soviet passports, valid for 5 years, in which we were described as "zsylni" [exiles]. Selling things did not suffice, and we had to go to work in the kolkhozes. No one, at least in our area, was allowed to do mental work. In the kolkhozes work was hard, entire days of farm labor, with cattle, "saman" [adobe], and many other jobs to which, of course, we were not accustomed. But we had to work, because we had to live. They even started forcing people to work, but one did not have to work if one had the excuse of old age or illness. As far as payment for "trudodni" [workdays], for which the norm was determined for each person, they promised it at the end of the year. But what they paid was the very minimum, a bit of wheat or flour. So we had to continue selling things or making extra money from "khoziajev" [farmers], digging up potatoes. We had to provide for everything ourselves, including fuel, housing, and livelihood, and that wasn't easy. They helped us with nothing, and they never cared about what we needed. We were left to our own devices. But they never forgot to watch us, and even in the settlement they arrested a few boys who seemed suspicious to them.

The local people supposedly had a friendly attitude towards us, but in reality they wanted only to take advantage of us, and when our host families realized that they couldn't get anything else out of us they would chase us from their homes without paying attention to anything else. So we all changed houses frequently. The atmosphere which surrounded us was foreign and hostile. The farmers behaved coarsely, worse than boorish: spitting, cursing, and screaming accompanied us everywhere. It was hard, but we had to control ourselves. Only the young ones would go to school; we older boys had to work. But I went to the local school for a few days. The level was very low and it rested on propaganda. They taught about communism all the time, about the happy Soviet land and the oppression abroad, in an antireligious and "antibourgeois" way. So I saw that such learning would not amount to anything. The young ones had to be brought up in the Polish mode, otherwise they would be bolshevized, especially since they were approached cunningly and given presents for "good learning," etc. After the fall of France I read an article in "Pravda" about the publication of 5 and 6 White German books. The article was very aggressive towards imperialist England and France, and also towards Turkey. It was very sympathetic towards Germany. The fall of France was a blow to us, but we did not lose our spirits. Even our material condition, which got worse from day to day, did not break our spirits. The winter of 1940–41 was extremely severe. "Burany" [snowstorms] raged, winds blew, and the frost would reach −50 degrees Celsius. Many of our families went hungry and would simply walk around in rags; Polish children would go around begging. In spite of this, they would rush us to work at the kolkhoz and they refused to give us protection. And so we, the exiles, would mutually support each other. Money, packages, and letters would come in from home, but a good part would be lost en route. A part was "hidden" by the post "commander" for his own use. We caught him in such manipulations a few times. There was no medical aid. There was Kim, a Korean veterinarian, perpetually drunk, in the village. There were supposed to be doctors in the center of the region, and in the drugstores one could get stomach drops or ointment for colds. It was hard to get everything. And one could not get anything. In the winter of 1940−41 a lot of merchandise came to the cooperative: candy and other sweets, petroleum, soap. They said that it all came from the Soviet-occupied countries of Lithuania, Latvia, Estonia, Bessarabia, and our own Eastern territories.

Then it all stopped, and again we had to care for everything ourselves. In the winter it came to this, that we sat around hungry. Hunger, cold, poverty, lice—and bare vegetating. We still waited for a change in our fate.

In the summer of 1941, as usually in the summer, it was easier to live because it was warm and we could always get flour, grits, and potatoes (in spite of high and ever growing prices; for instance, flour mixed with grits was 150−200 rubles). Afterwards, we started sensing from the news we received from the papers and home, a conflict between Germany and Russia. We were only hoping that it would happen and we were certain that it would. The war broke out, and we immediately prepared for a turn for the better in our lives. But no sign of such change was in sight. To the contrary, Wieliczko, the dignitary of "rajkom" [regional committee], denounced and accused Poles publicly and loudly at a meeting, and generally influenced the attitudes of the local people unfavorably towards us. In spite of the dissatisfaction of the local people with the Soviet authorities—they knew how to manipulate the people properly. The people were obedient in everything. But in the end, the Polish-Soviet pact was signed and the amnesty was issued. There were two waves after the amnesty. The first one was masses of prisoners released from concentration camps. They would wander around, traveling aimlessly. Ragged, wasted away, swollen, they traveled on not knowing what to look for. A period of searching, writing to the embassy and to offices began. The wave of prisoners ended by Christmas. The Polish Army was being formed. We (that is, mother and I) got in touch with father. He was in Kryl Orda, but then he left to join the Army. We were treated rather politely after the amnesty. Chaos prevailed on the railroads. The Germans were advancing, and the population quietly awaited them because they wanted liberation. Kolkhoz hands and workers were drafted continuously. Our exiles, to whom "documents of Polish citizenship" were issued instead of passports, started leaving to join the Army. A general conviction prevailed that this was our only salvation, aid, and protection. Afterwards, a "run for the South" started. Thousands traveled South, and our Army passed through there too. At first there were rumors that the Army was to be sent to the front lines, but then the rumors stopped. Instead, news came of epidemics which took thousands of lives—especially the typhus epidemic. Later, the authorities' attitude towards us changed. They began treating us more severely, forbidding us to leave. They even levied taxes on us (four different taxes), about which we had to complain at the embassy. Our correspondence with the embassy existed by virture of mediation through a local man of trust, a Delegate of our Embassy in our "oblast."

Just the same, travels to the south were very limited, and one could leave only if there was a special demand. People tried to leave for the South as they could. We were not successful, so we moved to the center of the region and awaited our opportunity. Finally, we boarded a stowaway night train to Pyetropavlovsk, having bribed a railroad employee. We stayed in Pyetropavlovsk for 10 days without reporting ourselves and in constant fear of being arrested. We were staying at the train station. Pyetropavlovsk was filled with troops. On June 1 we left for the South with a group of Polish families traveling on a "traveling ticket" under protection of a soldier. After 7 days we were in Tashkent, and afterwards we were in Yangi-Yul at our father's. We lived for 2 months in Yangi-Yul. We tried to bring our friends over to Yangi-Yul, but restrictions on travel were increasingly severe. News came about the arrests of our Delegates, and that our people who tried to avoid work were being tried. Unfortunately, there was nothing we could do to help them. It became certain that the troops and civilians would leave Russia for good. Polish-Soviet relations were uncertain and strained. Bolsheviks did not agree to let a large number of civilians go or to let the Polish Army continue forming there. They would also not agree to let Jews and Ukrainians from Poland go, considering them to be their own citizens.

We prepared to leave and left Yangi-Yul with the second transport. In the South we observed a sophisticated thievery which reached unheard of dimensions.

The last stage of our journey was the trip to Krasnovodsk. Here at the Caspian Sea a few more days of torment, dust storms, heat, and heavy labor passed. Finally that passed too. Behind us we left the "red paradise"—the country in which the worst and hardest years of our lives were spent. We kept repeating to ourselves at first, and finally out loud in Pahlevi: "Only to never go back there again."

DOCUMENT NO. 99

PAC/Box 50

NATALIA MAKAREWICZ
Born 1929
Krzemieniec county
Wołyń voivodeship

Great changes came with the arrival of the Bolsheviks. Stores were closed and looted by the Bolsheviks. They opened cooperatives which often had no merchandise. People spent nights standing in lines for fabrics, soap, salt, and sugar. Peasants, badly disposed towards the colonists, stole, took away land, grain, furniture, and clothes.

The Soviets were unfavorably disposed towards the Poles, considering them to be enemies of the Soviets. In November an election was held to choose deputies as local authorities. They removed the Polish authorities and replaced them with Soviets, Jews, peasants, and bandits released from prison. A peasant from Wiśniowiec, Stepaneczko, was elected head of our village. On April 1 they elected deputies to the verhovny committee [referring to the spring 1940 elections to the Supreme Soviet]. Bodasuk, a peasant from Wiśniowiec, belonged to the verhovny committee. Then began inquiries, depositions, and arrests of priests, policemen, and the best Poles. On February 10, 1939 [the correct year is 1940], the Soviets exiled us they took us away in tightly sealed freight cars they would not even allow us out to get water. Once every 24 hours they would let a woman out to fetch water because they were afraid that a man might escape. People fainted from thirst and were unable to even wash themselves. On account of this we were infested with lice. It wasn't enough that we were stung by poverty and grief, the lice stung us too. The Bolsheviks drove us to the Ural, placing us in wooded areas where we were forced to do the so-called zagotovka [norm of timber to fell]. Since then there was not Sunday or holiday for us. Survival in Russia was difficult. Missing work on a Sunday or a holiday was considered sabotage. Such people were often punished by prison sentences or fines. Despite the efforts of my parents and my older brothers and sisters, it was difficult to earn even enough for a morsel of bread.

When amnesty was declared the conditions for Poles improved

greatly. People were released from prisons. Our fathers joined the Polish Army and together we came to Iran.

DOCUMENT NO. 100

PGC/Box 123

JAN B.
Krzemieniec county
Wołyń voivodeship

How My Life Changed After 1939

Sept. 17, 1939, the Russian army crossed Poland's eastern border. After the Russians arrived, prisoners, beggars, and all the riffraff welcomed them happily. After their arrival the Russians closed the stores, took all the food, and gave out slips of paper with the price in worthless rubles for the things they took. They cursed the name of God, they destroyed churches and monuments, but some of the Russians got baptized after they crossed the border.

Feb. 10, 1939. I was deported with my parents to the land of Siberia. They treated us differently there more than once I was hungry and in danger while going around the Siberian marshes with a scythe looking for hay. My work was rated very poorly and they paid me even worse. Polish young people whose parents died or couldn't work for their children went gathering resinous branches in the woods or grubbing stems.

Some Polish young people went to school. What they taught first of all in school was that you call your teacher by his first name. The Russian people lived very poorly. In the forest there were a lot of human bones and skulls of people were deported in '35 as "kulaks." One thing cheered me that there was no order because the wood they paid to have cut down and collected just rotted on the banks.

DOCUMENT NO. 101

PGC/Box 120

WACŁAW P.
Born 1930
Łuck county
Wołyń voivodeship

When russian soldiers arrived and yelled at dad I didn't understand anything. I thought bandits came to us. At the station they loaded us into freight cars. In our car there were 21 families. Before departure they closed the doors with all their might and cut off one lady's head. In Russia we lived in a barracks. Here there was a lot of bedbugs. My 17 year old brother died, because he worked hard and ate little once for four days there was no bread. Brother got ill died and was swollen after death. I helped mama, I cooked lunch, because mama worked. I didn't go to school, because I didn't want to. During the day they drove five persons to the cemetery. A large cemetery was left with the Dead. Children and elders were ill with spotted fever and malaria.

Grade 2B.
Born in 1930.

DOCUMENT NO. 102

PGC/Box 118

CZESŁAW B.
Born 1927
Łuck county
Wołyń voivodeship

Near our settlement there were 2 other settlements 1,500 people in the three. 500 people died of enteric fever and dysentery. A few days before the amnesty some people were forced to sign documents that they were Russian citizens. People who resisted and they had it in for were arrested and only let out after they were supposed to leave. After the amnesty we left "siberia" and went to uzbekistan, my sister died of pneumonia and dysentery.

Before the men went off to the army sometimes we got a bit of barley flour but when they went off we got nothing for two weeks. In the kolkhoz there were 5 families and two single people. Two families one of 8 people the other with 4 people and a university professor Poznański died of hunger. One evening the Uzbeks came and wanted to kill us, we didn't unlock the door and only looked out a small window. That night we took our things and ran away from the kolkhoz on foot 26 kilometers to the station. The next day the Uzbeks came from the kolkhoz and wanted to take us back to the kolkhoz. There was a Polish government agency there and they didn't let us be taken, the agency commandant said they would find work at the station and they had food and we wouldn't die of hunger. They didn't want to go away. The agency commandant managed to get tickets and we left for Kermine. They waited all night they thought they would get us tomorrow morning but we left during the night and they didn't know when. The commandant wrote us a letter that they looked for us all day at the station and in all the clay huts.

DOCUMENT NO. 103

pgc/Box 117

ROMAN M.
Born 1926
Łuck county
Wołyń voivodeship

When the Soviets came to our village then the ukrainians started taking everything away from our homes and afterwards they started distributing our land among themselves, namely: to those who, because of laziness, couldn't even plow their own fields during the Polish times, went for ours very willingly. Afterwards the Soviets gave the Ukrainians 24 hours to do what they please with the Poles, so then the ukrainians from the village of Nawóz came to our settlement and started plundering and killing the colonists, they killed the following five colonists Tański, Kucharski, Strumiłło, Minkusik, Michalski, and 7 ran away or hid for a few weeks in the woods because one couldn't come out of the woods there were plenty of ukrainians everywhere with the "Moskale" [a derogatory word for Russians]. And ukrainians came to our house every night one after the other and looked for Dad but without luck because dad was hidden in the woods and then they didn't find anything else not even a chicken because the last ukrainians took even the smallest things away. Ukrainians didn't let us leave our houses, because they cursed us at every step and even little squirts threw sticks when I met up with them. After three weeks dad came back home, but he didn't sleep at home only he had to hide at night because they came every night and asked for dad. One night they came over to our neighbour Głowa and started searching so they could rob something and then they started asking my friend where father was, but the boy didn't say so they killed him (Władyslaw Głowa), a young boy he was only sixteen years old. The woman director Puszkarczykowa was murdered by the ukrainians and hung so they would have an excuse that it wasn't true. We were oppressed so since September 20 until February 10, on February 10 at night the ukrainians came with the "Moskale" and deported our entire settlement and even the neighboring settlements to Russia.

WITOLD T.
Łuck
Wołyń voivodeship

In the middle of September 1939 my family and I were staying in Janowa Dolina (Kostopol county), where my father soon joined us after being evacuated from Łuck with part of the voivode administration. On the morning of the 17th squadrons of bombers roared overhead flying toward the west. All day and part of the night you could hear an uninterrupted cannonade and an enormous glow appeared in the sky to the east. They said our units were putting up a stubborn resistance to the Bolshevik armies, which were trying to cross the line of border forts. Two days later the red divisions entered Kostopol, welcomed by the prefect as an allied army to help in the battle against the Germans. A few days later the prefect was arrested. The Ruthenian population of the nearby villages (in accord with the leaflets dropped from Soviet planes) came to "settle accounts with the Polish masters," disarming the police posts (I was a witness to one such occurrence) and smaller army units and plundering the Polish population. The Janowa Dolina quarries were handed over for a time to the administration of the robkom [workers' committee] formed among the local workers, headed by a politruk [political commissar] arrived from Russia. The highest and absolute authority was the Russian army commissar officiating in Kostopol.

When I went back to Łuck the change struck me at once, it even affected the way the city looked. The stores were actually still open, but for the most part empty, at best you could get apples, beer, and sausage of suspicious origin. The buildings were hung with banners portraits of Soviet dignitaries and posters mocking the defeat of Poland, sometimes in a vulgar manner. One of them particularly stuck in my mind, it showed a white eagle with a four-cornered Polish soldier's cap on its head and clawing at the back of a handcuffed worker. A bolshevik soldier was sticking a bayonet into the eagle. The background was a map of Poland. Our house was full of refugees from western provinces, among whom were several officers. My father stayed in the house because the voivode administration had been eliminated and the vice-voivode and all the department heads, except my father and the head of the administrative department, had been arrested. The voivode building was devastated and then turned into a weapons warehouse and military barracks. Our gymnasium, where I went back, was set up as the "4th Polish gymnasium"; but we studied in the afternoon with very poor light because of the lack of bulbs. Our building became the property of the Ukrainian gymnasium, which studied there in the morning. Our gymnasium was reopened by a director who was soon replaced by a Bolshevik politruk, and he knew a little Polish, but he tried stubbornly to speak to us in Russian or Ukrainian. But his attempts always ended in a fiasco, so that he finally had to capitulate. The school attitude to *meetings* was "simply hostile" as our communist teachers complained, we hooted at the meetings, we didn't want to join the cheering, we didn't sing the "international," so they wanted to close the school, because they considered it a hotbed of "counterrevolution." Arrests made among the students and teachers dampened the outer signs of our beliefs (we had to stop saying prayers aloud before lessons) but aside from that they achieved nothing else. They destroyed most of the library, both the gymnasium and the town library, where we borrowed books, they turned their particular "attention" to books dealing with achievements in the field of labor in the last twenty years and history and science books. Instead brochures appeared dealing with the Soviet system and pseudo-Polish newspapers. The study of the Soviet constitution was introduced and Russian and Ukrainian as compulsory subjects. The teachers were ordered to call us "citizens" and "comrades" or to address us (in Polish!) by given name and patronymic [i.e., after the Russian fashion]. They tried to inculcate atheistic doctrines and forced us to go to school on holidays, but we got out of that everybody sticking together and on religious holidays the school was empty. On Sept. 4 they arrested my father. Until then we had lived more or less on the money we had, but then we had to sell things, because the salary my mother got for working in the Gosbank (Polish Bank) was ridiculously small in comparison with the price of basic goods, of which there was constantly less and for which you had to stand in line sometimes all night. People often came to blows over their place in line, and the militia rarely intervened, composed as it was for the most part of Jews and Ruthenians. And you had to stand in line more and more often, not only for food, but even outside prison to deliver a package to my father. For permission to deliver a package you often had to try for months at the public prosecutor's, unless you were able to wheedle him with a bribe. Every package had a list of contents attached. They returned the list with the signature of the recipient. That was his only sign of life. Aside from that they dispensed no information about prisoners, or they gave false information, speaking to you at all depended on the good humor of the so-called prosecutor, who often ordered petitioners thrown out the door, or loaded them with a string of abuses. Among those arrested there were Ruthenians and Jews and both of these minorities started changing their, at first very warm-hearted, attitude toward the actions of the Bolshevik authorities. After several Communist Jews and Ruthenian nationalists were arrested, the more reasonable ones began to turn away from the Reds. The Jewish intelligentsia led by the rabbi evidently drew up a list of Jews involved in the actions of the red authorities. Nevertheless the attitude of both these minorities toward the Poles continued to be very unfriendly and annoyances were the order of the day. This hatred manifested itself particularly during elections to the "supreme soviet," when the Communists (mostly Jews) marked the Poles who dodged the balloting, they brought the urns to the beds of sick people, and also "accompanied" people to the polling place. After the first mass deportations to Russia in February 1940, when with 30°C below zero the military colonists and their families were deported in unheated freight cars, all the Poles expected the same thing sooner or later. And on Apr. 13 an "N.K.V.D." officer appeared in our lodgings in the company of two armed militiamen and one civilian agent, who was supposed to be a "witness" to our deportation, so that this act of violence at least had the appearance of legality. It was 4 o'clock in the morning. A Bolshevik locked the door, directed the search, after which he declared that "the Soviet government was moving us to Dnepropetrovsk," where we would join my father, obtain identity cards, and will lead the peaceful carefree life of Soviet citizens. We could take baggage with us—100 kilograms per person. We had two hours to pack. With an ironic smile he observed the disorder that reigned in the house and declared sententiously that bourgeois habits were too ingrained in our souls, and our stay in Russia would free us of them splendidly. A few hours later a truck came to take us to the station. The Bolshevik sealed the apartment, making up a list of things left behind (totally unnecessary, however, because as friends later informed us by letter, some Bolshevik family used our apartment and things). Cattle cars were all ready at the station platform and rang with the weeping and clamor of the people locked inside. They crowded us into one of the cars where there were already 40 people and their baggage. For three days the train stayed on a siding and horse and foot militia helped by the army kept people away from the cars who wanted to give something to their relatives or at least see them for the last time. During those three days they only let us out twice to get water from the town. We walked in the middle of the road surrounded by guards (with fixed bayonets) and on the sides a crowd surged with excited despairing people. Total strangers sometimes gave us money or bread, but the militia immediately confiscated it. On the fourth day the train finally set out and our journey began.

DOCUMENT NO. 105

PGC/Box 120

HENRYK S.
Równe county
Wołyń voivodeship

It was very very cold about 40 degrees C below. We rode in a small freight car there were 25 people. One child fell out the door and the train ran over him. At the settlement there were 5 families about 10 people in one isba [room].

I didn't go to school because I didn't have shoes In the summer I helped mama mowing hay from early morning still dark. We walked to work without food in the morning

Father was in prison

I am 12

DOCUMENT NO. 106

PGC/Box 120

ROMAN BARANEK
Równe county
Wołyń voivodeship

On the Sunday morning after the Soviet invasion troops entered the people did not know what had happened. Only when lightweight tanks passed through and infantry appeared did we learn what it was, because we saw tearing of the national emblem off the walls, destruction of the library which contained about 200 volumes and following this watches, rings and other valuables were taken away from our teachers. Horses and wagons were being taken from farmers without any questions asked, for instance when Soviet soldiers came to our house they put my parents standing against the wall and didn't let them move, and then themselves took the horses, horse gear, the wagon, food for themselves and for the horses, and afterwards they started doing a search, saying that if they find weapons or 'white' weapons father would be killed without any further excuses but the search was fruitless, because their aim was theft and plunder, because they took away the more valuable things. Then they told father that they can do whatever they want and nobody will contradict them. Then after about a 2 month stay a Soviet man came with an order and ordered to drive all colonists out of their houses. Well there were some Ukrainians who were in the prison at P.

for theft and murder so they came with a written order that they have an order from the Soviets to drive us out wearing whatever we had on, and so they drove us out. We had no relatives because my parents are from Cracow, and in spite of this although we had no relatives there we were received in a Ukrainian house, and for instance the village of Majaków was hiding Polish policemen from Russian searches, who thanks to that people escaped from Soviet hands and from labor at building roadways, because bolsheviks put policemen and military slaves to work at the roads for 16 hours a day. In villages such as Majków, Duliby, Lidawka, when gatherings or so called "meetings" were supposed to be held, then no one was there, and when bolsheviks threatened them with Syberia and started carting everything they had in their homes away in cars then they started coming to the meetings, but after the meeting was over, when the soviet yelled long live Stalin, etc., you could only hear his own and a few other voices and the entire crowd was silent, which was also a testimony to the hatred of Ukrainians in relation to the Soviets. On February 10, 1940, they took us and brought us under Soviet guard to a station at Ożenin, at which there were 49 of us in one car. and so we sat for two days under lock, thirsty because there was no water, and neither was there a furnace at which we could warm ourselves. They drove us to Vołogda, we rode for 8–9 days and during the entire time we got about 4 kilograms of bread per four persons and once we got hot water which they whitened with flour. From Vołogda we rode a 100 kilometers on sleighs for 3 days and for two nights to Shychenga next to Shujsk, during which journey half the people got frostbite on their hands, legs, and faces. Our house was very modest and cramped because there were four families 24 people, in addition there were plenty of bedbugs, cocroaches which simply dropped from the ceiling onto the floor. For 4 days we had no bread at all, only after 4 days we could buy 1.5 kilogram of bread for four, which cost 120 kopecks a kilo, a kilo of soup per ½ liter serv. 60 kopecks and one could only earn 1.5 ruble with great effort, there were also those who could not work at all, e.g. because of a sickness or they didn't have clothes, so those people even died of hunger, mostly after they swell they would be taken to the hospital and an announcement would be made that they died because of grave illnesses.

When the amnesty was already out they didn't tell us anything the NKVD just drove in and ordered us to sign a contract to work at a "lesopunkt" [an outpost in a forest] for a year, and if we don't sign the agreement they will drive us out, but we didn't agree to it, the following day they called a meeting at which they read to us that we were free, but told us that we were not allowed to go to any place other than Syberia and they kept forcing us to sign all that time, but when the majority did

War Through Children's Eyes

not consent they read out the names of 7 families which they said they were deporting to Syberia as punishment for "agitating."—Later we found out that they left them at Vołogda.

PGC/Box 120

MARIAN K.
Born 1925
Sarny county
Wołyń voivodeship

The Soviet army invaded, dirty and exhausted, and started praising their culture how good and prosperous they were. We didn't much believe them because you could see from their behavior, they invaded the stores took the merchandise or closed the stores and turned them into cooperatives where you could only get a small allotted portion. ·

In a small wood near the next village there was a skirmish between the Bolshevik army and a group of Polish soldiers, the woodsmen were immediately deported and their property was taken away on wagons and it was deported to Russia. They also arrested people who were well off and deported them and took their property and deported everything, they arrested Polish officers, leaving wives and children without any protection, the wives and children had to spend the night in a different household every night because they were afraid of being arrested. When they arrested someone they mainly took his whole family and even his relatives. They closed the churches and though they didn't ban praying they punished and reproached praying. They removed the pictures and crosses in the school because they began teaching in the Russian language now and against God because later it was forbidden to pray even in silence. They started to impose big taxes, it was forbidden to have more than just 1 cow and a patch of garden because the rest of the land was seized for the kolkhozes they were organizing. You couldn't find a Polish library, they eliminated the monuments and hard times began because from the age of 16 everybody had to work without exception boy or girl.

My father worked in the stone quarry food was very scarce so since I was 14 I went to work in the glassworks at the beginning I worked 4 hours but later I had to work 8 hours a day and as it happened day or night. When my father got a better job at the railway station he wanted to take me out of the factory but the authorities didn't permit when I didn't go to work so they went to court and I was sentenced to 1 year in the so-called correction home (colony) there I worked in a nickel-plating factory, work lasted 8 hrs. The food was not very adequate, so that you could barely get along, that was in Kiev when the Russo-German war broke out, when the Germans began to approach Kiev we were evacuated to Kirov there were 120 of us in a freight car the trip lasted 7 days we only got sustenance 5 times, there was no water although there were wells at every station very near the car but they didn't let you get any. I fainted 3 times from lack of water. Finally we reached the station where we got off but it was still 29 kilometers to the place we were moving to so we had to go on foot when we drank water from puddles along the way Here too work was waiting for us. On the Vyatka River in the north they rafted wood (logs) in the month of September walking barefoot in the water we towed the logs to shore everyone of us was frozen there were Russian children there it was a fright to look at their behavior and way of talking; food was this: 450 grams of black bread and a small cup of thin barley soup, so that you were very hungry. When the so-called amnesty came I was freed and I went to work in the settlement I found work for myself in the smith's, work was 12 hrs a day being 16 years old it wasn't light work for me because when I finished I couldn't feel my hands because it was 45°C below my feet hurt because I didn't have good boots or clothing and most of all the very poor food weakened your strength I was sad that I couldn't talk with my parents who remained in Polish territory even by writing and who cried when I left.

In the correction house in Kiev: There were about 130 of us Poles the rest were Russian boys the whole correction house had about 340 boys. The colony had a bed factory so we worked there as a learner I earned 30 rubles a month at first and for that the small amount of food of 450 grams of bread, and soup three times a day

We worked 8 hours a shift one shift was by day and another at night and the shift changed every 7 days When I was in Kiev I could still write letters to my parents. The Russian boys lived with us we didn't get along because 10-year-old boys were so wild that you can't imagine. Constant scuffles and quarrels.

We spent the day at work it wasn't hard but not easy either when you came back exhausted. I didn't get packages from home because you had to wait a very long time until the food spoiled.

When the Germans started to get near Kiev and bomb it, they took us to the station and loaded us on the freight car Poles and Russians and bigs thefts occurred when the Russian boys snatched almost everything we had and if anyone complained they were ready to beat you up and besides that they never left you in peace and they insulted us and made trouble.

STANISŁAW S.
Born 1927
Sarny county
Wołyń voivodeship

The Polish-German war broke out. On September 17, 1939. Russian soldiers came to our settlement, an officer with his adjutant came into our apartment. He asked that we let him rest and eat. Mommy gave them bread, butter, and milk because they did not have time to wait for anything more. I sat and watched how greedily they ate these things. When they finished eating the officer takes out money and wants to pay with Russian money, but Mommy did not want to accept it. He put the money on the table and says "don't give bread away like that because you will run out of it soon" we did not think that it could come to that. But soon we were convinced. One day I go to town to buy kerosene, salt, and other small items. I go to the store where I always buy things in the door stands a Russian soldier he stops me and asks what I am going in for in Russian, when I said that I am going for kerosene, salt, and sugar he was surprised that people could buy whenever they wanted and as much as they wanted. Some time later my older brother asks me to try to get him some shag tobacco. On one of the streets there is a store set up by the Russians. When I approached it I see a bunch of people I ask what there is there and I am told that they are selling Russian shag tobacco. So I stop and wait but one of my friends tells me that I should get into line because otherwise I will not get any. After a two-hour wait I reached the window and could buy one package of kurashka [shag]. One evening one of the Ukrainians comes to our house and begins to tell us that in Russia there is nothing that bread is sold only to workers and in rationed portions, I began to argue with him that it is not true that in such a large country there would not even be enough dry bread. It was worse every day. On February 10, 1940 at six in the morning three Russian soldiers came to us and tell us that we should pack because in two hours we are leaving. We ask where, He does not answer anything to this question, only says that we should hurry. At 10 we were loaded on sleighs and soldiers on the side do not let anyone anywhere, we set off for the station. At the station stands a transport numbering about 50 railway cars. Our sleigh draws up to one of the cars and stops. The soldiers open the doors of the car and order us to get in. They let us take only one package each and the rest is to go in the baggage car. We went into the car, we look and there are already 52 people there. It is a small freight car only benches are made in it. I go up on one of the upper benches. After a few hours I smell a terrible stench. The windows are open but what good does that do there are four windows while in the car there are 55 people. In the evening the train starts off. We go to the east but where no one says. I lie down and go to sleep. When I woke up it was already the second day I had a slight fever. The doctor comes to the car and asks what kind of trip we are having. I don't tell him that I have a fever, he walks up to me and checks my pulse, after some time he says 38,3 [normal body temperature is 36.6°C] he writes something down on a card and gives it to the orderly and goes out. On the next station the orderly brings two white rolls and a few pieces of candy gives them to me and tells me to eat them right away. And so we traveled for a whole week. After a week they began to give a little food, a piece of bread and a bit of gruel for the whole day. After 25 days of traveling we leave the train and board sleighs which take us to the settlement. At the settlement there are four barracks. 485 souls of us came to this settlement. After two days of rest the commandant of the settlement calls a meeting and says that the following day we have to go to work that Poland had fallen and there would not be a Poland any more. Hearing these words Czarniecki Stanisław a single young man of 24 stands up and says that what he says he should say to the Russians After these words the commandant telephoned the police station right away and two NKVD men came but Stanisław was quite strong when they came in an ordered him to go with them he did not say anything only nodded his head to his mother. But when they turned to go and walked away some 200 meters he took care of both of them so that one was found completely naked and unarmed and the other only dead and unarmed. After this incident no one heard anything about him. A few months later when we were spreading out into the surrounding areas, I went to a certain village. When I went into one of the houses I saw that a cross was hanging in the corner under a picture. I began to speak with a foreman who had been deported from southern Ukraine already in 1929 and after 8 years of prison got the foreman but he told me frankly what was in his heart. They didn't let him believe in God but he believed even if it was in secret. The Russian population sympathized with us and was sorry for us although they themselves almost died of hunger. At our settlement during a year and a half 128 people died of hunger. And so it was worse every day. After some time they took away by force children tó the age of 7. it is not known where. Whoever passed his 14th birthday had to work. The work was hard because in the forest the earnings were low a good worker earned 3 – 4 rubles daily. The food was so dreadful that everyone had a stomach sickness. And this is how it was until the amnesty. After the amnesty they let us earn more and live a little better but to let someone out of the settlement even no one from the commandery said a word. When we asked when we would leave there they said that it would be soon and this went on for two months. After two months I meet one of the foremen and ask why it's like that and he tells me what whoever wants to leave the settlement has to spend time in prison. So after this conversation I say to my brother that we have to escape. And this is what happened. On November 13, 1941, I, mommy, and my brother escaped from the settlement. There was no pursuit after us in three days I reached Vologda where there was a Polish outpost. From Vologda already under Polish care I made my way abroad.

DOCUMENT NO. 109

PGC/Box 119

CZESŁAW J.
Born 1927
Włodzimierz Wołyński county
Wołyń voivodeship

In the year 1940 on February 10 at two o'clock at night four NKVD men burst into our apartment, together with six peasants from a nearby village. We jumped up without knowing what was going on. They pointed a rifle at my father and he didn't have the right to even move his hand, and we were ordered to pack. They gave us 40 minutes to gather up our things and this forty minutes was not enough to gather even half of the things but we were not allowed to take them yet. After we came together one of the NKVD men read out an order to us that we were being deported to another voivodeship, that we were not to take anything with us because there would be enough of everything there. With our own horses we were taken to the nearest station of Bubnów. After an hour we entered small freight cars. There had to be 45 people in one car. And because it was so crowded we had to put our things in special baggage cars. We set out on our way they closed every freight car with a lock and there were bars in the window so that no one could escape. We are on our way for three days and they neither gave us food nor allowed us access to the cars where we stored our things nor do they give us anything to heat with. On the fifth day the men were taken out of the cars in pairs with pails right away the train guards led them away pointing their rifles at them a few minutes later they came back and brought oat soup and a bit of wood for heating. Throughout the journey this was repeated five times. The cars were full of holes they gave little heating material, it was cold and there was nothing before which one could heat up the bread that was frozen hard as a rock. We traveled like that for three weeks. We finally got to our destination in the Arkhangel Province, county of Niandomski, Sukhana settlement. After we left the train we asked for our things which we gave to be kept in the baggage car. They told us to come the next day. They put us in cold barracks and some of them were without windows and it was very crowded. The expected tomorrow came. My father and I took a sled and went for those things but there was no trace of them Our difficult days began. We had to go for hard work. My father went to "leso rubki" which means to cut wood, this did not go well because the snow was very high because one fell in up to the neck and more, and the cold was so great that it went down to 60 degrees. But cold or no cold, one had to go because if someone did not go for two days he went to jail and it was hard to get out of it. My mommy went to chop up branches. My older brother drove wood by horse carriage. Because if one did not go to work they did not give bread or food which one did not have money to buy. At the beginning a good worker earned 50 rubles and a bad one 40 rubles then they raised the money. The bread was black and underbaked so that in a kilogram there were only two pieces which cost 1 ruble per kilogram. And even so one couldn't buy it because for a worker they gave 1 kilogram and for a nonworker ½ a kilogram later even that was reduced A portion of soup cost 50 kopeck 1 ruble and more in which gruel chased gruel and could not catch it.

We slowly managed because there were no small children among us (I was the youngest) and what we had in clothing we sold to buy a piece of bread. Some people swelled up from hunger and died and some were afflected with "cyngo" [scurvy] (it is a terrible disease). The summer we were waiting for came. Then everyone was better off. Because we could pick mushrooms, blueberries, and various marsh berries that there were lots of in that place. In the summer there were terrible swamps so that one could not cross from barrack to barracks and had to make wooden walkways. After hearing about the amnesty that was proclaimed on October 5, 1941, we left for the German povolzhe [territories from which the Volga Germans had been deported] this means for German settlements in the Sarotov Voivodeship. But not the whole family because my mommy and older brother had to stay behind. Here we suffered the greatest hunger because we did not take even one piece of bread with us. We then traveled for a whole month. Not eating at all for three days at a time. In this difficult way we arrived at our destination Here already things were better for us because after the Germans there was left a lot of food, cattle, and generally what is on a farm. This is where I found out about the death of my mommy who at that time was not together with us. This was a terrible moment for me because I was not present when my mommy died. In this place I was for 4 months. I joined the junaks. After joining the junaks I was parted from my family. I only saw them in Pahlevi. I went that way to Narpoj where the junaks were gathering for going abroad. Together with the junak school on August 6, '42, we left Russia for Pahlevi, a Persian port. We traveled by ship for two days before we reached it.

DOCUMENT NO. 110

PGC/Box 119

APOLINARY H.
Zdołbunów county
Wołyń voivodeship

My experiences in Russia

Sitting at home, and it was Sunday morning, I heard a fierce cry of command the barking of dogs and calling. I left the house and saw troops walking along a road next to our house. It was the russian deluge. It was already too late to resist, to drive them back to their own lands. Only here and there Polish partisans were defending themselves, dealing mortal blows to the Russians.

In some places the bolsheviks were afraid of going through the woods even though they had tanks and armored cars, but instead they would circle about it and go around through the fields. Tanks would sink in mud not able to get out, they had to pull them out with tractors. A few dozen steps behind the tanks rode the cavalry, Instead of saddles they covered horses with blankets. Horses would fall under the riders, exhausted from tiredness. They were so thin that it was fearsome to look at them. One bolshevik whose horse fell down ran to the meadow where two were grazing, saddled them, and started slowly. And because the horse was big he climbed on it with difficulty. The farmer, when he saw it, grabbed a stick, grabbed the horse which stood by the well, and briskly started toward him. When the bolshevik saw the farmer with a stick on a horse, jumped from the horse and started running to his men. The farmer took his horses together with the saddle and rode to his farm. And the bolshevik had to go on foot. Having seen the store which was at the end of that street they fell upon it like wolves on a lamb, and started buying anything they found under their eyes. One bolshevik asked the shopkeeper "can we get sausage here," the shopkeeper replies that they can, "a skolko" [how much] asks the boshevik, the shopkeeper replies: one, two, because he didn't know they were so hungry, for there were few cases when a Pole would take more than two, "a bolshe mozhna" [can one take more] as many as you want says the shopkeeper. "Nyeuzhyeli" tak davaytie dvyenadtzat kilogramov" [really, so give me twelve kilograms]. He started eating right away. One could only hear "horoshaya kyelbasa" [good sausage]. Another one saw boxes standing on the shelves and not knowing what they were, asked for twenty boxes. He walked further, unpacked them, and started eating, but it didn't taste good to him. Only later he found out it was toothpaste. When they left the shop was already empty. There were still many incidents like this. They were asking what purpose yeast served, and when they found out it was for bread they ate it as if it was the most delicious cake. Everywhere in cities they burned documents, money, newspapers, books, and many different things concerning both military and civilian affairs. In the suburbs there was a large two-story building, surrounded with a fence, in which the police lived. In the morning when the police were asleep two divisions of russian army came to disarm the police. The guard standing at the outpost saw the bolshevik soldier stealing up through the fence to surround the gate, and open the way for the others, he hit him with a butt and pierced him with a bayonet. Leaving him by the fence he ran to the barracks to wake up the ones who were asleep. After a few moments everyone was on their feet and the bolsheviks crossed the gate. They gave a sign with a gunshot for Poles to surrender their arms. The policemen replied with fire from machine guns. Real fighting started. A greater part of russians fell and only one Polish officer remained. He quickly ran though all the rooms he took all the plans, documents, simply everything that fell into his hands, he put them all in one room and set fire to it. Annoyed bolsheviks broke down the door and burst inside and found nothing, because everything was already burned and the officer lay on the ground dead. A different movement, a different life prevailed everywhere. Russians and officers in particular bought out clothes, furniture and sent them to their families in Russia. Some never saw a bicycle before and would say "vot kakaya machina" [what a machine]. Anyone who was riding a bicycle would have it taken away from him and they were learning how to ride. In every ditch there were plenty of broken bicycles and a "boyetz" [soldier] would walk away with a broken head. After some time meetings and elections started, at which they voted for a representative who was chosen in advance. And when someone didn't want to on the same night he would be arrested and sent to prison. At one meeting they announced that everyone was supposed to bring their horses to the communal house for a checkup. I put my horses to the wagon and rode there. At the communal house a "boyetz" without saying anything took me off the wagon took the horses away and told me to wait. In a moment he returned and gave me kolkhoz horses, one large one which was falling down on the way, and a small one, a little fatter, which also barely stood on its legs. The days were getting worse. One could not sleep through one night in peace. Ukrainians attacked houses and robbed anything they found, and still threatened with death. One night I was awakened by some voice and knocking at the door. I got up from bed and looked at my watch, it was four in the morning. I was very surprised who it could have been walking about so early, for my parents were still asleep. I went to the window to see who it could have been. In the courtyard I saw sleighs with two horses pulling it. I thought that maybe one of my friends arrived, but I was disappointed because I saw a few men standing there with guns. I didn't know what to do. Knocking on the door wasn't stopping. I quickly dressed and woke up my parents. When everyone was up I opened the door. A few N.K.V.D. men burst into the room. The first question was "imyetie oruzhyo" [do you have weapons], then they ordered us to pack. Every one of us frightened, nervous, was asking where they were sending us, to paradise replied the russians. We were all busy packing our things. They only allowed us to take some linen and lard. One "boyetz" went up to the attic and brought a saw and an ax and says "vosmitye eto vam prigaditsa" [take it, you will need it]. The other ones stood in the line and were drinking cherry syrup from a bottle, which stood behind the wardrobe. In one hour we were all on the sleighs. My family consisted of four members. We started, and it was February 10. Even dogs howled plaintively because they felt that everyone would be leaving. At first they brought us to the communal house, where we stood for two hours until everyone was there and then we started on our journey. We rode for a rather long time. Snow mounds were in the way, and the road was not too good and the sleighs would overturn every once in a while. Finally we got to the station, where we were loaded into cars. The cars were overcrowded, there was no place to turn. The doors were closed and bolted and two militiamen rode with every car. At 10 o'clock a whistle was heard and the train started. Women and children cried only the men were keeping up our spirits that we were not going to Russia only to some other place. One hour after another passed and the train didn't stop. Only once in a while it would stop at a large station where we would get soup of hot water and a few groats swimming on the surface. After a week the train stopped and they threw us out to the woods into siberian taiga. We walked 2.5 kilometers to the settlement. There they distributed us among dirty bedbug-infested barracks, in which russians lived before our arrival. Everyone started on a job in a cow barn, covered up gaps in the windows, brought planks so that some beds could be built so one didn't sleep on the floor because one could easily catch a cold. And whoever got ill would have to leave his bones far away in North siberia. A doctor would walk from barracks to barrack with a wooden box, but in it he only had cotton and bandages. After two days the elders were taken to work, at removing snow and building roads. Hunger was already being felt. In the mess hall there was a soup made of beet leaves, which no one could eat, and flat cakes, so-called "sladie" [?], 2 centimeters in diameter, cost a ruble and a half each and no one could afford them because one's pocket didn't allow it. At the cooperative one had to stand 8–10 hours in a line to get bread, and even so one didn't always get it. Work quotas were so outrageous that no man was capable of fulfilling them. They gave bread in exchange for food coupons, 800 grams per worker, and 400 per non-worker. At first it was barely enough when there were still supplies from Poland and afterward when they ran out then it was hunger for good. Afterward they took everyone to the forest to fell trees. Everyone had to flounder in snow waist-deep, and was all wet by the time they got to work. There were no stoves, where one could dry onself. It was cold in apartments, the frost reached 70 degrees. Finally after the long torment of winter the spring came. Right away they took all men to raft down the river and women to sovchoz or to mine peat ("torforozrobotka"), and bigger boys to put bricks of peat together and dry them. After a short time a school was established to which Polish youths were dragged. They taught there that there was no God and that religion doesn't exist. And not being able to break us of that habit they relied on different skits. In the attic of the school sat a bolshevik and held a package with candies and there was a hole drilled in the ceiling. The teacher ordered children to yell: "Bozshe day konfyetov" [God, give candies] and then the soviet didn't throw candies. Then she ordered to yell Stalin day konfyeti [Stalin, give candies]. Then the soviet poured candies. Then the teacher said that there was no God because he doesn't give candies. In the middle of spring and it was at 10 o'clock everyone was asleep because they came from work. I woke up. the whole family was already on their feet. I didn't know what was going on. I got up and sat up on the bed, I saw the commander of the settlement with a revolver against the chest of my father and then a few N.K.V.D. men with sharp weapons. One of them yelled at me to get up. I got up quickly, got dressed and I am looking in all directions what is going on. N.K.V.D. started looking through all the things doing a search. Whatever they didn't take in

Poland they took in Russia. A golden band, prayer books photographs and all the money were taken by the commander "Markov." After the search they ordered father to only put on his pants, shoes on bare feet and a jacket. They said that he would go to the office. When they left the house I also left in a moment and saw how they were pushing him into a cab and they left in the direction of the city. In the summer we went to the woods and picked mushrooms to provide food for the winter. At the end severe winter came. The frost bothered us a lot and particularly when one stood in a line for a morsel of bread. And with time came also Christmas. They were not as joyful and as nice as in the native country. The bells didn't ring so loudly, calling the people to church, which went to pray and give their homage to God. You couldn't see carolers, walking with stars and singing carols and children riding sleds, skis and ice skating. Everywhere there were forests and marshes. When the Christmas holidays came every man, woman, and child tried not to go to work, to prepare at least a modest meal for Christmas Eve. Everyone tried to sell some of their clothes, or some other things, to buy milk or perhaps potatoes, to get which one had to walk 40 kilometers to the kolkhoz and one didn't always bring them back. On the other hand the policemen walked around the barracks with knouts and chased out of beds to work. Everyone also wanted to rest at that time after daily and so hard work. Finally the moment came when everyone sat down at the table to partake of that modest Christmas Eve meal. Before eating we all broke the wafer, which we brought from Poland, with each other, and then we wished each other all the best, that we could spend the next Christmas holidays in our Motherland, or at least in a different place and under better conditions. All evening long it was only crying and remembrances of better times. After eating our meal we all sang carols, which the commander couldn't stand and he came to the house every few moments to calm down the singers. And because there was no way he could calm us down because nobody paid any attention to him he threatened that he won't give any bread and would walk away to his office. So passed the evening full of sadness, for I spent it with our family not complete. 12 o'clock was coming, when everyone went to sleep. The following morning, everyone was still joyful with the dream that soon our captivity would be over and everyone will be able to breathe more freely in liberty. The second day passed similarly with carols and telling about various adventures. The third day passed a little more sadly, because everyone had to go to work, because they didn't dispense bread for two days and there was nothing left to eat. In the evenings some families gathered together and talked about what would happen later. So ended the Christmas holidays. Since that time everyone started working on, to earn for a morsel of bread and somehow survive that moment and return to Fatherland in good health. Month after month flew by ever more people started getting ill and worse times came. Finally the moment of liberation came. It was announced at the square next to the barracks. The commander said that everyone who wants to can leave. The joy was hard to describe. Everyone was very happy that maybe they can go somewhere and will be able to live that moment a little better. From the settlement we left for a kolkhoz in Uzbekistan. There it was also very difficult to get food as well as with clothing. There I joined the junaks and left for Teheran. A few months later my family as well. Only there is no news of my father. Here everyone breathed with full lungs because one felt that freedom of not being under a Russian bayonet.

DOCUMENT NO. 111

PGC/Box 120

ERNEST K.
Zdołbunów county
Wołyń voivodeship

Mommy and Little Sister and my brother earned 10 rubles each daddy stayed in Cracow. altogether we were 7. three went to work and four were at home and sometimes we went to pick berries. for two kilograms of berries they gave two rubles and this is what we lived on. when mommy got sick we had nothing to give her, In the winter we had no wood and we were cold I and my brother went to school in school they beat us instead of teaching us he turned his back to us and told the Russians to beat us in Russia my sister went to nursery school the Russian beat her and later she went to the hospital. when we were already leaving she died my teeth hurt in Russia but they did not treat them.

DOCUMENT NO. 112

PGC/Box 120

ROMUALD KOZŁOWSKI
Born 1926
Zdołbunów county
Wołyń voivodeship

On 9.17. 1939 the Soviet troops crossed the Polish border. Our weapons were taken away in the first place and a list was made of what we had on our farm, i.e., cattle, farm tools, etc. After a few weeks they started taking cattle and swine away from us, paying for them. So it could be said that it was "paid." They treated father the worst because he was a colonist so they imputed different things to him so long as they had an excuse to arrest him. On 2.10.1940 at 4 o'clock in the morning they surrounded our house and ordered us to get ready to leave for another "voivodeship." 30 minutes was the time we were given to get ready. We packed up certain things, crying. But it is known that when a person is in despair he doesn't know what he's doing. So the time passed and our things were not packed. The NKVD men threw some parcels on the sleighs and ordered us to get in and we went as far as Mohylany with only one stop on the way. There we were loaded into freight cars they put in the screws to lock the cars and only once in a while they would unscrew the doors and take two men from each car out to get water under escort. Or to search for "wood." After a few weeks we got to Russia, Vołogocki "oblast," Torfo-Razrabotka settlement. There I worked in a peat mine during the summer and at "Savkhoz" [collective farm] in the winter. It was very bad for me in the mine because in the mornings there was terribly cold water which leaked out of peat, and it reached below the knees even though they handed out cotton stockings only wide ones so-called "bakhily" [peasant work shoes] and "postoly" [bast shoes] in addition. But in a few hours they would soak through and legs simply grew stiff. When I came home from work they hurt a lot which I experience even now. At "Savkhoz" I scattered dung about the fields, etc.

Many people died of pneumonia too. I don't know even what to say about medical treatments. There was one "Nurse" who dispensed pills measured temperature and left. We lived in a house built of pine logs and walls of planks. Bedbugs drank our blood every night, and there wasn't even any way to help it. Father was in prison, Mother wasn't able to carry heavy loads after an appendix operation. My younger brother worked at laying peat bricks and heaping up mounds. Without consideration for my mother's illness they sent her out to hard labors such as carrying peat on "stretchers." And when I came back home from work hungry, because soup without anything but groats is not filling, and there was little bread so coming home hungry I had to watch my mother who came back from work and had to lie down on the bed because her side hurt terribly. And the next morning you had to go to work again because there would be "Progul" [vagrancy] and prison and so every day I had to suppress my own grief. looking at all this Russian people related properly the old ones particularly. But the youths were very hostile, for instance I was coming back from town I had 60 rubles on me. By the wood I was surrounded by "komosomol" [the Soviet youth organization] boys with knives. They stole my money and let me go. I reported this to NKVD men. But they asked if I was a Pole when I replied yes the commander of NKVD sneered and ordered me to leave. Of course there was no use protesting I went home with sorrow swearing vengeance even if afterward I had to die.

DOCUMENT NO. 113

PGC/Box 124

TADEUSZ B.
Zdołbunów county
Wołyń voivodeship

On the night after the invasion of the Soviets, the S Z R [probably USSR] troops started shooting at the neighboring settlement with machine guns. All the people ran away to the woods.

On Sunday they came to my father to have him drive up hay in the country wagon. after delivering the hay they stopped exchanged horses and took the wagon away and even took the whip away. Father walked with the horses for 2 kilometers 4 hours. On the second day one horse died and the 2nd had both rear legs knocked out of his joint. On February 10 5 in the morning 40 soldiers arrived they chased us from beds and ordered everyone to sit on the floor. afterward they loaded us into sleighs and drove to the village. there we stood until the evening. In the evening we started on the road to the station. After riding for 4 kilometers one country wagon overturned and into a terrible ditch covered with snow. Terrible crying started the wagon was picked up all the children were in the snow and they started riding again children were crying terribly. They loaded us into an 18 ton train car 48 people. In Moscow a woman got ill and started dying and her 7 year old son started crying terribly. Doctors came and took her away and left 2 children the boy was 7 year old and the little girl 3. At the settlement they assigned 8 hours for each person in the family to make 2 meters of the road. Every day that is to clear the ground of stumps along the line of 30 meters to dig two ditches cut up weeds and lay the road and put soil on top of the weeds. For not accomplishing this they didn't give any food products. Children up to the age of 10 had to perform that work because those above 10 had to work at chopping trees. There were plenty of bedbugs and rats in the apartment. Rats even bit off ears of two men. The commander Grybinshchykov said at a meeting that we will never return to Poland and when the germans and England weaken then they will go and take over the entire Europe

212

War Through Children's Eyes

They said that England is the worst enemy because there is most intelligentsia.

In the spring there was work close by but only for them because they chased us 15 kilometers so one only got wet and cold. People started getting sick and dying. After our liberation there was a meeting of communists I overheard. The commander himself was saying we only signed the Pact with the Poles so that England and America would help us.

After liberation we arrived at a station at which we were not allowed to sit only they chased us out onto the tracks and whenever a train comes it catches our torn louse infested rags still from Poland. We arrived at the place of destination they unloaded us next from the station to a field where we sat 1 month. after a month when terrible rains started falling they loaded our rags to buses and all families walked 20 kilometers carrying small children in their arms. In the kolkhoz they didn't give bread. only rotten potatoes and not even enough. There was no bath only in cold water you could wash the winter. We carried wood 3 kilometers and at night too. We left there in Omsk we stood in train cars 2 weeks. Afterward they loaded 30 Russian boys together with us who jumped with knives and started directly taking everything they turned off the lights and terrible moments started and a girl's voice was heard in the corner and afterward she got a knife in her chest and died. I broke away from the car and jumped up to a policeman who was standing by the door and listened and when I told him he waved his hand and left us in this car 4 of ours dead and all the money documents and also the good linen taken. Now were left completely stripped. I myself was walking around Tashkent and stole some beet and potatoes here and there and I couldn't even eat myself because I had to bring for my little 4 year old brother and for my 6 year old sister and when I brought they asked me to go once again.

Refugees

PGC/Box 123

KAZIMIERZ W
Born 1928

Then the lady commandant wrote down the people for work. The next day everybody went to work they gave 800 grams of bread and anybody who didn't work they took off to school and gave them 300 grams of bread in school they learned russian songs and poems and to read and to write and they said you won't be going back to Poland zdes vashi kosti zostanut [your bones will stay here] and we sayed that we were and the comminists sayed no. And they said there was no God and that we mustn't believe in God that he don't exist and they didn't let us wear religious medallions, but we had them in our pockets and around our neck anyhow and they said man arose from a monkey.

One day my brother went to work with the comminists one of them lost his watch or can't find it and he said my brother stealed that watch. next day my brother went to the woods for raspberries it was Sunday and he got lost in the woods and he missing for 7 days then they found him dead in the woods. We don't know if they killed him or he just died because the comminists said they would not spare his life because of the watch they took my brother of blessed memory and buried my brothers chopped the forest and my Father carried wood to the barracks to burn Father caught cold and got sick the doctors didn't allow him sick because they didn't know what sickness it was and so father lay sick for a very longer time then he died my brother made a plank coffin and buried my Dad because the russians didn't give planks they wanted us to bury my father without a coffin but my brother stealed planks at night and he made the coffin at night with the carpenter and they buried father my Mother was going to my father's burial and caught cold and cried and got sick too and after 10 days my mother died too. My father died May 27 at 6 o'clock and my mother died June 6 at 9 in the morning. My father was buried with my mother coffin to coffin. Then comminists were coming to the cemetery and pulled up the crosses and smashed them on the stone and threw them away and we found a small flat cross thrown in the bushes.

then when there was the Amnesty we left russia But it was very hard to get a horse and when they give a horse and cart from the kolkhoz the kolkhoznik still wants you to give him something more for the trip before we left my brother was sick and the kolkhozniks didn't want to take my brother in the cart they said us to leave my sick brother in the barracks and we go alone but we taked him with us we walked on foot the things and my sick brother rode in the cart I walked 75 kilometers then we came to the station and they let us into the building so packed that people sat on other people the train comed and we got onto the train but the conductor didn't want to take us we gave him 4 pieces of soap and then he let us on. On the way my brother got better and was well but at one station he went to get milk and he got cold and got sick and I got the measles too my brother died and I got better my brother died on the train and they took my brother on a sledge and they hauled him with a rope and don't know where they took him and I and my two other brothers goed on. 7 of us went to Russia and 3 came out alive. The end.

DOCUMENT NO. 115

PGC/Box 118

HELENA F.
Born 1926
Warsaw

I was deported to Russia on 4.13.1940 with my Mother and my two-year-old brother. The reason was that we were refugees and Mama is French.

On 5.3. of that year. We arrived in Zhana Semey in Kazakhstan.— On the second day everyone from the age of 17–16 went to work. Youngsters had to go to school, those who didn't go had to work. Because my brother was ill I was allowed to stay home.—Adults worked very hard in the factory, i.e., "Siesiomojka." Their work consisted of sorting and cleaning lambs hair.—Because the factory was active 22 hours they worked on two shifts. The hardest jobs were given to the Poles. It was carrying wool in steel baskets. An average work quota per woman was 7 tons. Not fulfilling this norm exposed one to the threat of prison. After work an overheated worker could take a shower but there was only cold water. It took two hours to get to the factory. Kazakhs would attack on the way back home at night.

Soviet authorities issued an order against walking at night, but the factory didn't allow workers to stay until morning. So the only way of solving that problem was to return at one's own risk, in case of a casualty the Soviet authorities were not responsible. Remuneration for work was 100 rubles monthly. One could buy a kilo of butter for fifty rubles.

A month after our arrival my brother got very sick and had to go to the hospital.

His illness was getting worse, his state was hopeless. Mama asked for a leave from work. She got the answer: "And who will be working in your place?" After long quarrels I was allowed to stay with my brother.

Sanitary conditions were terrible. In the ward there were children with active tuberculosis and dysentery. Medications were administered to all these children with the same spoon. The woman doctor would come to visit the children with a cigarette in her mouth. Oftentimes she was not sober. She would dispense medications in the morning. Syringes were dirty and not airtight.

Since I did not give my assent to this sort of treatment I was threatened that in case of death I would be responsible.

Mother managed to escape from work five days before the death.

At 10 in the evening my brother died.

There were 10 kilometers between the hospital and our home. A terrible storm started outside. The woman doctor declared to Mama that the hospital was for the living not for the dead so she must go back with the child. She was forced to go back home in the middle of the night, in a storm, with a dead child in her arms.

A few months later Mama procured a job in Semipalatynsk.

This time she worked as a dressmaker. The average quota was 7 dresses a day. Making each dress brought in 50 kopecks or 1 ruble. Often there was no fabric. At those times a worker was not paid.

July 1, 1941, Mama was "interned" by the NKVD as a Frenchwoman. I followed Mama of my own free will.

We spent an entire month at NKVD. Afterward they started driving us from prison to prison. In spite of my being a minor I was put together with the worst Russian elements. Men conducted close searches.

After four months of prison we arrived in a łagier [camp] in Novosybirsk.

In the łagier we found 500 German, Czech, and Latvian jews, and aside from them: 300 Hungarians, Frenchmen, and Russians who had some foreign relatives (who were long dead by then). We were fed very poorly. Per day: 400 grams of bread, three times a day a lukewarm watery soup and one herring. Our address, which we would list as a return address on our letters, was erroneous.

We were released on 2.3.1942, after Prof. Kot [Polish ambassador to the USSR] intervened on our behalf.

DOCUMENT NO. 116

PGC/Box 122

ZBIGNIEW R.
Warsaw

Recollections of my stay in Russia

In 1940 in February I left Warsaw in the direction of Lwów, smuggling headache pills which were expensive on the other side. I managed to get through the border with the help of the local Ukrainian popula-. tion. In Lwów I stayed at my aunt, who lived near the convent of the Carmelite nuns. At the convent I spoke with the sisters a few times, and found out that the convent had been turned into an old people's home, and the nuns had been ordered to leave it, with only two staying behind as washerwomen and two as cooks.

A few days after my arrival in Lwów, two NKVD men came to the apartment in the middle of the night and ordered me to pack. We took a minimal amount of bedding, clothes, and food and a half an hour later found ourselves in a railroad car. There were more than forty people in our car. It was a freight car with boarded up doors, with a hole in the floor where we took care of our needs. We were handed bread and water through small windows high up in the car. Hygienic conditions were dreadful since there was no water not only to wash but even to drink. So that vermin of all kinds felt very much at home. After traveling for nearly a month, we were unloaded and taken by car to barracks, to the settlement. There were already Russians there and Ruthenians who had been deported as kulaks during the formation of the kolkhozes. At the settlement my aunt and I worked on cutting wood cubes used for running car engines. After we had been there for three months, my aunt slashed her hand with a saw and was taken to the hospital. My uncle, who was working on the floating of timber, crushed his finger with a log and temporarily became unable to work. As a physically poorly develop-ed boy of 13, I earned between 3 and 4 rubles a day. Now there was not enough money for bread, since besides everything else, we were paid at irregular intervals. During this time we lived on mushrooms. I decided to escape back to Lwów and from there to my parents in Warsaw. And this is what I did. But on the third day after my escape I was captured and interrogated. From the interrogation I gathered that the place of my deportation and the destination of my escape were not known to the authorities so, fearing that my uncle might be held responsible, I con-cealed the truth. I was taken under escort to a so called prijomnik, that is a shelter, where I found other captured boys wandering over the coun-try, mostly Russians and partly also Tartars and Bashkirs. They were terribly dirty, lousy, and their ragged clothing barely covered their bodies. They were cleaned up a little and moved to a so-called clean barracks. At the shelter where was a constant atmosphere of struggle between the Russian and the Tartar boys because the Russians, being in the majority, persecuted the others. These were completely corrupted boys. When they were not in captivity, they lived mostly from stealing and blackmailing weaker boys. I tried to avoid any open conflict, but they were unpleasant to me in a systematic way. After a week another

War Through Children's Eyes

Polish boy came. We decided to escape together. But after jumping out of the second-floor window my friend hurt himself, so he stayed, but he urged me to escape. I saw from my hiding place how they tortured him in anger, smashing his head with bunches of keys, hitting and kicking him. I escaped. In this way I went through a number of shelters, until finally, morally exhausted, I gave up all further attempts to escape. In one of the shelters I met a group of Polish children. We were brought up in such a way that those who came from Podole and Wołyń were persuaded that they were Ruthenians and those from the Wilno region and Polesie were told that they were Belorussians. There was discord among us and the Russian boys took advantage of this, staging mass fights, and the authorities looked the other way at the results of their work. At the shelter we cut wood and gathered berries, which were sent off for processing, into barrels. The young Russians were brought up in such a way that they hated everything that was not communist and spewed hatred toward the so-called bourgeois countries. They tried to persuade us that we had been oppressed by our own government in Poland. After some time, I was transferred to a trade school, where they tried to make a blacksmith out of me. At this school, the following was the order of the day: Since we were the second shift, we got up at 7 AM. Our breakfast consisted of 200 grams of bread with tea. After breakfast began exercises, shooting, antigas, and physical education. At ten o'clock began two hours of study of the theory of metals. At noon lunch, consisting of 100 grams of bread and 3/4 liter of soup. The time from 1 PM to 4 PM was free. At 5 PM we went to a smithy, where we worked for 6 hours, with a one-hour break. On the way back, we were often trained during our march over especially selected marshy terrain and we often returned home at midnight or 1 AM. Exhausted, after a supper of 200 grams of bread and tea we threw ourselves on our bedding, thinking that tomorrow, like today, we would be faced with a quota of 120 ship nails in 6 hours. We slept in unheated or very poorly heated quarters, in which bedbugs feasted on our bodies. There was a shortage of bread, so the boys supplemented their diet with bread bought with food coupons and money stolen from the local population. I was persecuted just as I had been at the shelters. For instance, once, when I fell asleep at the anvil out of exhaustion, they threw a handful of hot coals into my shirt. The boys who did this were not punished. On our free days, which were every seven days we went, supposedly voluntarily, to work in the forest or at the kolkhozes. Relations between us and the people in charge of us were brutal. They always called us such names as a decent person would be ashamed to repeat, and those who did not fulfill their quota were locked up for the whole night. For instance, a 13-year-old boy was accused of desertion and sentenced to a year of hard labor because he went to a village some 60 kilometers away to visit his parents and was absent for three days. There was hunger among the local population (already after the war between the Germans and the Bolsheviks broke out), and there were incidents of eating cats and dogs. The population was greatly demoralized, lacking a feeling of shame and relations between men and women were brutal, shameless, and leading to the unleashing of man's lowest instincts (everything was done for profit). Religion and people who practiced it were persecuted. People lived like animals, with the goal to have as dissipated life as possible. This was the situation I found myself in when the amnesty came. I went to the local NKVD station demanding that I be permitted to leave freely as a free Polish citizen. But they answered that inasmuch as the Soviet government had taken care of me for two years, I had become a Soviet citizen. They started to persuade me that things had been bad in Poland, that the bourgeois oppressed me, took advantage of me, etc. When I refused to be persuaded, I was told with a mocking laugh that I would never be permitted to leave. Willful escape was punishable by hard labor, but when I learned that Polish outposts were being organized in southern Russian cities, I decided to escape, since I realized that if I managed to get there, Polish authorities would stand up for me.

In November, 1941, I escaped from the school and after a march of five days I arrived at the closest railway station where I mingled with a throng of refugees evacuated from territories occupied by the German forces, and traveled by rail to the city of Orenburg, where there was a Polish outpost. There I told my story to a Polish liaison officer, who made out identity papers for me. On my way to Orenburg I met a transport of prisoners, from the inside of the railway cars could be heard the cries of people in Russian: "People, whoever believes in God, give us water," but the escort did not allow anyone to relieve the thirst of the prisoners. When I received my documents, I became a free man once more after two years.

DOCUMENT NO. 117

PGC/Box 131

JÓZEF B.
14 years old
Majdan Kolbuszewski

My father was a butcher. We had a shop with kosher meat. There were four children in the family, Hirsh—21 years old, Rachela—19 years old, Jeremy—18 years old, I was the youngest. We lived well, so that older children didn't work, but studied. When the war broke out and German planes appeared that dropped a few bombs, the village was panic-stricken. Fortunately bombs fell in the fields and they didn't damage anything in the village. Nevertheless, people were leaving the village in a state of panic, moving to other places. After a few days, Germans arrived. Jews hid away. They ran to neighboring villages looking for hiding places with peasants they knew. The majority of Jews indeed found shelter in the villages, but many peasants refused to shelter even these Jews with whom for years they were involved in trade. Also Father with the family hid at a peasant he knew, from whom he bought cattle. But the peasant said that he is afraid of Germans and didn't want to keep us long. His wife, seeing our despair, said that she will hide us no matter what because she can't stand to see her old friends without any place to live. They hid us in a stable. We stayed there for a few days, afraid to go out and so that the neighbors would not see us. Seeing that the situation is prolonging, we decided to return home at night. At home we found the doors to be open and a looted apartment. Germans took our radio, a new wardrobe, and best clothing, and they turned the whole apartment upside down.

Germans in Majdan

During those few days that we spent in the countryside, Germans did things in Majdan their own way. Some most respected Jews and Poles they led out of town, and they tormented the rest of the population, dragging them to work and beating them without mercy. A few days after we returned to the village, they encircled the Jewish quarter, ordered all men to the town square, gave them containers with kerosene, took them to the temple, ordered them to pour kerosene over it, and set it on fire. They forced the Jews to dance in a circle around the temple. Germans stood splitting their sides with laughter looking at this spectacle. Every day Jewish sufferings increased. Seeing that we couldn't stand it for long, Father decided to go to the Russian side. With the help of smugglers, we went with the whole family to Niemirów.

At the Bolsheviks

In Niemirów we moved in with Father's friend, also a butcher, and we were planning to stay there. A few butchers formed an association and did business together. Older brother Hirsh also went into trade. He carried food products from Niemirów to big cities. Brother and sister were helping him. They earned more than Father in his butcher shop. Father, however, told every day about new restrictions in trade, especially concerning the trade in kosher meat. If the bolsheviks would force him to deal in non-kosher meat, he will never do it. He told us about elections and registrations. They decided not to go anywhere, be it registration or election. Once I overheard Father telling Mother that they were forcing people to take Russian passports. He consulted with Mother and they decided not to take passports because they did not want to become Soviet citizens and lose the chance to return home even after the war. Brother and Sister tried to persuade Father to take the passport, arguing that this will be of no importance after the war. One day Father told us that everybody refusing to take passports will be sent home, under the Germans, and he asked brother and sister to stop their business, because he wanted the whole family to go together. He told Mother to pack everything, because he was sure that something will happen any day.

In Exile

What we feared had finally occurred. One Friday night, in the middle of the summer, NKVD men appeared; they conducted a search and told us to pack. We were ready for this and we immediately stepped outside. We were taken to the station, loaded on windowless freight cars, fifty people to a car. We stood 48 hours in a sealed car in the station without food or drink. When the train moved all Jews in the car started to weep terribly. We the children seeing older people weep started to scream, but no one paid attention to our screams. We traveled for three weeks, and no one knew the destination. Mother and other women in the car lamented over the unknown future. During the whole trip we were not allowed out of the car. During the day they gave half a kilo of bread per person, at night some soup. There was a hole in the car where one could relieve oneself. One week after the journey began, we all fell ill with diarrhea and one had to wait in line to get to the hole. Children couldn't wait for their turn and relieved themselves in the car. Stink and dirt were unbearable. Women fainted and there was nothing to help them with. No one listened when we called for help. Guards were only watching the roof, to spot an opening through which one could get away. After three weeks we stopped at a station not far from the city of Troick. We left the car. We were divided into groups and taken by foot to Vostochna. We walked for the whole day even though we were weakened from illness and the journey. We arrived at night and were put up in barracks, 80 people to a barracks. We slept on the floor. We woke up in the middle of the night and a panic broke out. Mice were jumping over us, as big as cats. We chased them away, but they were not afraid. Impatiently we awaited dawn. When we complained about the mice to the commander he answered: "In Russia one can get used to everything." The next morning we were divided into groups. One part worked in the forest, another on the railroad tracks. I and Mother were relieved from work. When we reached the settlement it was still warm, but then winter came and cold reached 50°C. Though no one had warm clothing we were driven even when it was 48°C below zero. Those who worked received 1 kilogram of bread daily; we who did not work, only 400 grams. In the dining hall one could buy soup. It was warm water and it cost 2 rubles. Throughout our stay at the settlement we could never afford to buy soup. We were always hungry and we envied people who could afford to buy soup. I desired so much to eat something boiled that I begged people who bought soup to leave some for me at the bottom. After a few months we were taken to another settlement in the forest. Russian exiles lived there before, but I did not see them. My brother who worked as a loader met these exiles and said that there were many important personalities among them. There was no kitchen in the new settlement. One had to walk several kilometers to get soup. I went to fetch soup and for each portion I brought I received two spoonfuls. Because I was bringing five, six portions I was eating soup every day. One day I almost froze to death on the way to the kitchen. My hands froze and I could not move them for several weeks. I was forbidden to bring soup anymore. At this time my brother Hirsh got sick, we didn't know what it was and in a few weeks, without medical help, he died. We buried him in the middle of the forest.

War and Amnesty

We were not told anything when the war broke out. The guard told us about it one day, asking that we keep it a secret. Father said that he understands why our bread rations were reduced. After the amnesty we were all called together and they asked us to stay in place, that it will be better. Of course, we did not want to stay. We got documents and left for Samarkanda. We spent two weeks in Samarkanda, sleeping in the street, just as thousands of refugees. Many died on the street and there was no one to bury them. We lay among the corpses and we felt that we shall die here of hunger, and after many difficulties we managed to go to Turkestan. We weren't allowed to leave the train and we had to go to Kushata. We spent a night there and were sent to kolkhoz Burgen. We worked in the fields receiving 600 grams of bread and Mother and I, since we did not work, received 300 grams. The local inhabitants lived as miserably as we did. In the huts there was no furniture, only beds made of boards nailed together. We, the exiles, slept on wet ground.

Death of the Parents

Father and Mother got sick with typhus. Brother and sister tried to put them in a hospital. They did not even want to give us a cart to carry them there. After a few days of illness, without medical assistance, Father and Mother died on the same day. We mourned after them for a whole night and on the next day we buried them ourselves. After parents' death, brother and sister tried to have me accepted at a Polish orphanage in Turkestan. After long efforts, I was finally accepted at the orphanage. I spent eight days there. Polish children did not treat me well, but the teacher took my side. One day we were taken to Teheran. I stayed there for a few months until I left for Palestine.

DOCUMENT NO. 118

PGC/Box 131

ELIEZER H.
15 years old
Izbica

We lived in Izbica. My father was a tanner and made a good living. Until the outbreak of the war 1200 Jewish families lived in Izbica. First week of the war passed quietly in our town. Only during the second week a bombing began. My mother was just baking bread. She left everything and we escaped to the forest. Germans came on the next day. Three tanks and a lot of motorcycles. Everyone hid. There was not a soul in the street. One butcher, Chaim Falek, a Jew some forty years of age, was just closing a gate to his house. Germans shot at him and killed him. His son served in the Polish army and participated in many battles. He returned home safely. Around town, in the mountains, lights were burning. Neighboring villages were on fire. Polish Army fought the Germans for another six hours. In Izbica Germans called all men and kept them standing with raised hands for a whole hour. Then an officer came and told to go away. Suddenly this officer spotted an enormous, very tall Jew. This Jew was called in the village Josek's son. The whole family was so tall. They were the town's favorites. The officer shot and wounded the giant. Later they cared for him in the hospital, but he died, though he was taken to a hospital in Zamość. The whole town cried over the loss of this beautiful and healthy boy. The Germans stayed in Izbica for twelve days. Among the Germans were some Austrian soldiers who comforted the Jews by saying that the Russians will soon come. Bolsheviks came to town on Thursday, the Jewish population was relieved. There was a friendly reception. A fraction of Jewish youth joined the militia and wore red arm bands. The militiamen helped in searching for weapons. Bolsheviks took cattle from the landlords and carried it away on trucks. The Russians were for eight days only and then left, promising that they will return. They advised the Jews to leave with them. They said that in Russia no one will hurt us. You will become Soviet citizens, they kept saying. About 100 families decided to go with the Bolsheviks. We also went with them. We were taken by trucks to Włodzimierz and we took along some things.

We spent nine weeks in Włodzimierz. Other refugees came to town, it became crowded. The Russians announced that workers are needed for coal mines inside Russia. They advised to sign up freely, for otherwise they will take by force. We reported freely that we want to go into Russia. We were allowed to take all our things, we were taken by trucks to the railroad station where we were put on a train going in the direction of Łuck. We arrived to Asditish village. It was a nice village where only Jews lived. There was a Committee of Refugees' Assistance there. We were treated well and fed for four months. The NKVD functionaries from Moscow came and they said that there is no place for idlers in Russia. They registered and interviewed everyone. All refugees were rounded up and put on trains. We were taken to the town of Gorki. It was in winter, there were stoves burning on the train. In Gorki we spent three months.

Again NKVD agents appeared and they ordered us to work. Russia is big, we must help to build Russia. Who will not sign up freely for work will be deported to Siberia together with criminals. We signed up freely. We were sent to a large hamlet Pravdinsk, near Gorki. There were 18,000 people in this hamlet. There were 95 people in our group of exiles. A few Poles and a few Ukrainians. NKVD agents were saying that in Russia everybody is equal.

We were fed for three days and then sent to work. There was a paper mill in the hamlet, employing 12,000 people. Exiles were ordered to bring logs of the size of 2 cu. meters. Older people were folding paper. Children studied at school. I had my 13th birthday then.

My father earned 150 rb—the value of this was 2 dollars. Father brought bread from the mill. Mother stood in line to buy foodstuffs. Lines were long, sometimes 1,000 people stood in line. Russians would often let my mother go first. They said: you suffered enough from the war. They brought us bread at home. And candies for the children. At the mill there was a large dining hall for the workers, but the food was not kosher there, so my father couldn't make any use of it.

After three months posters appeared on the walls that refugees should no longer benefit from any assistance. They are already Soviet citizens. Then things started to get worse for us. Whole nights one had to spend in lines. People often hit each other in lines. After a whole night wait, one would walk away without bread.

We realized that we cannot stay in Russia because we will die of hunger. We wanted to reach Wołyń, where, we were told, life was easier. We sold some things, so that we could go to Wołyń. The way to Wołyń was through Moscow. In order to get to Moscow one needed a special permit from the head of the hamlet. All who asked for such a permit were sent, as a punishment, to Siberia. We went to Moscow illegally, not by train but by ship. We bribed the clerk at the ticket counter, paying 5 rb. extra for a ticket. We had to wait long for the ship, suffering from hunger. We were for three days in Moscow. We slept in the street. There was plenty of everything in magazine windows, even foreign products. Just as in Poland before the war. We easily got exit tickets and we departed in the direction of Kiev. It was summer. Kiev streets were full of refugees. Everybody, Ukrainians, Jews, Poles, wanted to return home even though Germans rule there. Letters arrived, that life is easier there, than in Russia. Then, it turned out that according to the Russian-Soviet agreement [i.e., the German-Soviet Boundary and Friendship Treaty] only Ukrainians are allowed to return. Some Jews who had non-Jewish names sneaked through and returned to the German occupation. In Kiev they again registered refugees, many enlisted for returning home. One day, at one o'clock at night, NKVD rounded up the refugees and took them away on trucks. You want to go to Wołyń, please do—said to us a NKVD representative. From his comforting words we thought that indeed they let us return home, but after a few minutes we ended up in jail together with several thousand refugees. A strong police guard was put around us. We thus waited long hours. It was a night of fear. One refugee tried to hang himself. An alarm was raised, he almost died. This night there was another registration and a part of the refugees was sent to Wołyń. We were relieved, after passing Shepietovka, the Russian border [i.e., the prewar Polish-Soviet border]. Now one could buy sugar, bread, and other products. One could live.

We traveled for about ten days. We passed through Kovno, Równe, and Ludomir. We returned home and moved into the same apartment as before. We left the luggage on the station. One night an NKVD man appeared and shouted that he is sending us to Siberia, to Kama. We cried, telling him how we suffered. Apparently he was moved. We were taken to the station, our luggage was checked, and nothing suspicious was found. We were taken back home and put under house arrest. But a few days later, at night, another NKVD agent appeared and walked us to the station. A large group of refugees gathered at the station. They were divided into four parties. Each party traveled in one hundred cars. We stood at the station from Friday until Sunday. We were allowed to take food.

The NKVD representative said: "If you want to go to the Germans, you will." Indeed we thought that we were returning to Poland, but it turned out that we were going inside Russia. Cars were locked, no one was allowed to leave. Armed sentries were in the cars. This way we arrived to Siberia.

We stopped at Assino station in Novosibirsk oblast. There were 30 people in each car so that about 3000 people came out of one hundred cars. Many were sick and weakened after the journey. Russian Red Cross gave assistance to the sick ones.

We spent two hours at the station. Other trains were coming. There were 15,000 refugees in Assino. One doctor from Warsaw died. We got 200 grams of bread daily. Every crumb was a treasure. Women wept because they could not feed the children. We had a heavy heart.

Railroad tracks ended in Assino. The nearest settlement was 300 km. away. We were put aboard a ship. The ship could take 700 people—2500 refugees were on board. People lay in cabins, one upon another. Several days we traveled by ship on a wide river. There was no bread, we were fed herring, 2 kgs. a day. Many people got sick on the way. There was a forest on both banks of the river. From time to time we saw some barracks. We were comforted that this infernal trip will soon come to an end.

We disembarked in Tygelder, where we stayed for two weeks sleeping in rotten tents. It was pouring cats and dogs, and all our things, carefully protected during the travel, rotted. Men were sent to work. One was taken by cart, 30 kms. into the woods, to fell timber. Mosquitoes were savagely biting, and people were swelling. Women rebelled demanding that we get transferred to a better place, and they prevailed. We were sent to Tshed, in taiga. Wealthy refugees were riding on carts, the poor ones had to walk. Even in Russia money means a lot. Tshed is an enormous camp with four barracks. Only the commander, a Russian, was in the camp. Russian exiles were sent to another place. We immediately noticed in this settlement an enormous cemetery where thousands of trotskyists were buried, and this made a big impression on us. We felt, what was in store for us? There was a branch of the Red Cross in Tshed, which took care of the sick. Immediately on the next day we were ordered to work. We had to build barracks for ourselves. We built huts from young trees, because there were no trees to make boards. Of course they offered no protection against rain. One Jew, 80 years old, from Włodawa died on the first day when chopping wood. There was no school, even small children worked. For two weeks of work one received 50 rbs. Workers were issued ration cards for a kilogram of bread, soup, and beans per week and a half a liter of oil and a piece of soap. The commander asked in one of his speeches that we work well, build a settlement, and we will be all right. My father, together with other Jews, organized prayers. The commander said that if he finds praying Jews again, he will send them to prison. This statement led to a rebellion among religious Jews. NKVD arrested some and sent them to some other place. This excited everyone even more. The trotskyists' cemetery, which was next to our barracks, kept reminding us: there is nothing to hope for, one should not take risks.

One hundred and fifty Poles lived in our settlement, but they did not interfere with our affairs and since we didn't trust them we told them nothing.

There was excitement in our barracks, like in a beehive. We got in touch with two other camps, Bukhatilov and Zavod, and were getting ready for a mass escape. We made a few hundred carts with wooden wheels—no one knew about this. One made a wheel from a log. Poles did not participate in this work, but they did not betray us. One day there was a Soviet holiday. NKVD commander and his deputy got drunk. We exploited this opportunity and set on our journey. Things were piled up on carts. Women tied children to their backs and a crowd of 12,000 people departed at night on foot. We walked silently through wood clearings and we covered 20 km. Suddenly NKVD agents came on horseback. They blocked the way. NKVD representative calmly advised us to return. He promised better conditions of work and better food. He promised everything, but the crowd wouldn't budge. Women were especially stubborn. NKVD arrested about 20 men, but this didn't help. The crowd did not want to come back.

We stood by the river. A big Russian freighter ship came. Refugees mounted on the ship and chased the captain and the sailors away. About 1500 refugees were on the ship. It sailed in the direction of Omsk. For half a day it sailed downstream. Soviet motorboats chased it. The ship had to turn back. Six planes arrived, and they circled over the crowd of refugees. They shot in the air to scare the people. Russians brought artillery. Refugees declared that they are not scared. Death is better than this kind of life. Rebellion lasted for four days. NKVD was negotiating, threatening, making promises. Supplies were exhausted. There was nothing to eat. Refugees surrendered and returned to Assino. We were treated better. We received much better food: noodles, potatoes and even those who didn't work received food. This lasted six weeks. Then the situation deteriorated again. Another rebellion was planned. This time the plan was to kill the commander and escape for sure. NKVD noticed that something is cooking. The camp was closed and refugees were sent into different localities. Our group was sent to Sverdlovsk oblast. The journey lasted two weeks. There were 1500 people in our group. We were put in Serov and Sasva together with 350 people. We lived there for an entire year. There was a lumber mill in Sasva, it produced boards for railroad cars and many refugees were employed at the mill. There were many Jews among NKVD agents. Some spoke Yiddish. We traded with them, we sold them watches and bought foodstuffs. Russian agents of the NKVD had nothing to do with this. The head of the mill was a convert, a certain Goldberg. Five thousand people worked in the factory and the pay was good, especially for producing ammunition cases. One earned 200 rbs. a month, a kilogram of bread cost one ruble. In a special dining hall one could buy good soup for a few kopecks. In addition, every refugee received half a morgue [1 morg equals 0.6 hectares] of land where one planted onions, potatoes, sunflowers. We also picked berries in the forest. We sold berries and bought various products. Our situation markedly improved. Refugees built a few big, sunny, beautiful barracks. We painted them white and blue to show that we remember about Palestine. The commander was very satisfied with us, foremen were brought who taught us various crafts. Wire was strung around the camp and one couldn't go out, but inside we were relatively free. Women tried to get some goats and chickens, but did not manage. From the Poles we found out about the Soviet-German war. Then, there were big demonstrations in the camp, with songs. The commander got really drunk, and workers got better food on the first day of the war. Bread rations were doubled. It was all right in the camp. We were told, that in other camps things were much worse.

Then amnesty took place. The commander gave us passports, bread for the trip, and we were released from the camp. We were told that we can go wherever we want. A group of five families, 35 people in all, rented a car to Bukhara. Everyone paid 55 rbs. for a ticket.

From Bukhara some refugees went to kolkhozes. My father and older brothers got work in a tannery. Father was an excellent specialist. He introduced new methods of work in the tannery, which were unknown there, and he used chemicals. At the beginning, he earned good money, then workers started to complain against the new "order." Father rebelled and we went to Tashkent. In Tashkent, even for money, one could not get any food. We were exhausted. Father died of hunger. Mother fell ill and also died. Seven of us began the journey and from the whole family, only two remained—myself and my 12 year old brother Abraham. We returned to Bukhara. We went into an orphanage. Out of 300 children, 100 died. Forty-seven Jewish children remained alive. Polish army took us to Teheran.

DOCUMENT NO. 119

PGC/Box 131

ZEEV F.
14 years old
Leżajsk

My grandfather Jezechiel Landau was a rabbi in Leżajsk. Because he was very old and could not carry his duties, my father used to replace him, i.e., his son-in-law, so that in actuality my father was the town's rabbi.

Our family was composed of five people, three among them children, of whom I was the eldest. My siblings stayed in Russia with my parents. Before entering the town, Germans bombed it; there was lots of damage, many victims fell. Three days before Rosh Hashana, on September 11, 1939, Germans entered Leżajsk and began their activity by maltreating Jews. Jews were caught and put to work, beaten up, their beards were pulled out together with their faces, and they lived in a constant horrible fear. On the first day, the Germans burned the temple Beth-Hamidrash; they wanted also to burn a second temple, but it was located in the middle of small houses where Christians lived, so they were afraid that the fire may spread to neighboring buildings. Jews caught in the street were used for such work as cleaning military barracks, washing the floors, cleaning apartments, and Germans supervised those who worked and beat them often with rods. Jews also had to clean the tanks, covered with mud and dust. After two weeks a regulation was issued, that in one day all Jews must leave the town and go across the border to where there are Russians. Father put us on a small cart, which he bought for a heap of money, and taking indispensable things with us we left. After one day we stopped in the hamlet Charłupka. There we met three Jewish families. We moved with them, for they received us very well, and we stayed until the holidays were over. During the last day of holidays we found out that the Russians are leaving town and that whoever wants to may leave with them. [The boundaries between the German and the Soviet zones of occupation in Poland were adjusted by a treaty in late September.] We went to Siniawa. There we met thousands of Jewish refugees and we couldn't find any place to sleep. It was difficult to find bread and other products. Father decided to continue the journey. After two weeks in Siniawa, father left in order to find a place where we could settle. He stopped in the village of Sterwic, near Brody, where our friends and relatives lived, who took care of us. They found a furnished apartment for us, and Father came back to fetch us, and we moved to this village. Father organized prayers in our apartment. During the daytime, older children came and with covered windows Father taught them from sacred books. In the evening, older citizens came, and they sat together with my father over the books. NKVD found out about these matters, and they started to persecute my father. Every day at daybreak, he was called for interrogation, he was warned to stop religious practices forbidden in the Soviet Union and threatened with Siberia. After each interrogation, my mother cried and begged Father to stop prayers and studies. Father didn't even want to listen, but he continued his mission with more precautions. Small groups continued to come every day, there was a watch standing outside, and not even for a moment did my father stop teaching. His situation continued to get worse. His every movement was spied on, people were afraid of him and shunned him in the streets. One day, NKVD called Father and Mother and told them that since they consider Father's activity to be hostile, they will give a choice: either to take a Russian passport [i.e., Soviet citizenship] and move 200 km. inside Russia, or to return under the German occupation.

In Exile

A week later, a group of NKVD men knocked on our door; they ordered us to pack things, 100 kg. per person. They took us by cart to the railroad station and loaded us on a car, 45 people in a car. They sealed the cars, so that one could suffocate. We received daily, when we moved, 400 grams of bread and soup, which we didn't eat because it was not kosher. First station Równe was besieged by thousands of people. Our train was attached to another train and an enormous transport set off. At Kiev we were allowed to disembark and get boiling water at the station. We were watched so that we didn't communicate with the local Jews who brought us food to the station. We stopped at Assino. We got off the railroad cars, we were sent to settlement in the taiga. In one settlement we were placed in a Soviet home where we were allowed to rest two weeks before we began to work. Mosquitoes and bugs bothered us constantly. The next day we had bleeding and swollen faces and we had to sleep in nets. Work in the forest consisted of cutting timber, loading wagons, and digging out stumps. No one in our family worked. Father was recognized as an invalid, Mother took care of three children. We lived from parcels that relatives sent us.

Revolt in the Camp

After four months of work, everyone was so exhausted that they could barely stand on their feet. Every day people died from exhaustion and illness. After a day of hard work, mosquitoes didn't allow one to sleep. Workers decided to leave their work and demand that they be transferred to another place. One day everybody put down their tools and went to the river in order to go to Assino. Alarmed NKVD men ordered the exiles to go to work. The exiles threatened the agents with saws and axes. NKVD men threatened with shootings. And indeed they shot in the air. "We prefer to die than live like this," shouted people while going in the direction of the river. Suddenly a plane appeared, which dropped leaflets calling everyone to return to work and promising that in the near future exiles will be transferred to another settlement where conditions of work will be much better. These leaflets made an impression, and exiles returned to work. On the third day, there was an investigation and a few Jews were arrested and sent to Assino. On the same day, a lightening killed a woman in the forest. During the funeral all exiles swore over the grave not to return to work.

For two days people didn't work at the settlement. The authorities didn't intervene, there was fear as to what the coming days would bring. On the third day an order came transferring us to another settlement. We returned to Assino, and we went by train to Kaminsk in the Sverdlovsk district. In the new settlement, life was indeed much better. Those who worked received daily one kilogram of bread, those who didn't—half a kilogram. In the mess hall one could buy rich soup for 30 kopecks. Mother went to town twice a week, sold our things, and brought back some produce.

Work in the lumber mill in the forest was not as tiring as in the old settlement. After a few months when we were ordered to leave the settlement no one wanted to go. We argued with the NKVD, but it did not help. Russian exiles, who had to be settled there, finally arrived. They chased us out of the barracks and beat up the persistent ones. The third settlement, which was designated for us was close to Siktifkar. They refused to recognize my father as an invalid there and he had to work. But the work was not too heavy. I brought branches and my father had to burn them. On Yom Kippur, Father organized a common prayer at our barracks. Soon NKVD men appeared and arrested him. During the trial he was not punished but it was put into his record that he is a religious offender. Father's brother, rabbi Joel F [——], lived with us in the settlement and he too was proclaimed a religious offender and during the whole time they were both persecuted by the NKVD.

War and Amnesty

When the war between Germany and Russia broke out and we found out that we can go wherever we want, our local authorities in vain tried to persuade us to stay. Neither we nor our uncle received exit permits because my father and uncle were marked as religious offenders. The exiles left, and we stayed alone among Russian exiles. Only four weeks later an older functionary from the NKVD, a Jew, came to us and moved by my father's tears promised that he would try to get for us necessary documents, and indeed a few days later arrived our red papers, specially designated for offenders, and we received permission to leave for Revda. In Assino we waited four days for the train and because it went only 140 km. past Assino, we had to wait another two days at the next station before we continued the journey. It was difficult to travel. There was no bread; potatoes bought in Assino and boiled at the stations were our only food. In Revda, Father got a job in a brickyard. He removed ashes from furnaces. He was often ill but there was no choice, we didn't have a penny. Then Jews fled from Revda because an airplane factory was opened there and people feared a German bombing raid. Father, weak and sick, decided to leave town. From Revda we traveled to Sverdlovsk. We were not allowed into town because refugees were forbidden to enter big cities. After a few days we went to Kermine. Before father befriended a few Jews from Bukhara who found an apartment for us we were homeless wandering in the streets. Finally, someone had pity on us, gave us his room, and moved to a stable himself.

A Delegation to see Gen. Anders

During this time we found out that besides the military, eminent rabbis also will be allowed to leave Russia. A delegation of rabbis led by rabbi Kaner from Cracow and my father went to Jangi-Yul to see Gen. Anders. The general promised that he will fulfill the rabbis' request. After returning from Jangi-Yul, father contracted typhus and could not participate in the drafting of the list of rabbis which was sent by rabbi Kaner. The plan to send rabbis away did not work. Only some individually left Russia. Among them was my uncle rabbi Joel F [——] and Halberstadt brothers. Others stayed in Russia. When a Polish orphanage was set up in Kermine, my father managed to have the three of us accepted there. I spent three months at the orphanage. When a list of children to be sent abroad from Russia was being prepared, an order came to put on it only ten Jewish children. A Jewish supervisor of the orphanage in vain tried to intervene, to increase the number of children. In the last moment we drew lots who is to be allowed to leave. I drew a winning lot. Ninety Jewish children, including my two brothers, stayed. I heard that the entire orphanage was closed. My brothers cried terribly when they heard that I was going and they have to stay. I told the supervisor that under no condition will I be separated from them. The supervisor talked me into going, in the end he brought an order from my father urging me to leave. In the letter my father wrote: "If I wasn't lucky to go to Palestine, let it at least be a consolation for me that my son is there." From Kermine through Ashhabad arrived a day too late, after the transport left. I had to wait five months for the second transport. We were the only Jews, just us, the ten children, in a large crowd of Christian children who bullied us terribly. Finally we left for Persia where I was sent to camp no. 2 under the care of the Jewish Agency.

DOCUMENT NO. 120

PGC/Box 131

ELIEZER K.
13 years old
Leżajsk

My father was a butcher. My mother died a few years before the war. We were four children at home: Bajla, 18 years old; Brukha, 15 years old; Hana, 14 years old; and me. My father didn't want to marry again. My older sister was taking care of the household, and my father worked as a butcher until the beginning of the war. On the third day of the war, the gunshot fire was heard from a little grove not far from our little town. There was shooting in the neighboring village and we heard that the front line was there. People said that in that village many were killed and among them a lot of Jews. They said that one Jew was hit by a bullet while he was praying. When Germans came to the village Jews started to run away. Germans were firing at them. One deaf Jew didn't hear Germans ordering him to stop and got a bullet in his belly. All his intestines came out of him. With the intestines outside, he ran to his house and collapsed dead on his threshold. When Germans came to our village, all Jews went into hiding, afraid of going out in the streets. Since Germans were cutting beards of all the Jews, my father didn't leave the house even later when it was already possible to move freely. At the beginning the Germans didn't do us any harm. Seeing that nothing is happening to us, people started to leave their hiding and return to their regular occupations. The Germans stayed in our little town only for a few days, then they left and the Russians came. When after a few days it was announced on the radio that the Russians were leaving the town and that anyone who wanted could go with them and knowing how much Jews suffered in Lubaczów, where 40 Jews were burned alive, we fled from the little town with the Russian army and arrived at the village Czitków. My father had nothing to do in the village so he took to trade. He dealt in tobacco, matches, vodka. He was taking foodstuffs to the town and from the town he was bringing things which were scarce in the village. My sister worked in the first kolkhoz (open there). There was no shortage of anything in that kolkhoz, Russians were bringing there everything. People in the village said that they did it so that other villages would want to become kolkhozes too. But after some time they stopped backing that Kolkhoz and all of its participants quarreled with each other and moved into different villages. My father was not at all successful in his trade. His every step was followed. It was difficult to buy stuff and difficult to sell it. In the villages people sold foodstuffs unwillingly. There were continuous searches in the trains and sometimes my father had his packages confiscated and he was told that if he were caught again doing illegal trade he would be sentenced to prison. So Father interrupted his trade and we were living off the things we still had. Our situation was very bad. So it is not strange that when the registration to return home was announced, my father was one of the first to register. Some weeks later, one Saturday evening, we were awaken by the knock of rifle butts at our door, the agents of NKVD arrived and declared that we are going home. We were taken to the station, put on the freight train, the doors were closed and after some hours we started towards Lwów.

In Exile

In Lwów they packed into our car still more people, attached some new cars and the whole train a day later started to move in an unknown direction. All that time since we left our home until the Russian frontier they didn't give us anything to eat or drink. It was hot in the car which was very crowded. Again and again somebody would faint and before we crossed the Russian border some people in our car died. Only then they started to give us a piece of bread each and a little bit of soup. On every station they let us go to relieve ourselves for 15 minutes and under heavy guard. My father didn't want to eat the soup because it wasn't kosher. All the month he didn't eat anything else but bread and water. After a month we arrived at a station. I don't remember its name. We were let out of the car and after two days at the station we were packed into automobiles which had to cross the mountains, forests, so that a car could hardly travel. In the middle of a big forest there was a barracks number 74. I was told later on that we were in Troick region. There was only one barracks in that place, there were no other deportees. We were the first Polish citizens in that place. Only some weeks after the second barrack was built and a hundred deported Russians brought in. We had no contact with these exiles. They were kept separately and we were not permitted to talk to them. Father worked felling trees and he received in compensation 200 grams of bread daily and watery soup which cost 30 kopecks. When people started to complain to the commander that they can't bear it any longer, that they ask for more bread, the commander replied that they should either get used to it or die. Older sister worked at removing snow from the roads. The commander thought the quota produced by my sister and other women is too small and he established record quotas for meeting which one received bigger rations of bread. From this competition at work my sister caught cold, came back ill to the barracks, and two days later died of pneumonia. She was buried in the forest. Our situation deteriorated to the point where every day a few people died. One day a tree broke both legs of one of our friends and after a few weeks he returned on crutches from the hospital. We were chased to work during the most bitter cold. It was very cold in the barracks. We, children, lit some wood in order to warm up and a fire broke out. Before we knew it, the barracks was on fire. We tried to put it out with snow, but it did not work. The barracks burned down together with all our possessions. We built new barracks but we had to sleep on bare boards because our pillows were burned and we had nothing to use for cover. We also did not have our underwear and we suffered because of this.

War and Amnesty

Our situation deteriorated before the outbreak of the war. Bread rations were decreased, work quotas were increased. Father was so weakened from hard work and starvation that he could barely walk. Every day I went with him to work, to help him. We couldn't afford soup in the dining hall. Father earned little and we had nothing to sell. After a few weeks the commander gathered everyone and declared that Polish citizens are free and that they can go to warmer areas. He gave us a few rubles and a certificate and we started in the direction of Samarkanda. In Samarkanda we had no place to go. We slept in the street. There was no bread. After a few days Father decided to go to a kolkhoz. Kolkhoz was called "Dymitrov." We worked in the cotton fields, even children worked, and we received 200 grams of grain daily and we had to live on it. One day we received some rye flour. It was a big holiday for us. We lived in kibitkas and slept on a clay floor. It was even worse here than in the settlement. We were constantly hungry and we could barely work. After a few weeks Uzbeks told us that they can't keep us any longer because they had no food for us. We begged them to allow us to stay a few days more. One day bandits raided us and started to shoot through the window. One woman ran out with a bucket of water, but they fled thinking that we will start shooting too. After this accident we were afraid to remain in the countryside, and with the only other Jewish family, Fiszel from Łódź, we returned to Samarkanda. There was nowhere to go, we slept in the street. The NKVD men were constantly chasing us out to kolkhozes. After a few weeks, Father found a stable where we moved in. One day I found out that there is a Polish orphanage in Samarkanda. Father did not permit me to go to this orphanage but I was so hungry that I disobeyed him, I went there alone, I said I was an orphan and I was accepted. Afraid of Father's anger, I was coming home every night, so that Father wouldn't know that I am in the orphanage. I was very happy there. There was plenty of food, only Polish children often beat me up. But I did not really mind, because there was no bread at home. Not only was I full but every evening I took home a piece of bread so that my two sisters could stay alive. Father kept asking where I spent all my days and where do I get bread. I answered that I work for one Jew in Samarkanda who not only feeds me but also allows me to take some food home. One day I was told in the orphanage that in the evening a certain number of children will be sent to Teheran. But since one heard such rumors constantly, I did not believe. As always I went home to sleep. When I came back in the morning I found out that all the children had left at night. I started to cry. The principal, who was Jewish, calmed me down and said that another group of children will go and I could join it, but I can't go back home for the night. This lasted several weeks. The principal rounded up children among whom there were 20-year-old boys claiming to be minors. We, Jewish children, stopped speaking yiddish between ourselves so that no one on the way would suspect that we are Jewish. One day we set out. When the train stopped at the station in Bukhara we saw all Jewish children who left with the first transport. It turned out that they were ordered to return to where they came from. They cried and begged to be taken with our transport, some wanted to throw themselves under the train. But it was all in vain, they were left at the station, and we continued the journey. It turned out that all Jewish children from the first transport were ordered out of the station and were left at God's mercy. From Bukhara through Kvasnovodsk we went to Teheran where in the beginning I lived in a big camp and then I was transferred to a Jewish Orphanage and sent away to Palestine.

Notes

PREFACE

1. Following the 1943 discovery at Katyń of the mass graves of Polish officers taken as prisoners of war by the Red Army in 1939, the Polish government requested the International Red Cross to send a commission to investigate the circumstances of this mass murder. In response, the Soviet government severed its diplomatic relations with Poland (*DPSR*, pp. 523–38). On Katyń, see Janusz K. Zawodny, *Death in the Forest: The Story of the Katyn Forest Massacre* (Notre Dame, Ind.: University of Notre Dame Press, 1962).

2. This ratio can be established on the basis of two independent "samples" listing Polish deportees in the USSR. The first list was prepared very early on the basis of token information coming from Russia to Japan by the Polish embassy in Tokyo (see Poland. Ambasada [Japan], "Zesłańcy Polscy w ZSRR," manuscript [Tokyo, 1941]). At that time the locations of 8,700 Polish citizens in the USSR were known to the Polish authorities; in this group there were 2,205 children under the age of fourteen (25 percent). In addition, the final report, "Number and Distribution of Polish Citizens in the USSR" (HI, PAC, Box 41, Folder 330), prepared by the Polish embassy in the USSR according to data available as of April 25, 1943, lists 265,501 people as still remaining in the Soviet Union. Of these, 76,146 (29 percent) are listed as "children."

3. Roman Buczek (who had access to the archives of Stanisław Mikołajczyk, prime minister of the Polish government in exile [acquired by the Hoover Institution in 1978]), in his well-documented article published in *Zeszyty Historyczne*, estimates the total number of deportees at 1.5 million. This is a somewhat inflated figure in view of the sources he quotes. The specific numerical estimates quoted in his article total 1.15 million. Furthermore, 100,000 of this total is probably due to a printer's error, for except for one entry, Buczek's data tally with a table appearing in the document, "Computation of the Polish Population Deported to the USSR Between 1939 and 1944" (HI, PGC, Box 588, MSZ, London, 15.III.1944). The number of deportees from Wołyń in Buczek's text is 250,000, but in the MSZ document it is 150,000. Thus, the correct total should be 1.05 million. Considering that about 150,000 were mobilized into the Red Army, we arrive at the figure of 900,000 as the approximate number of deportees into Russia. Unfortunately, Buczek does not cite references for the 1.5 million

estimate or for the breakdown of deportations by region appearing in his article. It is likely, however, that we had the same document in hand, for on pp. 49–50 of his article, he offers statistics on the occupational structure of the deportees, compiled on the basis of 120,000 personal files from the Polish Red Cross in Teheran. The authors of the MSZ document used the same source to compile statistics on occupational stratification. The MSZ data are as follows:

OCCUPATIONAL STRATIFICATION OF THE DEPORTEES

Category	Percentage
1. Clergy of all denominations	0.5
2. University professors, scientists	0.6
3. Primary- and secondary-school teachers	4.0
4. Doctors and qualified medical personnel	3.1
5. Judges and prosecutors	0.8
6. Defense attorneys	1.3
7. Engineers, technicians, agronomists	4.7
8. Journalists, artists, writers	1.2
9. Employees of the Forestry Service	3.7
10. Artisans	24.6
11. Merchants	4.4
12. White-collar private employees	3.2
13. Professional soldiers	8.0
14. Police and frontier guards	4.0
15. White-collar state and local government employees	5.0
16. Peasants	27.6
17. Workers	3.3
Total	100.0

Buczek (p. 50), on the other hand, groups statistics into five categories:

Category	Percentage
a. Workers, artisans, peasants, Forestry Service	50.2
b. Soldiers and judges	16.0
c. Clergy, professors, and scientists	11.0
d. Defense attorneys and engineers	7.0
e. Primary- and secondary-school teachers	4.0
Total	88.2

Category (e) in Buczek's table corresponds exactly to (3) in the MSZ table, and the percentages tally. His other categories are composites of several categories listed in the MSZ document: (a) = (9) + (10) + (16) + (17); (b) = (5) + (13); (c) = (1) + (2); (d) = (6) + (7). In all four cases Buczek quotes numbers which he could not have obtained by simple addition.

Buczek's percentages	Correct percentages (according to the MSZ document)
a. 50.2	59.2
b. 16.0	8.8
c. 11.0	1.1
d. 7.0	6.0

The explanation for these discrepancies does not immediately suggest itself. We would not bother with it in such detail except that Buczek's data is the only published source on the social composition of deportees. The ethnic composition of deportees tallies in Buczek's article and in the document from the MSZ (52 percent Poles, 30 percent Jews, and 18 percent Ukrainians and Belorussians).

4. With characteristic capriciousness, the Soviet authorities from time to time forbade the sending of parcels from certain areas of the occupied territories. In the autumn and winter of 1940, for example, parcels could not be sent from Lwów or Tarnopol. People hired messengers who traveled with a few parcels to some other town, Kołomyja or Białystok, and expedited them from there (Letters to Danuta Polniaszek; HI, PGC, Box 927, File "Lwów"). After Polish-Soviet diplomatic relations were severed in April 1943, the Polish authorities in London kept a record of 271,000 Polish citizens still remaining in Russia who received help from the social assistance network set up in the USSR in 1941–1943 by the Polish embassy (HI, PGC, Box 49, File (in English) "Numerical Record and Location of Polish Citizens in Soviet Union"). They decided to continue to assist these Poles by sending parcels of food and clothing from Iran. In January 1944, the Soviet authorities ordered a stop to mail delivery of these parcels. Altogether, by May 1945, the Komisja Wysyłki Paczek (Commission for the Expedition of Parcels) sent 41,308 parcels to Russia. From late 1944 on, they were dispatched mostly through the American Jewish Joint Distribution Committee (JOINT) channels and reached mainly Jewish addressees (HI, PGC, Box 410, File "Refugees in USSR"; Box 409, File "Care and Assistance for Polish Citizens in USSR").

5. On the state of health of Polish deportees in the Soviet Union, see Dr. Seweryn Krzysztof Ehrlich, *U podstaw armii polskiej w ZSSR: Walka z chorobami zakaźnymi w 1942 r.* (Rome: Włochy, Nakładem Towarzystwa Wiedzy Wojskowej 2. Korpusu, 1946).

6. Ibid., pp. 53–54, 59.

7. As the Soviets' role in the Allied military effort grew in importance, their position vis-à-vis the Polish government hardened. In the end, on January 16, 1943, the People's Commissariat for Foreign Affairs sent the following note to the Polish embassy in the USSR:

> In connection with the exchange of Notes in the years 1941–1942 between the People's Commissariat for Foreign Affairs and the Embassy, concerning the citizenship of persons who previously lived in the Western districts of the Ukrainian and White Ruthenian Soviet Socialist Republics, the People's Commissariat for Foreign Affairs informed the Embassy on December 1, 1941, that all inhabitants of the above-mentioned districts who found themselves on the territories of these districts at the time of their entry into the Union of Soviet Socialist Republics (November 1–2, 1939) had acquired Soviet citizenship in accordance with the decree of the Supreme Council of the USSR dated November 29, 1939, and the Citizenship of the USSR Act of August 19, 1938.

In its note of December 1, 1941, the People's Commissariat for Foreign Affairs informed the Embassy that the Soviet Government were prepared, by way of exception, to regard as Polish citizens persons of Polish origin living in the territories of the above-mentioned districts on November 1–2, 1939. The People's Commissariat for Foreign Affairs is bound to state that despite the good will of the Soviet Government thus manifested, the Polish Government has adopted a negative attitude to the above statement of the Soviet Government and has refused to take the appropriate steps, putting forward demands contrary to the sovereign rights of the Soviet Union in respect to these territories.

In connection with the above, the People's Commissariat for Foreign Affairs, on instructions from the Soviet Government, gives notice that the statement included in the Note of December 1, 1941, regarding the readiness to treat some categories of persons of Polish origin on an exceptional basis must be considered invalid and that the question of the possible non-application to such persons of the laws governing citizenship of the Union of Soviet Socialist Republics has ceased to exist. [*DPSR*, pp. 473–74.]

8. Władysław Anders, *Bez Ostatniego Rozdziału* (London: Gryf Publishers, 1959), pp. 112–22, 132–34.

9. Large numbers of Polish children ended up in Soviet orphanages (Docs. no. 18, 57, 116). They were often put there against their will, for no apparent reason—those vacationing at summer camp in 1941 were hurriedly evacuated east after the Russo-German war began and placed in Soviet *dietdoms* (Irena Wasilewska, *Suffer Little Children* [London: Maxlove Publishing Company, 1946], p. 69). The Polish embassy received scores of letters from children put in these establishments, many of which Wasilewska preserved. Treatment was brutal, and besides the harsh discipline to which all inmates were subjected—beatings, hard work—Polish children experienced additional hardships because of their nationality. The Russian children were encouraged to tease and beat them, and the staff resorted to equally unsophisticated methods of russification. One fifteen-year-old described the punishment for speaking Polish in an orphanage in Irtysh. Girls were ordered to undress and stand naked (older girls were allowed to keep their underpants on) in a busy spot, such as the "red corner" or the entrance to the dining hall, for everyone to see (HI, PAC, Box 24, File "Dzieci"). No wonder many Polish children who left Russia, particularly the younger ones, could not speak Polish or understand it; they were often demoralized as well. Older children, apparently, had greater resistance to sovietization on both accounts.

10. A memorandum prepared by Irena Wasilewska (whose book on Polish children in Russia, *Suffer Little Children*, is by far the best among works dealing with this subject) states that 21,688 children were evacuated from the Soviet Union. This, apparently, was what the Polish Red Cross files in Teheran revealed (HI, PAC, File no. 266, "Notatka . . ."). In her book, however, Wasilewska used the number 15,000.

11. Alumni organize periodic meetings, keep in touch with each other, publish a newsletter, and have issued memorial volumes dedicated to their schools. See Związek Szkół Młodszych Ochotniczek, ed., *Książka Pamiątkowa Szkół Młodszych Ochotniczek* (London, n.d.), and Koło Junackiej Szkoły Kadetów, ed., *Junacka Szkoła Kadetów* (London, 1972).

12. We have interviewed some authors of the compositions as well as some whose compositions have not been preserved or included here. Many said that

the misery and unhappiness of their life in Russia was counterbalanced by a feeling of adventure, liberation, and change from sheltered family life. We found no expression of such feelings in the compositions.

13. The Soviet occupation brought substantial institutional changes to the universities, other schools of higher learning, and to the primary and secondary school system: new administrators were appointed; new curricula were developed; new teachers were hired; Ukrainian and Belorussian were introduced as languages of instruction; and the student body changed its ethnic and social composition and acquired new rights vis-à-vis the teaching staff. The rather complicated Polish system of primary and secondary, private and public schools was replaced by the so-called Soviet ten-year school (*desjatiletka*).

The main focus of the reform in primary and secondary schools was secularization and elimination of subjects dealing with the Polish cultural and historical heritage: religion, Latin, and Polish history and geography were banned from the curriculum; Polish-language classes were drastically limited (Docs. no. 4, 40, 75, 95). New teaching staffs were appointed, especially in newly established Ukrainian or Belorussian schools (Milena Rudnycka, ed., *Western Ukraine Under the Bolsheviks* [New York: Shevchenko Scientific Society in the USA, 1958], p. 179); teachers were brought from the Soviet Union and many Polish teachers dismissed. Before the war, school was an important tool of polonization in these territories; now it was given Ukrainian, Belorussian, or Jewish national "form" (language of instruction, new courses, and new teachers and students), and it was to become a tool of sovietization. The new authorities were especially concerned with indoctrinating young people; the younger they were the more attention was devoted to giving them a socialist education. Many extracurricular activities were organized: various youth organizations were established, such as Pioneers, Circles of Atheists, or Red Corners; choir, orchestra, and sport competitions were organized; there were many evenings of entertainment, amateur theater productions, and the like. Secularization and antireligious propaganda were foremost on the agenda. For the benefit of the youngest children, the following proof of God's powerlessness and Stalin's might was staged: children were encouraged to say a prayer asking God to give them bread. After a while, when there was no bread in sight, they were told to pray to Stalin. When they finished, candies, bread, and butter were brought or dropped on to the classroom floor through a hole in the ceiling (HI, PGC, Box 10, Lwów: 6558; Białystok: 78–81; Łomża: 99; see also Docs. no. 31, 46, 84, 110). The Soviet Commissariat for Education must have approved this scenario, for it was used throughout the occupied territories as well as in Russia itself.

Young people were encouraged to liberate themselves from obedience to the traditionally sanctioned authority of school and family. Students at schools and universities were invited to denounce the political unorthodoxy of their teachers or schoolmates and to inform on their parents (HI, PGC, Włodzimierz Wołyński: 40–41; Białystok: 78–81; Box 10, Lwów: Czarnecka). Along with the politicization of the student body a new and strict discipline was imposed on all educational establishments. Everything had to be carefully planned: each teacher had to draft a detailed lesson plan for each class; each professor a detailed timetable for each lecture and research project. Attendance was scrupulously recorded, and teachers were made personally responsible for the satisfactory progress of all their students (Rudnycka, *Western Ukraine*, pp. 167–69, 186–89). In an effort to stamp out the roots of bourgeois mentality,

Polish literature and history books were often withdrawn from school libraries and burned (HI, PGC, Równe: 36, 37; Białystok: 82; Łuniniec: 53, 54).

14. One of the most moving, beautiful, and sad examples of a child trying to understand the war is the diary of Dawid Rubinowicz (*Pamiętnik* [Warsaw: Książka i Wiedza, 1960]), a thirteen-year-old Jewish boy from Krajno near Kielce in Poland. The most terrible day-by-day description of death from starvation can be read in the diary of a sixteen-year-old boy from the Łódź ghetto, Dawid Sierakowiak (Warsaw: Iskry, 1960). The comparison of these two books and also of the compositions presented here with the diary of Anne Frank dramatically illustrates the differences between death in Eastern and in Western Europe during the Second World War.

INTRODUCTION

1. Article 2 of the secret protocol reads:

In the event of a territorial and political transformation of the territories belonging to the Polish State, the spheres of interest of both Germany and the USSR shall be bounded approximately by the line of the rivers Narew, Vistula, and San. The question whether the interests of both Parties make the maintenance of an independent Polish State appear desirable and how the frontiers of this State should be drawn can be definitely determined only in the course of further political developments. In any case both Governments will resolve this question by means of a friendly understanding. [*DPSR*, p. 40.]

2. During the military preparations against Hitler, many KOP officers were transferred to other units dispatched to the western front, and in some cases, entire KOP detachments were incorporated into Polish armies fighting the invading Germans.

3. On September 10 and September 14, Count von Schulenburg, the German ambassador in Moscow, had conversations with Molotov, which he immediately reported to Berlin:

I explained emphatically to Molotov how crucial speedy action of the Red Army was at this juncture. Molotov repeated that everything possible was being done to expedite matters . . . Then Molotov came to the political side of the matter and stated that the Soviet Government had intended to take the occasion of the further advance of German troops to declare that Poland was falling apart and that it was necessary for the Soviet Union, in consequence, to come to the aid of the Ukrainians and the White Russians "threatened" by Germany . . . For the political motivation of Soviet action (the disintegration of Poland and protection of "Russian" minorities), it was of the greatest importance not to take action until the governmental center of Poland, the city of Warsaw, had fallen. Molotov therefore asked that he be informed as nearly as possible as to when the capture of Warsaw could be counted on. [*DGFP*, p. 44, 61.]

4. For further information, see Wiktor Sukiennicki, "The Establishment of the Soviet Regime in Eastern Poland in 1939," *Journal of Central European Affairs*, July 1963, p. 196.

5. A linguistic pun is involved here. In Polish, the customary form of address to everyone except close friends is either *pan* (mister) or *pani* (madam). *Pan*, however, means "master" as well. In Soviet folklore the word *pan* often appears jointly with the word "Pole," meaning snobbish, aristocratic, haughty—

in a word, class enemy. A very popular Russian song from the 1920 Polish-Soviet war concerns Budenny's army, Polish *pany*, and the fate they deserve. Also, there are Russian jokes to the effect that everything Polish has that "alien" quality; even Polish slippers have it, for while the Russian word for slippers is *tufli*, the Polish is *pantofle*.

6. The territory of Poland was divided into sixteen voivodeships. In official publications they were often clustered into four groups: the central, eastern, western, and southern. In September 1939 the Soviet Union occupied all the eastern voivodeships (Wilno, Nowogród, Polesie, Wołyń), three of the four southern voivodeships (Lwów, Stanisławów, Tarnopol), and one central voivodeship (Białystok).

7. See Władysław Pobóg-Malinowski, *Najnowsza Historia Polityczna Polski* (London, 1956), 2:539, 638.

8. One of the principal stipulations of the agrarian reform carried out during the *dwudziestolecie* called for redistribution of land from the largest estates. In eastern Poland all private estates of over 300 hectares were subject to redistribution. Of the 2.3 million hectares redistributed between 1919 and 1935, about 6.1 percent (143,000 hectares) was given to approximately 8,000 military colonists. Over 6,500 of the colonists were either privates or noncommissioned officers. About two-thirds of the colonists lived on their land; the rest either abandoned it or leased it to local peasants. Almost half of the colonists received plots of land in Wołyń voivodeship. There were also civilian colonists living in the area. In 1936 the Association of Colonists had 8,000 military and 8,000 civilian members.

The settlement program was part of a comprehensive policy of polonization of the eastern territories, which were populated predominantly by minorities (in the Wołyń voivodeship ethnic Poles constituted only 16 percent of the population; in the Polesie voivodeship, only 14.5 percent). Military colonists in the area assisted the organs of public security in putting down "attempts at disturbance of the public order" (Piotr Stawecki, *Nastepcy Komendanta* [Warsaw: Wydawnictwo Ministerstwa Obrony Narodwej, 1969], pp. 136−40), which time and time again pitted the local non-Polish population against Poles employed by or assisting the state administration and police.

9. Total Red Army casualties, as reported by Molotov in a speech to the Supreme Soviet on October 31, 1939, were 737 killed and 1,862 wounded (*Russia and the War* [London: Modern Books, 1939], p. 9). Polish sources confirm that there were no major Polish-Soviet battles in 1939.

10. This point needs to be rigorously demonstrated, lest we be suspected of a certain naiveté in accepting hyperbolic descriptions of militia activities in the reports of the victimized population, who understandably spoke ill of them. But the evidence on this issue consists of more than epithets: it includes names and independently corroborated information.

The factual evidence is overwhelming, especially since it is provided by many independent testimonies from a large number of small rural communities throughout eastern Poland. The origin of these testimonies is significant, for in small communities people know each other's affairs intimately. Although in a few instances they might have erred, exaggerated, or even lied about their neighbors, they could not have done so consistently in independently given testimonies about a thousand or so rural communities scattered throughout nine voivodeships. The accounts we read contained not merely rumors but vivid recollections of facts and events familiar to the witnesses since the militiamen they mention had been living among them long before the Soviets came to Poland (HI, PGC, Łuniniec: 7, 8; Brasław: 3, 11; Postawy: 7; Dzisna: 7, 8; Mołodeczno: 16; Skałat: 10, 11; Kostopol: 7; Zdołbunów: 8; Kowel: 11–13; Szczuczyn: 4, 13).

11. Not necessarily as measured by the number of victims, but primarily in terms of psychological discomfort and the lost sense of security. These were greatly affected if one's neighbors, with their intimate knowledge of local relationships, rather than a foreign, and therefore more distant and abstract, invader, were to be feared.

12. One such incident on a Równo street was described by a miller from Tuczyn: "I saw with my own eyes how Soviet soldiers caught a Polish colonel in the street, took out his revolver from the holster, shot him with his own revolver, and then left his body lying in the street and went away" (HI, PGC, Równo: 7).

13. Several hundred policemen, who had surrendered, were ordered to march outside Lwów to be interned at a POW camp. While leaving the city limits, at Zielona Street, they were shot with automatic weapons and machine gunned from tanks. Almost all were killed, but a few witnesses and survivors lived to tell the story. (HI, PGC, Box 10, Lwów: 776, 2404, 3644.) Near Łuniniec a KOP detachment, some policemen, and a number of civilians who participated in skirmishes with the Soviets were taken prisoner. They were ordered into several barns and then all the policemen and KOP officers and NCOs were called out and shot. (HI, PGC, Łuniniec: 4.) Undoubtedly, there were other incidents of this kind.

These mass murders, in contravention of international law and the rules of warfare, are particularly disturbing since they were committed so early in the war, in September 1939, long before Nazi bestiality and Japanese cruelty were to turn the Second World War into an unprecedented experience of lawlessness and horror. Because they were systematic, these incidents should be interpreted, we think, as an indication that the Red Army came to Poland less to wage war than to carry out a social revolution. Indeed, the battle orders of one Soviet unit captured by the Poles designated KOP detachments as a "band of Polish officers" (GSHI, Orlik-Rückemann, 1940).

14. See also Milena Rudnycka, ed., *Western Ukraine Under the Bolsheviks* (New York: Shevchenko Scientific Society in the USA, 1958), p. 61.

15. Throughout the occupation, the population preserved its sense of humor. It was always eager and able to notice the ridiculous aspects of its occupiers' behavior. Under the German occupation, one finds an identical tendency, as if oppression by fools were somehow easier to bear than tyranny by serious and practical men. Seen in this light, the occupation seemed perhaps less permanent, more arbitrary or accidental, and therefore destined to pass as quickly and unexpectedly as it had occurred. It was rather hard to believe that a ruling class whose most compelling desire was for watches, whose members thought Greta Garbo, Amsterdam, and oranges were industrial products, and whose most fashionable women wore nightgowns to the opera would prevail for long.

16. On December 21, 1939, the ruble was declared the only legal tender in this area (Doc. no. 67).

17. Apparently a shortage of money was not a consideration. We do not know whether they received special bonuses in rubles or whether they were allowed and encouraged to take along their savings (if they had any), or whether the prices were so ridiculously low that when ruble-złoty parity was introduced, their pay was sufficient to launch them on this buying spree.

18. Soviet administrators, slowly pouring into the newly occupied territory, were poor and destitute. They were overwhelmed by the new variety of things that they could acquire, and they wanted to acquire them all (Rudnycka, *Western Ukraine*, pp. 74, 80). According to the recollections of a Ukrainian journalist who came to Lwów from Kiev, about two weeks after the Red Army occupied the Western Ukraine and the first foreign-made cars and elegant pieces of clothing made their appearance in Kiev, excitement swept over the republic's capital. Everyone wanted to go to Lwów or Tarnopol to buy things, and *komandirovka* (travel authorization) to some town in the newly occupied territory became the most sought-after document. (Ibid., pp. 34–52.) People were literally starved for material objects. Aleksander Wat observed a similar attitude in Vladimir Mayakovsky during his visits to Warsaw in the interwar period (*Mój Wiek* [London: Polonia Book Fund, 1977], 1: 139–40).

19. "Through the railroad stations at Uściług and at Włodzimierz Wołyński, day and night, freight cars filled with all kinds of objects were going into Russia. From Włodzimierz Wołyński they took a hospital, an electrical plant, military barracks, and furniture from officers' and NCOs' apartments. Likewise, inventories of landed estates confiscated in the area were sent east. Through Uściług military trucks were carrying things away as well." (HI, PGC, Włodzimierz Wołyński: 13–14.)

20. *Pravda* reported the following figures on redistribution in Lwów voivodeship: 717,000 hectares of land, 17,700 horses, 37,700 head of cattle, 12,000 pigs and sheep (November 26, 1939).

21. Interviews with Polish citizens evacuated to Iran confirm that the Soviet authorities tried to organize kolkhozes throughout the area. Two methods were used: setting up kolkhozes on large confiscated estates or forcing individual peasant landowners to join kolkhozes by imposing very high taxes on their holdings. However, almost without exception, interviewees were unable to give the exact locations of kolkhozes in their counties or provide other specific information about them. One gets the feeling that the Soviets were proceeding cautiously, waiting before engaging in full-scale collectivization of agriculture. Our guess is that collectivization was to be carried out only after the deportations had depleted the local populations to the point of rendering them incapable of substantial resistance. Interestingly, while carrying on an intensive anti-religious propaganda campaign, the Soviets were equally cautious not to offend too openly the religious feelings of the local populations (Rudnycka, *Western Ukraine*, pp. 126, 139, 142). Again, taxes were used to force the closing of churches (Docs. no. 40, 75). In other instances, arbitrary decisions of the local Soviet authorities were applied. But on the whole, priests and churches were dealt with more subtly than, say, political parties or professional organizations and their leaders. There was neither an explicit ban on religion nor a systematic closure of churches, nor were clergymen summarily arrested. "The Soviets demonstrated unexpected moderation towards bishops, the clergy, and religious services in general" (*Actes et documents du Saint Siège relatifs à la Seconde*

guerre mondiale, vol. 3 [Vatican: Libreria Editrice Vaticana, 1967], p. 25; see also Dennis J. Dunn, *The Catholic Church and the Soviet Government, 1939–1949* [Boulder, Colo.: East European Quarterly, 1977], pp. 49–51).

22. This technique had been practiced in the Soviet Union before. When Stalin was given the task in the early 1920s of ensuring that Ural and Siberian peasants would "sell" grain to the state, he formed executive commissions (*komsods*) composed of the poorest peasants in the area. These commissions were given 25 percent of the grain they confiscated from kulaks who refused to sell at state prices. (Abdurakhman Avtorkhanov, *Tekhnologia vlasti, protses obrazovania KPSS* [Munich: Posev, 1959], pp. 34–35.)

23. Absenteeism and tardiness were considered sabotage and were punished by fines and imprisonment. No one was allowed to change jobs without official authorization (HI, PGC, Box 10, Lwów: 5075, 5758, 6324; Kostopol: 9; Kowel: 63; Białystok: 75–77), although workers could be reassigned to factories or to jobs within factories without being consulted. Entire factories, along with their workers, were shipped to the Soviet Union (HI, PGC, Białystok: 30, 31; Łomzà: 97).

In the early months a propaganda campaign was conducted to induce people, especially those with technical training, to sign up for work in the Soviet Union (HI, PGC, Box 10, Lwów: 5723, 8908). On October 21, 1939, *Pravda* proudly announced that the first group of unemployed, 1,010 people in all, was leaving for the Donbas (Doc. no. 118).

24. In a construction company in Lwów, workers earned eighteen rubles a day. "One day a normsetter came to a construction site. He asked an engineer to select the best bricklayer and ordered him to put up a wall. After half an hour he counted the number of bricks that the man had already aligned and then, multiplying them by sixteen, set a new quota for an eight-hour day. The engineers argued that an average rather than superior bricklayer should have been chosen for this trial and that work productivity is highest in the first hour on the job, but to no avail. A new quota was set, and as of that day workers could earn no more than fourteen rubles per day." (HI, PGC, Box 10, Lwów: Feldman.)

25. Bank accounts and safe deposits were impounded and only small withdrawals permitted—one hundred to two hundred złotys per month. During the winter of 1939–40, safe deposit holders were called into banks, safes were opened, and all valuables confiscated. Depositors were permitted to take along only family papers and souvenirs. In pawnshops all objects valued at 100 rubles or more were confiscated. (HI, PGC, Box 10, Lwów: 5915, Obertyńska [4796], Weleszczuk.)

26. Mrs. Danuta Polniaszek-Kossakowska, who was deported to the USSR in 1940, preserved her correspondence with high-school friends writing to her in Russia from Lwów. From one letter we learn that high-school certificates were not distributed at the end of the 1939–40 school year because there was a paper shortage and they could not be printed (Letters to D. Polniaszek).

27. The so-called Paris, behind the Great Theater in Lwów, became very fashionable, wrote another friend of Danuta Polniaszek. Tram conductors used to announce in the vicinity: "Gentlemen speculators, getting out." Anything could be bought there, but the people had little money to spend: "Ninety percent of all present were selling something, 8 percent were just looking, and only about 2 percent were buying." (Letters to D. Polniaszek.)

28. Rudnycka, *Western Ukraine*, p. 82.

29. Ibid., pp. 21, 30, 82; and Wat, *Mój Wiek*, 1: 281. "I find shabbiness most repulsive in communism," wrote Aleksander Wat, who lived in Lwów under the Soviet occupation, "shabbiness as a moral-aesthetic category rather than a merely aesthetic impression—the fact that communism makes towns, things, and people's characters shabby" (1: 307).

30. But the new names of streets in Lwów belonged, with few exceptions, to the Russian or Soviet tradition. Sistine's Street was changed to October Street, Potocki's Street to Pushkin's. There was a newly named Komsomol Street in town, a Lermontov Street, and a Street of the First of May. (Rudnycka, *Western Ukraine*, pp. 91–92; HI, PGC, Box 10, Lwów: 8479, 10190.)

31. From Białystok someone reported a different inscription on a poster: "Who is not with us is against us. Our opponent is our enemy, and we shall destroy our enemies." (HI, PGC, Białystok: 19.)

32. Painters were organized into an association of creative artists and a cooperative of artisans. Members of the cooperative were subject to the discipline of work: they started painting every day at 7:00 A.M. and ended at 2:00 P.M. They were, like everyone else, subject to fines and imprisonment for absenteeism or tardiness. Most of their time was spent painting portraits of the Soviet party and government officials. However, the cooperative also produced various inscriptions, posters, and advertisements, which were later displayed in city streets. The techniques of painting, sizing, and laying out of portraits were "normalized." Prices varied depending on demand, the greatest boom coming when Bessarabia and the Baltic states were incorporated into the USSR (HI, PGC, Box 927: File "Lwów"). Bruno Schulz, for example, a renowned Polish writer teaching drawing in a school in Drohobycz, was at times commissioned to do such commercial paintings (Bruno Schulz, *Księga listów* [Cracow: Wydawnictwo Literackie, 1975], pp. 122–127 *passim*).

33. Rudnycka, *Western Ukraine*, pp. 74–75.

34. At first, only officers, NCOs, and policemen were ordered to register, but then virtually everyone was required to do so, including refugees, professionals, civil servants, students, teachers, all eligible voters, all unemployed persons, all males over sixteen years old, and all those interested in repatriation to the Generalgouvernement, the German-occupied part of Poland (HI, PGC, Box 10, Lwów: 3926, 4633, 5723; 7261; Białystok: 22–25; Równe: 12–13; Brasław: 4; Wilejka: 22, 23; Kowel: 32; Lida: 15).

In October 1939, all officers were called to register. No one was exempt from this procedure; even reserve officers and pensioners were ordered to appear. Everyone had to bring two photographs and was asked for personal data, address, employer (former and present), military rank, and financial status. Then a detailed interview concerning military service followed: what units one had served in, at what rank; whether one had had any connection with the intelligence or the police; whether one had served in the 1920 war (against the Bolsheviks) and in what formation; what medals one had received for this campaign; whether one had taken prisoners in this war and how one had treated them; was one mobilized in 1939 and did one fight against the Germans or the Soviets? Then there were questions concerning political activity: past membership in professional, political, and other voluntary organizations had to be revealed. People were asked whether they had belonged to a secret underground military organization or whether they knew something about its existence. They had to give the names and addresses of their relatives and were asked whether they had any friends or relatives in the USSR. (HI, PGC, Box 10, Lwów: 4085.) Finally, they were asked if they would like to serve in the Red Army.

35. Rudnycka, *Western Ukraine*, pp. 90, 157–58, 186, 192, 211.

36. Ibid., pp. 93–95.

37. See also ibid., p. 25.

38. Ibid., p. 193; Volodymyr Kubijovych, *The Ukrainians in the General-gouvernement* (Chicago: Mykola Denysiuk, 1975), pp. 47, 60, 181–82.

39. Sometimes candidates would be drawn from among those who identified themselves in the first days as supporters or friendly hosts of the invading Red Army (Sukiennicki, "Soviet Regime," p. 200). At other times the population was asked to propose candidates, who were then questioned by the presiding Soviet official. Only the poorest candidates or those who had served time in jail passed the scrutiny and got the official's approval (HI, PGC, Łomża: 13; Łuniniec: 21). If no one wanted the job, the Soviet official would appoint someone, threatening him with arrest if he refused to serve, or send a replacement from another village (HI, PGC, Łomża: 13, 14). In any case, as a rule the existing Polish authorities—village and *gmina* heads (*sołtys* and *wójt*)—were dismissed and sometimes arrested, and a village committee appointed in their stead.

40. See, for example, Michał Borwicz, "Inżynierowie dusz," *Zeszyty Historyczne*, no. 3 (1963): 145–49, on the literary milieu in Lwów under the Soviet occupation, particularly his description of this procedure in the Union of Writers.

41. Rudnycka, *Western Ukraine*, p. 72; HI, PGC, Box 10, Lwów: 4090.

42. In a front-page article, it was said that the Lwów Temporary Administration had issued an appeal for the organization of elections to the National Assembly of Western Ukraine "a few days ago." On October 12, an identical formula was used to inform readers about a similar initiative of the Białystok Temporary Administration in Western Belorussia. The very imprecision of "a few days ago" departs strikingly from *Pravda*'s usually disciplined style of reporting important events. On the basis of information published in local Lwów newspapers (*Vilna Ukraina* and *Czerwony Sztandar*), Professor Sukiennicki points to October 4 and October 5 as the dates on which the regional temporary (interim) administrations in Western Ukraine and Western Belorussia issued calls for summoning the national people's assemblies in those two provinces ("Soviet Regime," pp. 210–11). But it is of secondary importance whether the city or the regional temporary administration appeared as titular initiator of the elections; neither could decide such an important issue on its own.

43. Sukiennicki, "Soviet Regime," p. 206.

44. In larger towns, every apartment building might have its "agitator"; in smaller towns every few houses; and in the villages, one man was put in charge of ten families (HI, PGC, Łomża: 41, 41a; Białystok: 32; Równe: 24; Skałat: 24; Box 10, Lwów: 1248).

45. It was dangerous not to come to these meetings. Repeated absence inevitably led to arrest. Sometimes the punishment for absence was most imaginative. In the village of Orzechowice, a Ukrainian was fined one ruble for failure to come to a pre-election meeting. The fine, very small indeed, had to be paid in even smaller installments of two kopecks a day (100 kopecks equal

1 ruble), but in person at the county seat, which was five miles away (HI, PGC, Skałat: 24).

46. A lot of imagination and effort went into the preparation of these lists. Responsibility for their accuracy rested typically with doormen or house committees (HI, PGC, Box 10, Lwów: 8595, Białystok: 38). In Białystok local militiamen went from house to house compiling lists for the purpose of distributing firewood, which everyone wanted to stock before the winter. Those lists were later used to compile voters' registers. (HI, PGC, Bialystok: 39.) In Lwów a similar stratagem was used: ration cards entitling people to purchase 100 grams of sugar were distributed by agitators compiling voters' registers (HI, PGC, Box 10, Lwów: 7047).

47. "In the pre-election period numerous meetings were organized during which capitalist countries were repeatedly condemned and the Soviet regime in the USSR highly praised. And because of that, we were told, we should vote for Nina Gnaciuk." (HI, PGC, Równe: 26.) This is a rather typical non sequitur.

48. In a *Pravda* article of October 11, the Lwów Temporary Administration, calling for elections to the National Assembly of Western Ukraine, enumerated the four most pressing issues to be resolved by this assembly: the establishment of Soviet authority in Western Ukraine; the unification of Western Ukraine with the Soviet Ukrainian republic; confiscation of landed estates and their redistribution among individual peasants; and nationalization of banks and large-scale industrial properties. This was an unusual statement, however. The next day, when the Białystok Temporary Administration's call for elections to the National Assembly of Western Belorussia was reported in *Pravda*, none of these issues was mentioned. The report merely stated that the ballot should be universal, equal, direct, and secret. The purpose of the vote was not even revealed. In scattered articles over the following days, one could find occasional reports of how, during pre-election meetings, some speakers called for the installation of Soviet authority in Western Ukraine and Western Belorussia. But the issue was downplayed, and it was not clear whether installation of Soviet authority meant political integration with the Soviet Ukrainian and Belorussian republics. Indeed, we were unable to find a single article in *Pravda* before the elections (except the October 11 article previously mentioned) calling for integration.

49. Molotov put it very diplomatically in his speech on October 31:

We know, for example, that in the past few months such concepts as "aggression" and "aggressor" have acquired a new concrete connotation, a new meaning. It is not hard to understand that we can no longer employ these concepts in the sense we did, say, three or four months ago. Today as far as the European great powers are concerned, Germany is in the position of a state which is striving for the earliest termination of the war and for peace, while Britain and France, which but yesterday were declaiming against aggression, are in favor of continuing the war and are opposed to the conclusion of peace. Roles, as you see, are changing. [*Russia and the War*, p. 4.]

50. Beata Obertyńska, a well-known writer, recalled one such meeting in Lwów: "The speaker, a young Jew from Lwów, was talking complete nonsense. He claimed, for example, that every count, officer, and landowner could cast six to ten votes in elections in Poland, while a peasant or a worker had no right to vote at all." (HC, PGC, Box 10, Lwów: Obertyńska [4796].) In another propa-

ganda mishap, the case of Professor Studyński was described in leaflets intended to illustrate the persecution of Ukrainians: the Polish government, it was stated, discriminated against Studyński by changing his title to that of ordinary [i.e., full] professor, although he had once been an extraordinary [i.e., associate] professor of the Lwów university (HI, PGC, Box 10, Lwów: 6095, 8556).

51. "Who would like to get more land? Who has an old house and would like to get a new one? Who would like more cattle, or a horse?" an agitator would ask during a meeting, taking down names of people who responded to his queries and promising that they would get all they wanted after the election. (HI, PGC, Łomża: 39.) In some factories, stores were set up where, after the meeting, those attending could buy various desirable items (HI, PGC, Białystok: 35). A group of refugees from Silesia were told during a meeting that they would be deprived of food ration cards and kicked out of their apartments if they did not vote. "When the meeting ended, we were all called to Zielona Street and given ten złotys each. We were told that after the elections we would receive ten złotys every week and free food until we were allowed to return home." (HI, PGC, Box 10, Lwów: 7178.)

52. "In Rawa Ruska a certain Perepełycia was nominated as a candidate. She was a maid at the lawyer's house before, and they dressed her in karakul furs and drove her in a car from one meeting to another, calling her 'the most beautiful daughter of the nation.' " (HI, PGC, Box 10: Dogilewski.)

53. Borwicz, "Inżynierowie dusz," p. 141.

54. Sometimes people did raise objections. During a pre-election meeting at the Lwów Polytechnical School, after the chairman asked the "Who is against?" question, a few students raised their hands. "I stood up and told him [the chairman] that I wanted to propose someone else's candidacy. The chairman asked me what I held against his candidate—Did he kill someone, or steal something, or isn't he noble-minded? I replied that I could not reproach his candidate with any of these because I did not know him. In response the chairman instructed the candidate to read aloud his own autobiography. This is how the candidate got 'elected' by our meeting." Not surprisingly, there is a postscript to this story: this student did not have to vote for the candidate; he was arrested on October 18. (HI, PGC, Box 10, Lwów: 11262.)

55. Wanda Wasilewska, certainly one of the most articulate candidates (she was a communist and a rhetorically gifted Polish writer) recalled a conversation with a large group of women after one of the pre-election meetings: "We all like you very much and we shall all vote for you," said one of her interlocutors, "but there is one thing that we all beg of you—please save us from these Bolsheviks" (Borwicz, "Inżynierowie dusz," p. 141).

56. "When threats proved not sufficient, they bound people up, put them on carts, and took them to vote," recalled a peasant from Wołyń (HI, PGC, Włodzimierz Wołyński: 26). In another part of the country (Sokal), Stanisław Widomski spent October 22 in jail, together with a group of Ukrainian boys being held as hostages so that their parents would behave on voting day (HI, PGC, Box 10; Lwów: Widomski).

57. In Zambrów village, near Łomża, those showing up early were promised sausage. "In the beginning they were giving out half a pound of sausage and a handful of candies, later less, and in the afternoon nothing at all." (HI, PGC, Łomża: 63.)

58. In some mountain villages, where there were no pencils and peasants

were illiterate anyway, some voters wrapped cow and horse manure into paper ballots and then stuffed them into ballot boxes (Stanisław Vincenz, *Dialogi z sowietami* [London: Polska Fundacja Kulturalna, 1966], p. 174).

59. An entire hamlet from *gmina* Przytuły, Łomża county, hid in the forest. The NKVD found only one old man there (HI, PGC, Łomża: 65). The "hamlet Zamorze, populated by Mazurs, refused to participate in the elections. Later, they were all deported" (HI, PGC, Łuniniec: 40). "The village Demiczów was known in Równo county for its strongly nationalistic Ukrainian sympathies. On the election day Ukrainian flags were put out in Demiczów, and not a single person went to vote. The very next day sixteen people from the village were arrested and sent to Russia." (HI, PGC, Równe: 32.) Many more Ukrainian villages collectively refused to participate in the elections (HI, PGC, Równe: 38, 40; Włodzimierz Wołyński: 43, 44), and they, too, were quickly punished by deportation. Such collective refusals seem to have occurred predominantly in ethnically homogeneous villages—whether populated by Ukrainians, Mazurs, or Poles (like those in Łomża county, for instance)—where the Soviets could not manipulate national hatred to secure the cooperation of one ethnic group against another. But to verify this hypothesis more data will have to be systematically gathered and analyzed.

60. *Pravda*, October 27 and 29, 1939.

61. Anti-Semitism, already endemic among the Poles living in eastern Poland before the war, was reinforced during the Soviet occupation due to the visible support many Jews offered to the new authorities. While the Polish army was being formed in the USSR, the Soviet authorities exploited the ethnic antagonism between the Poles and the Jews. The Soviets, in practice, denied permission for Jews to be conscripted into the Polish Army (see, for example, the Soviet interpretation of the concept of Polish citizenship), but they initially allowed some Jews to join and later spread rumors that the *Polish* military authorities were preventing Jews from joining the army. On the other hand, the Polish military authorities, as a rule, were not very receptive to Jewish volunteers (Shimon Redlich, "The Jews in the Soviet Annexed Territories, 1939–1941," *Soviet Jewish Affairs*, no. 1 [1971]: 81–90; PGC, Box 129, File "Dział II"). On November 14, 1941, General Anders issued an order prohibiting all manifestations of anti-Semitism in the army. Two weeks later, on November 30, in order to placate the discontented troops, he issued a clarification of his statement so that his strong condemnation of anti-Semitic attitudes in the Army would be understood properly. For the moment, he said, the Polish reason of state requires "that the Jews not be irritated." Military commanders were instructed to warn all those "too hot and vigorous" that "right now all manifestations of struggle against the Jews are completely inadmissible and will be severely punished as actions hurting our cause. When we finally become masters in our own country, after the campaign is won, we will settle the Jewish problem in the manner required by the greatness and sovereignty of our Motherland and of simple human justice" (Stanisław Kot, *Listy z Rosji do Gen. Sikorskiego* [London, 1955], pp. 465–66). So much for anti-Semitism in the Polish army. Moreover, of the 115,000 Polish citizens evacuated from Russia, only 5,000 to 7,000 (less than 5 percent) were Jews (including 850 children). This is significant, for between 30 and 40 percent of all the deportees into Russia were Jewish.

On the other hand, the material assistance provided to Polish deportees by the network set up by the Polish embassy reached the Jews without discrimination. In fact, as a report prepared by the Polish embassy reveals, 33.9 percent of all Polish citizens who availed themselves of the embassy's relief apparatus in 1943 were Jewish. On April 25, 1943, out of a total of 3,847 people employed in the embassy's relief apparatus, 1,828 (47.5 percent) were Jews (PGC, Box 128, "Report on the Relief Accorded Polish Citizens by the Polish Embassy in the USSR"). It seems that the Jews, whose survival skills were well developed after centuries of persecution, were, on the whole, better informed than the rest of the Polish deportees as to where to seek assistance, how to reach the embassy's outposts, and, apparently, how to make themselves useful.

62. Vincenz, *Dialogi z sowietami*, p. 125.

63. One especially grim chapter was written during the last week of June 1941, after the Russo-German war broke out. During the evacuation of prisons and POW camps, the NKVD killed political prisoners—peasants who did not deliver quotas on time, workers arrested for absenteeism, people who refused to vote or accept Soviet passports, and the like—and Polish soldiers who could not be transported east. A precise count is unavailable, but the number of victims undoubtedly runs into the tens of thousands. The massacre in Lwów prison is probably the best known (HI, PGC, Box 927, File "Lwów"; Rudnycka, *Western Ukraine*, pp. 442–44), but the fate of prisoners in many other towns was identical. We have found sworn depositions from witnesses of massacres perpetrated on prisoners in Berdyczów and in Głębokie (HI, PGC, Box 22, Protokół przesłuchania, 6.V.1942; Box 689, File "Uchodźcy z ZSSR," Note dated Kujbyszew, 28.X.1942). Altogether about two thousand people were killed in these two massacres. On the massacre perpetrated during the evacuation of the Stara Wilejka prison, see HI, PGC, Wilejka: 61; AC: 2489, 3556, 4966, 5908, 11004, 12398, 12558, 12599, 12693, 15523. On killings during the evacuation from the Stryj prison, see HI, AC: 2422; and during the evacuation from the Tarnopol prison, HI, AC: 3477. For descriptions by survivors of mass murders during the evacuation of POW camps from southeastern Poland into Russia, see HI, AC: 15, 478, 481, 607, 621, 659, 725, 2562, 3147, 4507, 4711, 4807, 5084, 5193, 12578.

Bibliography

ARCHIVES

Hoover Institution Archives, Stanford, California (HI)
    Władysław Anders Collection (AC). Papers (in Polish), 1939–1946.
    Polish Government Collection (PGC). Poland. Records (in Polish), 1918–1945.
    Poland. Ambasada (USSR) Collection (PAC). Records (in Polish), 1941–1944.
    Polish Armed Forces Collection (PSZ). Poland. Polskie Siły Zbrojne. Miscellaneous records (in Polish), 1940–1945.
General Sikorski Historical Institute Archives, London (GSHI)

BOOKS, ARTICLES, AND COLLECTIONS OF DOCUMENTS

Actes et documents du Saint Siège relatifs à la Seconde guerre mondiale, vol. 3, *Le Saint Siège et la situation religieuse en Pologne et dans les pays Baltes 1939–1945*. Vatican: Libreria Editrice Vaticana, 1967.

Anders, Władysław. *Bez Ostatniego Rozdziału*. London: Gryf Publishers, 1959.

Avtorkhanov, Abdurakhman. *Tekhnologia vlasti, protses obrazovania KPSS*. Munich: Posev, 1959.

Borwicz, Michał. "Inżynierowie dusz." *Zeszyty Historyczne* (Paris), no. 3 (1963); 121–63.

Buczek, Roman. "Działalność opiekuńcza ambasady R.P. w ZSSR w latach 1941–1943." *Zeszyty Historyczne* (Paris), no. 29 (1974): 42–115.

Dunn, Dennis J. *The Catholic Church and the Soviet Government, 1939–1949*. Boulder, Colo.: East European Quarterly, 1977.

Ehrlich, Seweryn Krzysztof. *U podstaw armii polskiej w ZSSR: Walka z chorobami zakaźnymi w 1942 r.* Rome: Włochy, Nakładem Towarzystwa Wiedzy Wojskowej 2. Korpusu, 1946.

General Sikorski Historical Institute, ed. *Documents on Polish-Soviet Relations, 1939–1949*. London: Heinemann, 1961.

Koło Junackiej Szkoły Kadetów, ed. *Junacka Szkoła Kadetów.* London, 1972.

Kot, Stanisław. *Listy z Rosji do Gen. Sikorskiego.* London, 1955.

Kubijovych, Volodymyr. *The Ukrainians in the Generalgouvernement, 1939–1941.* Chicago: Mykola Denysiuk Publishing Company, 1975.

Molotov, Viacheslav M. *Russia and the War: Molotov's Speech to the Supreme Soviet of the Soviet Union, October 31, 1939.* London: Modern Books, 1939.

Poróg-Malinowski, Władysław. *Najnowsza Historia Polityczna Polski, 1864–1945.* Volume 3. London, 1956.

Poland. Ambasada (Japan). "Zesłańcy Polscy w ZSRR." Manuscript. Tokyo, 1941 (HI).

Redlich, Shimon. "The Jews in the Soviet Annexed Territories, 1939–1941." *Soviet Jewish Affairs,* no. 1 (1971): 81–90.

Rubinowicz, Dawid. *Pamiętnik.* Warsaw: Książka i Wiedza, 1960.

Rudnycka, Milena, ed. *Western Ukraine Under the Bolsheviks, IX. 1939–VI. 1941.* New York: Shevchenko Scientific Society in the USA, 1958.

Schulz, Bruno, *Księga listów.* Cracow: Wydawnictwo Literackie, 1975.

Sierakowiak, Dawid. *Dziennik.* Warsaw: Iskry, 1960.

Sontag, R. J., ed. *Documents on German Foreign Policy, vol. 8.* Washington, D.C.: Government Printing Office, 1954.

Stawecki, Piotr. *Następcy Komendanta: Wojsko a polityka wewnętrzna Drugiej Rzeczypospolitej, 1935–1939.* Warsaw: Wydawnictwo Ministerstwa Obrony Narodowej, 1969.

Sukiennicki, Wiktor. "The Establishment of the Soviet Regime in Eastern Poland in 1939." *Journal of Central European Affairs,* July 1963, pp. 191–218.

Vincenz, Stanisław. *Dialogi z sowietami.* London: Polska Fundacja Kulturalna, 1966.

Wasilewska, Irena. *Suffer Little Children.* Translation of *Za winy niepopełnione,* 1945. London: Maxlove Publishing Company, 1946.

Wat, Aleksander. *Mój Wiek.* London: Polonia Book Fund, 1977.

Zawodny, Janusz K. *Death in the Forest: The Story of the Katyn Forest Massacre.* Notre Dame, Ind.: University of Notre Dame Press, 1962.

Związek Szkół Młodszych Ochotniczek, ed. *Książka Pamiątkowa Szkół Młodszych Ochotniczek.* London, n.d.

Index

Administration, local: Polish, 5, 6, 9, 18, 20; Soviet, 26. *See also* Militia, Village committees
American Jewish Joint Distribution Committee (JOINT), 241
Amnesty, xxii–vii *passim*
Amsterdam, 12, 246
Anders, Władysław (Gen.), xxiv, 253
Arrests, 16, 20–26 *passim*
Austria-Hungary, 7

Baltic states, 3, 249
Barbara, xxvi
Berdyczów: prison evacuation from, 254
Berlin, 4, 244
Bessarabia, 3, 249
Białystok, 7, 13, 15, 24, 25, 241, 245, 249; Temporary Administration (Soviet) in, 250, 251
Buczek, Roman, 239, 240, 241
Buzuluk, xxiv

Canada, xxv
Caspian Sea, xxiv
Chkalov, xxiv
Churches, closing of, 247
Circles of Atheists, 243
Colonels' regime (in Poland), 7
Colonists (Polish), 8, 10, 13; Association of, 245
Constitution (Soviet), 17, 23

Cooperatives, 15; of artisans, 249
Czerwony Sztandar, 250

Death, xiv–xxiv *passim*, xxv, xxviii
Deportations, xiii, xix–xxiii *passim*, xxvii, xxviii, 16, 19, 22, 26, 239, 241, 247, 248; occupational stratification of, 240
Donbas, 248
Drohobycz, 249
Dzalal-Abad, xxiv

Egypt, xxvi
Elections, 18–24 *passim*, 250, 251; candidates during, 23, 25, 252
England, xxv, 22, 251
Ethnic minorities, 4, 7, 18, 19, 245; deportations of, xxiii; children, xxiii, xxvii; Belorussians, xxvii, 4, 6, 7, 9, 14, 17, 18, 19, 241, 243, 244; Ukrainians, xxvii, 4–10 *passim*, 14–19 *passim*, 26, 27, 241, 243, 244, 253; Jews, 7, 18, 19, 24, 27, 241, 243, 251, 254; communist sympathizers among, 9; refugees, 15; anti-Semitism, 26, 253; collaboration of, 26, 253
Evacuation: from the USSR, xxiii–vi; of prisons, 254
Executions, 26

France, 22, 251
Frank, Anne, xiii, 244; *Diary*, xiii

Garbo, Greta, 12, 246
Generalgouvernement, 19, 23, 249
German-Soviet Boundary and Friendship Treaty, 13, 19
German-Soviet Treaty of Non-Aggression, 3, 5, 6
Germany, xiv, xxi, xxvii, 3, 4, 5, 6, 7, 8, 244, 251; Soviet shipments to, 13
Głębokie: prison evacuation from, 254
Grzybowski, Wacław (Polish Ambassador in the USSR), 4
Guzar, xxiv

Hitler, Adolf, 3, 13, 26, 244
Hoover Institution Archives, xxi, xxvii, 239

Iran, xxiii–vi passim, 241, 247
Iraq, xxvi
Irtysh, 242

Japan, 239

Karabalti, xxiv
Kara-Su, xxiv
Katyń, 239
Kazakhstan, xxiv
Kermine, xxiv
Khrushchev, Nikita, 21
Kielce, 244
Kiev, 247
Kirghizia, xxiv
Kolkhozes, xxv, 11, 247
Kołomyja, 241
Komisja Wysyłki Paczek (Commission for the Expedition of Parcels [Poland]), 241
Komsomol, 21
KOP (Frontier Defense Corps), 3, 6, 8, 244; shooting of officers, 246
Kotlubanka, xxiv
Krasnovodsk, xxiv
Kremlin, 4
Kuibyshev, xxiv

Labor camps, xxii

Labor unions (Soviet), 21
Lithuania, 3
Łomża, 252
London, xxi, xxvii, 241
Lugovoe, xxiv
Łuniniec, 246
Lwów, 10, 12, 16, 17, 19, 20, 24, 25, 241, 245–54 passim

Margilan, xxiv
Mayakovsky, Vladimir, 247
Militia (in Soviet-occupied Poland), 9, 14, 15, 16, 20, 24, 25, 26, 245; common criminals in, 10
Mikołajczyk, Stanisław (Prime Minister), 239
Molotov, Viacheslav, 4, 5, 26, 244, 245, 251
Moscow, xxii, xxiv, xxvi, 4, 21, 26, 244
MSZ (Ministry of Foreign Affairs, Poland), 239, 240, 241

Narew, 3, 244
National Democratic Party (Poland), 7
Nazareth, xxvi
NKVD (Soviet State Secret Police), 9, 20, 253, 254

Obertyńska, Beata (author), 251
Officers (Polish), 10, 11, 16, 18, 239, 244, 249, 251; shooting of KOP, 246
Orlik-Rückemann, Wilhelm (Gen.), 6
Otar, xxiv

Pahlevi, xxiv
Palestine, xxvi
People's Commissariat for Foreign Affairs (Soviet), 241, 242
Pieracki, Bronisław (Interior Minister), 8
Piłsudski, Józef (Marshal), 7
Pioneers, 243
Poland, xxii, xxiii, xxvii, 3, 4, 6, 10–26

passim, 244, 246, 251, 254; collapse of, xiii; partitions of, xiv, xxi, 5; Twenty Years, 7, 8, 245; Jews returning to central, 19; administrative division, 245
Polesie, 7, 8, 245
Polewka, Adam, 23
Police (Polish), 6, 10, 13, 18, 20, 240, 246, 249
Polish army (in USSR), xxii–vi *passim*, 253
Polish embassy: Japan, 239; USSR, xxii–vi *passim*, 239, 241, 242, 253, 254
Polish government in exile, xxi, xxii
Polniaszek-Kossakowska, Danuta, 16, 248
Ponomarenko, Pantelejmon, 21
Potemkin, Vladimir, 4
POWs, xxii, 239, 246, 254
Pravda, 4, 5, 21, 24, 247, 248, 250, 251
Prisons, xxii, 254
Propaganda, 11, 14, 16, 21, 22, 23, 26
Property: confiscation and redistribution of, 12–20 *passim*, 26, 248, 251
Przemyśl, 13

Rawa Ruska, 252
Red Army, xxii, 3–12 *passim*, 21, 22, 239, 244–50 *passim*; reception of, 9; shabby look of, 11; gifts to, 13; collaboration with, 19; during elections, 25; casualties, 245
Red Corner, 242
Red Cross: American, xxv; International, 239; Polish, 240, 242, 243
Refugees, 15, 249
Registration, 18, 21, 249
Równe, 15, 17, 246
Rubinowicz, Dawid, 244
Rubles, 12, 246–51 *passim*
Rudnycka, Milena, 15

San, 3, 244
Schulenburg, Count Werner F. (German ambassador to USSR), 4, 5, 244
Schulz, Bruno, 249
Settlements (posëlki), xxii–viii *passim*
Shakhrisabz, xxiv
Shortages, 12, 15, 17, 247
Siberia, xxiii, 23
Sierakowiak, Dawid, 244
Sikorski, Władysław (Gen., Prime Minister), xxii
Skałat, 17, 18
Slave labor, xiv, xxiii
Social revolution (in occupied Poland), 8, 14, 19, 21, 246
Sokal, 252
Stalin, Joseph V., 3, 4, 243, 248
Stanisławów, 245
Stara Wilejka: prison evacuation from, 254
Starvation, xiv–viii *passim*
Stryj: prison evacuation from, 254
Studyński, Kirilo (Professor), 25, 252
Sukiennicki, Wiktor (Professor), 250
Supreme Soviet (USSR), 241, 245
Szkoły Junackie (Junaks' Schools), xxvi
Szkoły Młodszych Ochotniczek (Schools of Young Volunteers), xxvi

Tarnopol, 6, 241, 245, 247; prison evacuation from, 254
Tashkent, xxiv
Tatishchevo, xxiv
Taxes (under Soviet occupation), 13, 247
Tchok-Pak, xxiv
Teheran, xxiii, xxiv, 240, 242
Tockoje, xxiv

USSR, xiv, xv, xxi–viii *passim*, 3–14 *passim*, 19, 23, 27, 239–53 *passim*; incorporation into, 18, 20, 22, 26
Uzbekistan, xxiv

Velikoe-Alekseevskoe, xxiv
Versailles Treaty, 7
Village committees, 9, 10, 13, 14, 18, 19, 20
Vilna Ukraina, 250
Vistula, 3, 244
Voroshilov, Kliment, 4
Vrevskoe, xxiv, xxvi
Vyshinsky, Andrei, xxii, xxv

War: 1920 Polish-Soviet, 245, 249, Russo-German (1941), xxi, xxii, xxiii, 242, 254, Second World (1939), xxi, xxviii, 244, 246
Warsaw, 244, 247
Wasilewska, Irena, xxiv, 242
Wasilewska, Wanda, 252

Wat, Aleksander, 247, 249
Western Belorussia, 4, 13, 14, 21, 26; (People's) National Assembly of, 18, 20, 25; elections in, 22, 251
Western Ukraine, 4, 13, 14, 21, 26, 247; (People's) National Assembly of, 18, 20, 23, 25, 250; elections in, 22, 251
Wilno, 245
Włodzimierz Wołyński, 247
Wołyń, 239, 245, 252

Yangiyul, xxiv

Zbaraż, 6
Zdołbunów, 6
Złoty, 248, 252